MW01273320

V

DATE DUE

The Natural Limitations of Youth

The Predispositions That Shape the Adolescent Character

Developments in Clinical Psychology

Glenn R. Caddy, series editor
Nova University

The Natural Limitations of Youth

The Predispositions That Shape the Adolescent Character

by

John J. Mitchell
University of Alberta

Ablex Publishing Corporation
Stamford, Connecticut
London, England

Copyright © 1998 by Ablex Publishing Corporation

Printed in the United States of America

Library of Congress Cataloging-in-Publication Data

Mitchell, John J., 1941-
  The natural limitations of youth: the predispositions that shape the adolescent character/John J. Mitchell.
      p.   cm. — (Developments in clinical psychology)
  Includes bibliographical references and index.
  ISBN 1-56750-372-1. — ISBN 1-56750-373-X (pbk.)
  1. Adolescent psychology.   I. Title.   II. Series.
BF724.M563 1998
155.5—dc21   97-40928
                                                                CIP

Ablex Publishing Corporation   Published in the U.K. and Europe by:
100 Prospect Street   JAI Press Ltd.
Stamford, CT 06901   38 Tavistock Street
                                       Covent Garden
                                       London WC2E 7PB
                                       England

This book is dedicated to my wife, Jenelle, and to my daughter, Renel.... Strong, intelligent, dignified, and loving women who enrich my life and elevate my spirit.

Contents

Acknowledgments

My father, Robert Vincent Mitchell, edited the original manuscript and, as always, his suggestions were thoughtful and helpful. This is the tenth of my books he has edited, and each one shines a little brighter because of his helpful eye and disciplined temperament. Thanks, Dad.

As background research for this book, I interviewed more than 200 adolescents living in Alberta, British Columbia, Washington, and Oregon. These young people provided me with a wealth of first-hand data on how they think and what they feel. As well, as part of my ongoing research here at the University of Alberta, I have analyzed written statements from more than 1,000 university students describing, in compelling detail, the experiences that shaped their adolescent lives. To all of you who volunteered time and testimony, I say "thank you."

J.J. Mitchell
Edmonton, Alberta
April, '98

Introduction

The Mystery of Youth

In this book I am going to try to explain why this is the right place and the right time to embark upon a more realistic understanding of youth—an understanding grounded in both the strengths and weaknesses of the adolescent character. For those of you steeped in the popular theories that canonize all things youthful this may prove painful. Current adolescent theory is so completely intertwined in the dogma of *inevitable* growth and the doctrine that potentiality *naturally* flows into actuality that it has turned a blind eye to the forces that inhibit growth and stunt maturity during adolescence.

Romanticized notions of youth hide an elementary fact of human development: All potential is not upward. Every human has the potential to regress as well as to progress, to backslide as well as to march forward, to spiral downward as well as to rise upward. Our culture has so indoctrinated itself with the glory of upward-and-outward that it is blinded to the adolescent's capacity for life-diminishing rather than life-enhancing choices—to sink rather than to swim. A cherished illusion is that youth have a built-in beacon that wisely directs, but this simply is not the way it is. Youth have dignified inner whisperings, to be sure, but no clarion call, no unfailing instincts, no persistently right urges to chart their direction.

The romantics congratulate themselves on their lofty image of youth; and I congratulate them too, for without grand images we all are diminished. But I do not congratulate the romantics who refuse to tally the teen suicides; who turn their eyes away from the prison walls; who deny what runaways are running away from; who deny the juvenile sex trade; who see in teen pregnancy only healthy babies but not the broken mothers, the damaged infants, the abusive fathers. But the truth is not always as we wish it to be, and the truth is that adolescent potential *has no guaranteed direction*; for the natural talent of youth to mature it must be aimed and trained. The upward potential of youth is given wings by the encouragement, the wisdom, and the leadership of adults far more than by any stirrings inherent to the adolescent's nature.

The sad reality is that of all people youth are the most easily corrupted. On their own they lack the experience, the intellectual judgment, and the moral fiber to resist the forces of corruption. From these facts no one who loves youth can turn away. This book, however, is not about the corruption of youth; instead it is about their corruptibility. The differences may appear slight but they are not. Corruption has to do with the outside influences which have a corrupting effect, whereas corruptibility has to do with characteristics *inherent to* the person being corrupted.[1]

More than anything I seek an honest understanding of the predispositions which shape the adolescent character. Youth-as-Titan is comforting to adults afraid to lead by example. But Youth-as-Titan, just as Titan himself, is myth, and a rock or two needs to be thrown at the glass houses that protect adults from the adolescent need to be pulled upward to a higher maturity.

THE ADOLESCENT MORATORIUM

Erikson coined the term *moratorium* to mean a period of permissiveness between the juvenile incompetencies of childhood and the full responsibilities of adulthood; it is a delay of adult commitments characterized by a selective permissiveness on the part of society. The moratorium provides a protected period of experimentation to help young people become better able to assume personal obligations and to make meaningful commitments to their loved ones and to their society. Moratorium, then, is the "in-between" world in which teens grow, mature, and prepare to meet the world. "The functional reason society takes this stance is to give adolescents time to mature and experience so that when it is time for them to enter the adult world, especially the occupational world, they will be ready, emotionally and educationally" (Manaster, 1989, p. 163).

The moratorium is defined by laws both written and unwritten. The *written* laws require the parent society to provide basic health care, to educate, and to protect the young. The *unwritten* laws of the social contract claim that, in exchange for receiving food, shelter, emotional support, and schooling, the adolescent *should*: (a) remain in school until age 16; (b) avoid pregnancy; (c) avoid state-financed dependency (i.e., welfare, drug rehabilitation, prison) and; (d) work toward acquiring a mature identity.[2]

THE MORATORIUM AS WASTELAND

There exists an unspeakable human wasteland in North America peopled by almost 10 million youth. This wasteland has been meticulously documented by sociologists, educators, penologists, urban planners, and most recently by The Carnegie Council on Adolescent Development. Those of you who don't want to believe the bad news I recommend that you simply drive to the parts of your city you don't allow your children to go to and spend a month. The first-hand evidence is extremely compelling. My concern in this book, however, is not with the undisputable fact that some of our youth are corrupted by deplorable social conditions and that some of them are broken by depraved human connections, but rather, I am concerned with *how easily youth are corrupted and how readily they are broken.* I am concerned with the raw product of the adolescent character.

Researchers at the Carnegie Council have done as much as anyone to document how youth fail to comprehend what is involved in mastering the adult roles they will shortly inherit, and their tendency to believe that someone will assume the roles for them if they are too difficult; further, these investigators have described in grim detail the tendency for many young people to think that it simply won't matter if they do not carry out their future roles effectively. At this moment in North American history, Hamburg (1989, 1992) concluded, *the primary obligation of adults is the preventing of youth casualties.* Fateful choices, shared destinies. Here is a man who knows first-hand the vulnerability of youth in modern culture. The Carnegie Council, under Hamburg's direction, has been investigating the millions of youngsters who inhabit the moratorium wasteland. Here are a few of their findings.

In North America about one in four adolescents does not graduate from high school. Statistically, the one dropout is far more likely to receive public assistance and to engage in crime than the three who graduate. One in ten girls becomes pregnant during adolescence. This one girl is more likely to experience long periods of unemployment, to drop out of school, to remain on public assistance for more than three years, and to require hospitalization than the nine teenage girls who do not become pregnant. The Center for Population Options estimated that adolescent child-bearing cost the United States $16 billion in 1988; current projections (1998) are closer to 24 billion.

Illicit drug use is thought by most experts to be greater in the United States than in any other "moratorium" country in the world. Estimates indicate that about 20 percent of American teens smoke cigarettes daily and about 6 percent consume alcohol daily.

Adolescents, because of their need (and desire) for experimentation, are vulnerable to a host of risks. In the short-term they are susceptible to sexually transmitted diseases and accidents related to alcohol; delayed consequences include cancer, cardiovascular disease, and obesity in adult life, all of which are encouraged by their high-calorie, high-fat, junk food diet.

By age 16 substantial numbers of youth show signs they will reach adulthood unable to meet the requirements of the workplace, the commitments of relationships in families, and the responsibilities of participation in a democratic society. These youth are among the estimated 7 million young people—one in four adolescents—who are extremely vulnerable to multiple high-risk behaviors and school failure. Another 7 million may be at moderate risk, and they remain a cause for serious concern.[3]

Bad news comes so rapidly when describing the adolescent wasteland that it is instructive to repeat a few of the major points. Approximately one of out every four American adolescents approaches adulthood:

- without the occupational skills to obtain and hold a job;
- without the interpersonal skills to maintain a family;
- without the social skills to carry out the duties of a citizen in a democracy; and,
- without the confidence, or skills, to overcome these limitations.

With predictable consistency these kids hate school, achieve poorly, and do not acquire the literacy skills required for economic advancement. The bottom line is that they lose whatever natural zest for learning humans usually possess during the wonder years, they become alienated from everything that healthy youth are attached to, including their parents, their schools, their community, and their churches. They are lured to drugs by other damaged peers, by the glory of intoxication, or simply by the desire to retreat from an environment that the vast majority of people reading this book would never allow their own children to enter even for a day. About 70 percent of them drop out of school, sealing their economic fate.

Taking all of this into account, what do we mean when we speak of the natural limitations of youth? Basically, we mean:

- that young people readily become less than what they are and that their potential is *easily* eroded;
- that their natural zest for life can shift into indifference and scorn, that their eagerness to contribute to their family and to their society is easily suffocated;
- that their self-esteem network is vulnerable to fables and illusions;
- that without active assistance from adults and peers they have a very limited ability to cope with their most pressing problem, the prevention of pregnancy;

- that their ability to formulate long-term goals is weak, and weakened even further when their ambitions are superficial and contrived; and,
- that without decent adult intervention in their personal lives youth lessen in their civility, regress in their behavior, and backslide in their sociability.

I want to emphasize that this book is neither "pessimistic" nor "cynical," the labels that youth-watchers invariably give to commentary that doesn't blame family, school, or society for every adolescent hardship. Rather, this book, in my opinion, is realistic and honest in that it portrays youth as they are, not as we pretend they are, and that it opens to investigation inherent traits that need realistic appraisal. Hopefully, this portrayal will help to bring about a much needed increase in our understanding of the adolescent personality, and help to bring into sharper focus the young person's need for guidance and stewardship in our moratorium culture.

NOTES

[1] There is no need to overview the theories of human depravity which claim that we humans are driven by genetic (or evolutionary) forces that, somehow, cause us to be criminals and corruptors of each other's humanity. As near as I can surmise, there is no real benefit to reducing the less worthy in our nature to genetic and biological forces; not merely because to do so contradicts our capacity to govern our lives as self-directing agents but, more importantly, because the scientific evidence which supports such a determinism is paltry and unconvincing. There is no one-way street between behavior and biology, and everyone, even the sensationalizers, knows it. Ornstein, in *Roots of the Self*, summarized it succinctly:

> Whenever the news trumpets some version of "biology affects behavior," it obscures the fact that biology and behavior form a two-way street. Hormones affect sexual drive, for instance, but sexual activity affects hormone levels. An active brain seeks a stimulating environment, but living in a stimulating environment literally changes and enriches the brain. Fatigue and boredom cause poor performance on the job, but stultifying job conditions produce fatigue and boredom. Scientists and writers who reduce our personalities, problems, and abilities to biology thereby tell only half the story, and miss half the miracle of how human biology works. (1992, p. 55)

[2] *Youth's obligation to the parent society:* The moratorium makes several demands on the young. First, it requires them to attend school. Most demands, however, are of exclusion. For example, youth cannot intern or apprentice for meaningful employment in any systematic way. Historically, young people's work had direct continuity with the work they would perform as adults; this is not true today.

Secondly, youth cannot leave their home without parental permission before the age of 16. We no longer tolerate what Friedenberg called "therapeutic runaways"—youth who leave the deplorable conditions of their household to pursue a better life. Third, youth cannot join trade unions, nor can they, by legitimate means, access well-paying jobs before graduating from high school.

[3] A 1994 U.S. Justice Department report claimed that youth between the ages of twelve and seventeen are five times more likely to be the victims of assault, rape, and robbery than are adults thirty-five years and older. Each year nearly 1.3 million adolescents are raped, robbed, or assaulted in Canada and the U.S. The U.S. saw over 2,200 murder victims under the age of eighteen in 1991. In the same year over 5,000 youth were killed by guns (Farris, 1996).

I

Adolescent Intelligence

1

The Rise of Intelligence During Adolescence

> All rising to a great place is by a winding stair.
> —Francis Bacon

Although it is not customary to begin with a confession, I would like to do so to set the record straight: Anyone who claims to know exactly how adolescents think, or for that matter, exactly how anyone thinks, is an imposter. To report what adolescents say or do, or to describe the mistakes they typically produce, is not too difficult; but to know exactly *how* they think is another thing altogether. It is fair to report, however, that we do not know a good deal about how adolescents think, especially with regard to the problem-solving strategies associated with formal thought.

In this chapter I want to tell something of the story about the incredible potential that graces adolescent intelligence. Steinberg (1989) once claimed that there are three chief ways that the thinking of adolescents is an improvement over the thinking of children. First, adolescents are better at thinking about the possible—they do not limit their thoughts to what is real. Second, adolescents are better at thinking through (and devising ways to test) hypotheses. Third, they are better at analyzing abstract concepts. These three points, however, do not exhaust the ways adolescent thought soars beyond that of children.

Since Jean Piaget first began to explore this mental territory in the 1920s, the intellectual advances that take place during adolescence have been known as "formal thought." In the balance of this chapter my focus is on what goes into, and what comes out of, formal thought. As the chapter title suggests, this is a period when intellectual power increases by leaps and bounds. In later chapters I will try to explain why adolescents sometimes use this power with flare and vitality and why, on other occasions, they use it frivolously, even stupidly, and why, on still other occasions, they don't seem to use it at all. For now, however, our concern is with the upside of adolescent intelligence.

FORMAL THOUGHT: ITS CONSTITUENT PARTS

> Our rational component is our guardian angel. It is that component that tells
> us something is awry and leads us to correct our mistakes in
> spontaneous judgement.
> —Massimo Piattelli-Palmarini (1994, p. 43)

Psychologists have looked at formal thought from many angles over the past several decades. My approach is rather straightforward in that my primary concern is with the *specific abilities and competencies* which, taken in their entirety, produce a higher plane of thinking during the adolescent years. These include increased capacity for abstraction, increased comprehensiveness, increased capacity for self-analysis, increased facility for analyzing propositions, and increased preoccupation with the future. In the next few pages we will see how they give wings to adolescent thought.

The First Feature of Formal Thought: It is Increasingly Abstract

Donaldson (1978), in her splendid work, *Children's Minds,* which Jerome Bruner (1986) claimed was "One of the most powerful ... books on the development of the child's mind to have appeared in twenty years," made an insightful observation on abstract thinking, which is of special value to anyone trying to grasp the differences between "concrete" thinkers (this usually means children) and "formal" thinkers (which usually means adolescents).[1]

> It is when we are dealing with people and things in the context of fairly immediate
> goals and intentions and familiar patterns of events that we feel most at home.
> And when we are asked to reson about these things .... we can often do it well.
> So long as our thinking is sustained by this kind of human sense, and so long
> as the conclusion to which the reasoning leads is not in conflict with something
> which we know or believe or want to believe, we tend to have no difficulty. Thus
> even pre-school children can frequently reason well about the events in the stories
> they hear. However, when we move beyond the bounds of human sense there
> is a dramatic difference. Thinking which does move beyond these bounds, so
> that it no longer operates within the supportive context of meaningful events,
> is often called 'formal' or 'abstract.' (Donaldson, 1978, p. 76)

Moving "beyond the bounds of human sense" to ideas that have nothing to do with our own immediate lives is the challenge of abstract reasoning. And this is the first quality that separates the thinking of teens from the thinking of children—the capacity to *systematically* manipulate abstract concepts.

The Second Feature of Formal Thought: It is Increasingly Comprehensive

When solving problems children do not usually recognize that an unexplored possibility could be as correct as a more obvious possibility. Adolescent thought, on the other hand, is less susceptible to leaving out critical facts, less prone to errors of omission, and less likely to believe that the right answer has been found when one of the options seems immediately reasonable. In sum, formal operational reasoners not only consider many possibilities, they try to consider all possibilities; this, in turn, "allows them to achieve a broad overview, to plan in considerable detail what they are going to do, and to interpret whatever they do within the total context. In contrast, concrete operational children tend to reason on a case-by-case basis and to plan less thoroughly. This sometimes leads them to misinterpret what they see and to leap to conclusions too quickly" (Siegler, 1986, p. 41).

Comprehensiveness requires the ability to consider the effects of two, three, even four variables at the same time, a skill known as *combinatorial thinking*. This skill exists in only a subdued form in childhood, but blossoms brightly in adolescence.

Combinatorial thinking is important in systematic hypothesis testing (versus trial and error) with regard to complex problems. This more sophisticated approach to problem-solving requires that the individual be able to consider all possible combinations of all factors of a problem and to test these in such a way as to permit only one factor to vary at a time; in other words, to observe the effects of one variable while holding all other factors constant. (Lloyd, 1985, p. 75)

Without comprehensiveness, the thoroughness demanded of scientific reasoning is not possible.

The Third Feature of Formal Thinking: Thought Becomes the Object of its Own Investigation

To children a thought is a thought is a thought; but adolescents come to realize that a thought may be born to rich or poor parentage. And whereas children possess very few standards by which to judge whether one thought is more valid than another, adolescents become increasingly adept at it.

When we say that thought "becomes the object of its own action," we mean that it has the ability to double-check itself and to retrace its own steps to see if mental errors have been made along the way. Walking back through one's own thoughts is one of the most profound breakthroughs in the adolescent's mental life. Now the thinker can actually interrupt the thought process at any given moment to ask: "Am I thinking this through clearly." "Have I left anything out?" "Have I paid too much attention to one side of the issue at the expense of the other?" After such a rethink the thinker might even say: "Let me go through this one more time." The net effect is that the thinker is no longer simply accepts mental conclusions "as delivered." The thought process becomes accountable to its own internal audit and, as a result, more and more ideas are rejected as unfit. This capacity to reject an idea because of its lack of coherence represents a great advance over the child's intellect which, generally speaking, cannot double-check its own conclusions nor evaluate them by a higher standard.

Like all of the constituent parts of formal thought, this capacity does not operate at peak efficiency all of the time; indeed, it appears to not work at all some of the time, and in some individuals it seems to never work. To operate efficiently it must be beckoned; it is not a given and is not primary to the thought process; it does not act in us spontaneously and without effort (Piattelli-Palmarini, 1994). Like all of the constituent parts of formal thought, its efficiency is influenced by the discipline and the training of the thinker in whom it resides. In future chapters we will pay close attention to the forces that interfere with double-checking the thought product. We do this for a simple reason: In the absence of double-check mental errors go undetected and prejudices unexamined. Thinkers who do not reassess their own conclusions cannot escape their own intellectual entrenchment; for all intents and purposes, thinkers who do not double-check their own thought-processes are thinking as a child thinks.

A Fourth Feature of Formal Thought: It Becomes Increasingly Propositional

A proposition is any statement capable of being believed, doubted, or denied. Propositions can be debated, analyzed and dissected; they are not bound to as-is reality, indeed, the most exciting ones are grounded in as-if speculation. Propositional thought allows one to investigate ideas beyond reality *as it is presently understood.* To go back to Piaget: "Reality becomes secondary to possibility."[2]

Propositional reasoning goes beyond everyday experience to investigate things never directly experienced, to quiz remote abstractions, to speculate about the unreal. Propositional reasoning also allows one to reason about false hypothese and to draw logical conclusions from them. Here, again, Wadsworth helps us:

If a logical argument is prefixed by the statement "Suppose coal is white," the concrete operational child, when asked to solve the problem, declares that coal is black and that the question cannot be answered. The child with formal operations readily accepts the assumption that coal is white and proceeds to reason about the logic of the argument. *The older child can submit to logical analysis the structure of the argument, independent of the truth or falseness of its content.* (1989, p. 118, emphasis added)

In contrast to the formal thinker, children focus on the perceptible elements of a problem and speculate rarely about possibilities that do not bear directly on the matter at hand. They eagerly wade into a problem with no real strategy, no "game plan." When they solve a problem correctly they may not know how they solved it, or when faced with a similar problem, they may not be able to beckon the strategies that only a few minutes before they used so effectively.

Political thought undergoes significant transformations during adolescence precisely because the formal thinker is able to investigate theoretical scenarios never before considered and is able to examine ideological and dogmatic propositions inconceivable to a less mature mind.[3]

Ordinarily the youngster begins adolescence incapable of complex political discourse.... By the time this period is at an end, a dramatic change is evident; the youngster's grasp of the political world is now recognizably adult. His mind moves with some agility within the terrain of political concepts; he has achieved abstractness, complexity, and even some delicacy in his sense of political textures; he is on the threshold of ideology, struggling to formulate a morally coherent view of how society is and might and should be arranged. (Adelson, 1972, p. 106)

Eventually, the mental furniture of concrete thought, so neatly arranged and tightly spaced, gives way to a much more expansive exercise of reason. And although first flexings are modest, propositional thought is a giant stride forward; indeed, without propositional thought philosophy is impossible.

A Fifth Feature of Formal Thought: It is Increasingly Future-Oriented

Concrete thinkers are not chained to the present, but neither are they free to take flight from it; their mental center is "here and now" not "there and then." Formal thinkers, on the other hand, are more liberated from the clock, even the calendar; they glide through light years, infinity, timelessness in ways that concrete thinkers cannot even begin to contemplate. As Bleiberg expressed it: "In their heads, using only thoughts and words, adolescents can project themselves into the future (the realm of the possible), and in so doing can explore the full range of possibilities inherent in a problem" (1994, p. 40).

With formal thought immediate time is recognized as a flicker of eternal time, clock time is differentiated from experiential time, geological *and* astronomical time take hold. The adolescent's transformation to future-oriented thought is profound for many reasons but perhaps the most important is that thought is inherently narrow when bound to the present.

The capacity to speculate about the future infuses new mystery into the identity project. "It must be clear that without the skills of hypothesis-raising, conceptualization of the future, logical problem solving, and the ability to anticipate consequences of an action, *work on identity formation could not really begin.*" Indeed, most identity questions are shrouded by the future and cast in terms of one's relationship to it.

> Without the capacities of formal thought, identity would be tied to the observable, the readily measurable or manipulable dimensions of experience. But with the door of abstract reasoning opened, *identity becomes a vision of what might be possible as well as what has already been experienced.* Because of formal thought there is chance to conceive of an identity that is a unique integration, a new combination of past, present, and future that takes a person along a new course. (Newman & Newman, 1988, p. 366, original emphasis)

Without future-oriented thought the grand disciplines of theology and cosmology cannot be. And, to keep our focus on the issue at hand, neither can a young person's personal identity be meaningfully constructed without an eye trained on the future.[4]

FORMAL THINKING AND SCIENTIFIC THOUGHT

> Decision making has certain basic elements: Stop and think; get information; assess information, including consequences; consider options, or formulate options; try new behavior and get feedback. These are fundamental elements of decision making that contribute to healthy adolescent development.
> —David Hamburg (1992, p. 244)

Formal thinkers form hypotheses, experiment with them, control variables, describe and record the outcomes of these experiments and, from these steps, draw conclusions in a formal manner. This combination of mental qualities brings Santrock to observe: "The adolescent's thought is more like a scientist's than a child's ... the adolescent often entertains many possibilities and tests many solutions in a planned way when having to solve a problem" (1990, p. 130).

Scientific reasoning, because it compares differing effects with differing outcomes, requires one to think about the interactive effect of several variables at the same time. Most adolescents can determine the effect of one, all, or some combination of a set of variables. Such mental bookkeeping is beyond the grasp of children, who reason best when only one or two variables are manipulated.

If I can pursue this point just a bit further. Aristotle laid down an axiom of logic that is now known as "the principle of contradiction." He described it this way: "It is impossible for the same attribute at once to belong and not to belong to the same thing in the same relation." This princilpe allows us to conclude, among other things, that a thing cannot be itself and its opposite at the same time. I have spent a number of years teaching this principle to teens, and I have found that, despite its obtuse language, it is quite understandable to most of them. Concrete thinkers, on the other hand, wrestle with this axiom, but they never seem to pin it down; it is too elusive and too cumbersome for them. And in this example we confirm one further difference between the concrete and the formal thinker.

In the end we come to see that the advances of formal thought, taken in their totality, dignify human thought by empowering the intellect to:

- go beyond the real to investigate the ideal;
- go beyond the physical to investigate the hypothetical;
- go beyond fragments to investigate wholes;
- go beyond "what is" to investigate "what if";
- go beyond the present to investigate the future.

IMPORTANT DIFFERENCES BETWEEN THE CHILD-AS-THINKER AND THE ADOLESCENT-AS-THINKER

One of the challenges facing anyone who investigates the adolescent thought-process is to do so without making teens appear, on the one hand, incompetent or trivial or, on the other hand, unduly masterful and profound.[5] Neither extreme is accurate yet both are correct some of the time. If we were to condense a great amount of research into one brief sentence, it might read like this: The thinking of adolescents is profoundly richer than the thinking of children, but it remains less profound than the thinking of adults.

The point to be seized is that the thinking of children is locked into its own primitive mechanics. Children think transductively, which is to say that they infer a particular fact from another particular fact. Usually only an isolated part of a problem is seen. As Goldman (1965) explains: "What may be central in an incident to an adult may be relegated to an obscure and unimportant detail to the child, while what are obscure and unimportant details for the adult are often seen by the child as of the greatest importance" (p. 52). The child, for the most part, deals with only one problem at a time, and will oversimplify situations too complex for singularity of thought. All of which "leads to unsystematic and fragmentary thinking, which in turn leads to illogical and inconsistent conclusions because all the evidence has not been considered. But the major disability is the lack of reversibility of thought, the inability to work back from an inconsistency to check on the evidence in the light of conclusions reached" (Goldman, 1965, p. 52).

In practical terms, teens acquire mental abilities that allow them:

- to think about the possible as well as the real;
- to think about implications as well as facts;
- to think about alternatives as well as givens;
- to think about hypotheses as well as descriptions;
- to think about "what if" as well as "what is."

All in all, the probable, the possible, and the theoretical rival material reality as the object of thought. Thinking is no longer bound to what is or what is not; formal thinkers investigate treasures of the mental universe unknown to concrete thinkers.[6]

POSTSCRIPT

> The adolescent who insists upon a critical examination of conventional wisdom is making himself into an adult.
> —Leon Eisenberg

When talking about the adolescent's great capacity for rational and systematic thought, I want to bring to your attention the tremendous *potential* for reason, the *potential* for rationality, and the *potential* for intelligence that live in every young mind. Without an appreciation of this vast potential, we simply cannot embrace the heroic possibilities of youth. Yet, equally true, without an honest recognition of how easily this potential may go untapped, we are blind to the deficiencies and limitations of youth. There is a considerable distance between the adolescent's actual intellectual level and that adolescent's potential level under adult guidance or in collaboration with more capable peers. This distance is what Lev Vygotsky (1978) called the "zone of proximal development," and it interests us because its focus is the same as ours—the extent to which the adolescent thought-process can be improved and upgraded.

We all agree that at their height formal thinkers calculate with Newtonian precision and infer with Napoleonic swiftness, but we also all agree that formal thinkers are not always "at their height." Formal thoulght is an ability teens do not always use, and when they do use it, there is no guarantee that they will use it effectively. Formal thought, as David Elkind observed, "*Is a capacity which we possess but which we use in very special circumstances*" (1985, p. 221, emphasis added). Individuals capable of formal reasoning sometimes reason on a formal level, sometimes on a concrete level, sometimes on an affective level, and sometimes not at all. And to further complicate things, when adolescents do employ formal thought, they may do so effectively in one are and clumsily in another.

> It is an additional mistake to presume that a person who is formally operational in one area is formally operational in another. The young person who thinks abstractly in areas of math or science may think in concrete terms in history and literature. Another young person may operate in an opposite way. Even within an area we may find ourselves using formal thought in one situation and reverting to concrete thought in another, depending on our mood, the complexity of the situation, or some other factors. (Ingersoll, 1989, p. 148)

Formal thought is not the exclusive instrument of reason and intelligence: In many youngsters it actually works more aggressively in the service of emotion than reason. As we will see in upcoming chapters, some youth use their intellect not as scientists or philosophers, but for self-advantage and self-promotion.

In conclusion, adolescents are lifted by formal thought and transported to a higher intellectual plane because of it, but this does not mean that their thoughts (or their lives) are always under its influence. If this were the case you would, at this moment, hold in your hands a much briefer book.

2

Egocentrism and Egocentric Thought

Egocentrism is the mental force that causes one to interpret data from one's own point of view without balancing or double-checking it with other perspectives. Perhaps its purest and most natural form is seen in the narrow-mindedness of young children.

Jean Piaget, the giant on whose shoulders we stand when surveying this topic, described egocentrism as an *embeddedness* in one's own point of view that colors everything from the inside out. In young children this embeddedness exists without their awareness; hence, they unselfconsciously think that what they saw at the parade is the same as what everyone else saw, and they presumptively infer that the scenes in the movie that made them sad made everyone sad. The egocentric child sees the world from his own position in it without realizing that it is a position, and therefore, "both on the social and on the physical plane, *he is egocentric through ignorance of his own subjectivity*" (Looft, 1972, p. 75, original emphasis). (Ignorance of one's own subjectivity is not unique to children, but in them it is created by limitations and immaturities *natural* to their developmental age. Ignorance of one's own subjectivity during adolescence requires a set of explanations beyond mere developmental immaturity.) At any rate, ignorance of one's own mental operations is a fact of the child's mental ecology. Not until the onset of formal thought (at about age 13) is much progress made in overcoming it.[7]

Young children sometimes give the impression that they do not know that perceptions of reality other than their own exist. Suppose, for example, that a three-year-old knows candy is hidden behind the books on a bookshelf and then another child (who does not know this secret) enters the room. If an adult were to ask the first child what the second one thinks is on the bookshelf, the first child will usually answer "candy." Because the first child knows candy is behind the books, he can't imagine the other child not knowing. (This of course is not the case with 5-year-olds, who have an increasing grasp of private knowledge.)

Piaget spoke of the young child's egocentrism as the innocent absence of self-consciousness.

> There is nothing in ego-centrism which tends to make thought conscious of itself (since this self-consciousness only arises through some shock with another mind), and this unconsciousness enables the objects of thought to succeed one another in an unrelated fashion. Juxtaposition is therefore the result of absence of direction in the successive images and ideas, *and this absence of direction is itself the outcome of that lack of self-consciousness which characterizes all egocentric thought.* (Campbell, 1976, p. 29, emphasis added)

Donaldson (1978) adds to this a deceptively simple passage: "The child does not appreciate that what he sees is relative to his own position; he takes it to represent absolute truth or reality—*the world as it really is*" (p. 20, original emphasis). The failure to recognize that what one sees is relative to one's position is not restricted to children; indeed, its adolescent equivalent is an awesome thing to behold.

Egocentrism produces a narrow-mindedness of which children are both victims and beneficiaries: victims because they cannot stand back to evaluate their own thoughts, and therefore are at the mercy of them; beneficiaries because it provides a clarity without which they would be swept away in the swirl of infinite data their mind is charged with organizing. Egocentrism carries this two-sided sword up through the adolescent years.

THE DEVELOPMENTAL PROGRESSION OF EGOCENTRISM

Piaget believed that the first two decades of life see four distinct stages of egocentrism, three during childhood and one during adolescence. Each of these stages builds on the advances of the previous stage, each contains its own modes of reality analysis, and each contains *unique modes of reality distortion.* As we would expect from even a cursory knowledge of childhood growth, each of these stages is associated with advances in mental strategies; equally important, each stage is characterized by a particular differentiation *failure,* which is not effectively overcome until the child progresses to the next stage. Let's take a quick look at these four stages to prepare for future discussions.[8]

1. The Conquest of the Object (Birth to Age 2). The thoughts and actions of infants are grounded in a radical egocentrism so complete as to make it virtually impossible for them to differentiate the self from the larger world. (An idea akin to, but not the same as, Freud's concept of primal narcissism.) Egocentrism at this age is based on the child's "belief" that sensory impressions are essential to the existence of the object. *Sensorimotor egocentrism begins to decline when the child recognizes that objects have their own existence independent of his [or her] perception of them.* This, in essence, is the child's first acknowledgment of the "as-is" world. Transcendence of this egocentrism arises from the emerging capacity for mental representation.

2. The Conquest of the Symbol (About 2-6 Years). The egocentrism of this age makes it difficult for the child to differentiate between symbol and referent. The child at this stage does not seem to understand the relationship between the signifier and what is signified because symbols are viewed as identical to their referents.

> When explaining a piece of apparatus to another child, the youngster at this stage uses many indefinite terms and leaves out important information.... Although this observation is sometimes explained by saying that the child fails to take the other person's point of view, it can also be explained by saying that the child assumes words carry much more information than they actually do. This results from his belief that even the indefinite "thing" somehow conveys the properties of the object which it is used to represent. In short, the egocentrism of this period consists in a lack of clear differentiation between symbols and their referents. (Elkind, 1967, p. 1027)

When symbol and referent are confused thinking about the world *is always in terms of one's position within it.* Children at this age believe that their perspective is shared by others, and that their understanding of an event is the only one possible.

3. The Conquest of Classes, Relations, and Quantities (About 7-11 Years). At this age the child can perform elementary syllogistic reasoning and propose concrete hypotheses. These abilities transport the child from more primitive levels of comprehension, but they also introduce new deficiencies. For example, children at this age do not understand that their hypotheses need to be tested, examined, and verified in order to determine if they are true, or even *likely to be true.* At this level "children too readily accept their own hypotheses as something factually given and believe that the facts must adapt to fit their hypotheses" (Muuss, 1988, p. 267).

The egocentrism inherent to this stage makes it difficult for 7- to 11-year-olds to differentiate between perceptual events and mental constructions; hence, *they cannot think independently about their thoughts.* Hypotheses that require untrue assumptions ("snow is black") cannot be investigated with much proficiency. However, with the attainment of formal operations this form of egocentrism diminishes.

Here children are blind to the realization that *errors take place within the thought process itself,* a blindness that impedes their ability to solve problems, but that empowers them to believe in the rightness of their thinking and to tackle mysteries they do not even begin to comprehend. *"The inability to differentiate between an assumption and a fact is what constitutes concrete operational egocentrism"* (Muuss, 1988, p. 267, original emphasis). And as we will soon see, the inability to differentiate an assumption from a fact carries far more significance during adolescence than it does during childhood.

4.   The Conquest of Thought (12-20 Years). "Formal thought" is a synonym for the higher plane of intellectual functioning that blossoms during adolescence and that allows the young person to reason more accurately and to conceptualize more objectively. Chapter One described the particulars of formal thought in considerable detail; therefore, we will not go further into it here. The egocentrism of adolescence expresses itself in many ways (e.g., the personal fable, the imaginary audience, idealistic reform, and self-referenced speech) all of which in their distinctive ways move the adolescent away from reason and toward egocentric self-priority.

HOW IS EGOCENTRISM LESSENED DURING ADOLESCENCE?

When I was a boy of fourteen my father was so ignorant I could hardly stand to have the old man around. But when I got to be twenty-one, I was astonished at how much he had learned in seven years.
—Mark Twain[9]

In our culture, common knowledge says that adolescents are self-conscious and self-centered, so it comes as no surprise when experts claim that they are egocentric. What is something of a surprise, however, is how unpredictably egocentrism expresses itself, and how it ebbs and flows not only during the course of a year, but even during the course of a single day. Egocentrism is always present in the thought process, but it is not a constant presence.

Egocentrism begins to subside when the thinker begins to double-check mental conclusions that present themselves to consciousness. "Present themselves" is critical. Younger children accept their mental conclusions without much awareness that they spring from the thought process itself. Children treat mental conclusions as facts of nature. They simply are, and what they are is. Thoughts are not double-checked because children tend not to grasp the relationship between process and product, which is to say that they do not understand how conclusions work their way to the top of the thought chain. They don't recognize how self-centered their thought is; indeed, as I suggested earlier, younger children don't seem to recognize that degrees of egocentricity exist; therefore, they cannot think of themseves as more (or less) egocentric than anyone else.

Adolescents are more advanced. They know that conclusions derive from mental processes, and they also know that these processes are not error-free. From these insights into their own thought process they learn to double-check and to verify their conclusions. From the moment of this insight (that one's own thought process is prone to error, and that errors can be discovered and corrected) young people live in a strained dialectic with their own intelligence.

Egocentrism persuades the thinker to accept an idea by whether it agrees with what "I" want, or with what "I" need, and in this persuasion, it impedes objective analysis and impartial thought; and as much as any single force, it contributes to fabled thinking.

THE DIFFERENCES BETWEEN EARLY ADOLESCENT AND LATE ADOLESCENT EGOCENTRISM

If we go back to the premises that guide this investigation we will recall that mental growth naturally moves from an egocentric orientation toward a sociocentric orientation, that thinking becomes increasingly decentered, and that with increased maturity the individual comes to recognize that other people have their own independent existence. Most current research supports the idea that adolescents undergo a gradual migration away from the egocentrism, which dominates the lives of children. Indeed, one of the gravest concerns that we have for late-adolescents as they approach graduation from high school, or as they prepare to leave for university or assume their first full-time job, is that they have not yet lost the egocentrism which typifies early and middle adolescents. (To arrive at one's 19th birthday locked into the egocentric patterns of a 13-year-old forewarns of a host of problems.)

We infer that egocentrism is lessening as a force within the personality (and the intellect) when sociocentric tendencies take a stronger position in day-to-day life, and when the individual experiences an ascendance of outside-the-self investments. About this there is not much dispute, as the issue is partly definitional (i.e., egocentrism is in decline when opposite characteristics are on the increase). The *causes* of egocentric decline, however, are not clear. We've observed for decades that the decline is correlated with increasing age, but age itself does not account for it. (As we will see in upcoming chapters, some young people become increasingly egocentric, increasingly narcissistic, and increasingly selfish with each successive adolescent year. This of course is something to be reckoned with.)

When we look at the behavior profiles of late-adolescents, we see that they as a rule are less egocentric than younger teens. A brief look at some age-based trends gives us a better feel for the differences between early and late adolescent egocentrism:

- During late-adolescence youth perceive more accurately the traits which define their personal uniqueness; as a result, their need for fables and fictions lessens.

- Late adolescents are developing their own standards of self-importance; therefore, they are less likely to think well of themselves merely because they are loved by their family or respected by their peers.

- Late adolescents become more accepting of the positive as well as the negative aspects of their nature; as a result, their sense of identity tends to be more consistent and freer from transient influences—hence, they are more capable of enduring commitments.

- Late adolescents are more adept than their younger brothers and sisters at *perceiving the unique personhood of others,* forcing them less frequently into accepting prejudices and stereotypes. They see more clearly the individuality of parents and relatives, and for this reason adults find them easier to get along with than younger adolescents, who for the most part lack insight into and empathy toward the adult personality.

- During late adolescence the trend is toward more continuous investments, partly in response to increased cultural demands for long-term decisions such as job and marriage, and partly in response to a personal identity more secure with itself and more certain about what is meaningful in the long run. This deepening of interests precipitates greater interest in "larger" issues, and mapping out long-range goals. Some psychologists claim that a general humanizing of values takes place at this age. Kimmel (1974, p. 81), for example, reports: "They are creating their value system out of their growing understanding and synthesis of their own feelings ... with more empathy to the needs of others while at the same time they are creating their own unifying philosophy of life." All this accords with an *expansion of caring,* a growing empathy with others, and a greater concern for their feelings.

- During late adolescence there is a greater tendency to identify oneself in terms of beliefs, morals, and ideologies. Late-adolescence is an age for committment, or at least for coming to grips with the necessity of commitment—a realization facilitated by the ability to see beyond immediate concerns.

- During late adolescence youth become more bound to the long-term calendar. A preoccupation with the future is possible only after hypothetical reasoning and a probabilistic view of future time are acquired.[10]

THE IMPACT OF EGOCENTRISM ON
ADOLESCENT SPEECH

> How can I know what I think till I see what I say?
> —G. Wallas

It is literally impossible to grasp the nature of youth without taking into account their egocentrism. In the next chapter I will describe how egocentrism shapes the adolescent's belief system, how it predisposes teens to believe they are performing before an audience, to believe that they are completely unique, to believe that society should be reformed to better gratify their particular needs, and to believe that they are immune from undesired consequences. Here, however, in the final moment of this chapter, I want to briefly describe how egocentrism influences speech.

The speech of 3-, 4-, and 5-year-olds almost always reflects their own immediate perspective, their own immediate desires. Their use of language is so privately grounded that they often use words and symbols completely meaningless to everyone else. It is not even clear that 4-year-olds have a conception of what a "point of view" means. Because their communications are self-based, preschoolers may speak right past each other without paying any attention to what kids next to them are saying. Elementary teachers know it is impossible to communicate effectively with first- or second-grade children without first sharing their frame—seeing with their eyes—for these children cannot, with much proficiency, climb out of their own frame or see through the eyes of the teacher.

Here is how Miller described the "collective monologue" of children:

> Children who apparently are talking together while playing in a group may actually be talking, but not necessarily together. Each child's remarks are unrelated to anyone else's. There is a collective monolog, of sorts, rather than a conversation. For example, one child's statement, "I think I saw Superman in a phone booth yesterday," might be followed by "this sweater makes me itch" from another child. (1989, p. 58)

Children assume that the listener will decode the intended meaning of a statement without the benefit of precise language. (Anxious adolescents make the same assumption.) Thus the child may blurt to the mother, "She dropped it on him," without explaining who "she" is, what "it" is, or who "him" is. Mothers understand these sentences by adding the necessary information the child left out, which, of course, they do with remarkable facility.

Before we begin our look at adolescent speech, we should make clear that adolescents are effective conversationalists in most situations, especially non-threatening ones. In most settings their command of the rules of conversation (known as pragmatics) is commendable; they take their turn in conversation far better than children, and they are usually able to recognize when speech might be lost in the hubbub of confusion or distraction. They know how to use questions to convey commands (Why is everyone talking so loud at the dinner table?); how to deploy articles such as "the" and "a" in ways to enhance understanding (She is *the* person to see if you want a job); and how to tell stories, jokes, and anecdotes to entertain guests of varying ages. Despite these allocentric qualities, their speech is frequently encumbered with egocentric peculiarities, and they are the focus here.

Donaldson hit the mark perfectly: "For a conversation to go smoothly, each participant needs to try to understand what the other knows already, does not know, needs to know for his purposes, wants to know for his pleasure" (1978, p. 18). Donaldson describes a sophisticated, listener-based style of communication that shares a good deal with what Grice called "effective communication."

Effective communication, according to Grice, is governed by four maxims:

- The maxim of quantity: Speak neither more nor less than required.
- The maxim of quality: Speak the truth and avoid falsehood.
- The maxim of relevance: Speak in a relevant and informative way.
- The maxim of clarity: Speak so as to avoid obscurity and ambiguity. (Grice, 1975, p. 45)

Effective speech is objective and listener-grounded, whereas egocentric speech is subjective and self-grounded; effective speech takes into account the perspective of the listener whereas egocentric speech is entrenched in private perspective.[11]

Egocentric speech produces sluggish thought. "Late" is superior to "1:30 a.m.," because any time can be late but only one time can be 1:30 a.m. "Out," is superior to "at John's house" because out can be many places but John's house only one place. Collectively, "out late" is much preferred to "at John's house until 1:30 a.m." The value of imprecise speech is easy to see: It expands freedom. Imprecise speech decreases accountability; precise speech increases it. Egocentric speech preserves self-priority.

Why are adolescents drawn to egocentric speech? Egocentric speech makes everything pertaining to "me" more important than anything that isn't. Its allure is in its narcissistic utility.

During the course of the adolescent years egocentric speech generally decreases in frequency and declines in power; when it does not we suspect developmental delay, anticipate an increase in the adolescent's narcissistic tendencies, and usually we observe a reluctance to accept the responsibilities of approaching adulthood. Perhaps the most positive thing we can say about egocentric speech is that it keeps the growing person centered in himself (herself), and helps him (her) to face challenges that can otherwise be overpowering.[12]

INDICATORS THAT EGOCENTRISM IS IN DECLINE

> When I was 13, 14, and 15, I hated both of my parents, I hated their rules, and everything else about them. They didn't understand me at all. At around 16 or 17 my views started changing (I moved to college when I was 17). Near the end of my 17th year I got closer to my parents and, now at 19, my parents are my best friends. I tell them almost everything, and even though they are three hours away from Edmonton I talk to them every other day.
>
> —19-year-old university students response to the question: "Did your attitude toward your parents change during adolescence?"

One may assume that egocentrism is losing its influence when the adolescent begins:

- to recognize that others have a private existence that parallels "my" existence, and that others have rights that parallel "my" rights.
- to recognize that adults possess their own private individuality, and their own unique history; when adults are not perceived as merely part of the impersonal "other."
- to lessen his (her) demands that others always see things from "my" point of view. (No small accomplishment if we believe, along with philosopher Thomas Nagel, that "the capacity to put oneself in another person's shoes is behind most altruistic behavior" (1975, p. 64).)
- to realize that others share parallel feelings and life experiences, and although these parallels are not perfect duplicates of one's own experience, they are close enough to be meaningfully shared.
- to understand that he (she) shares important commonalities with others; when the fable of complete singularity begins to fade.
- to join social gatherings without assuming that his or her arrival carries great significance.

In my experience over many years of working first-hand with teens I have found that very few *early* adolescents attain much distance from their egocentric nature; *middle* adolescents master several of the above indicators, but rarely all of them. *Late* adolescents exhibit a far greater facility, and are thereby transported away from the intense egocentrism of their younger brothers and sisters. Indeed, this march away from egocentrism is one reason older adolescents have the potential to be such good counsellors to younger teens.[13]

POSTSCRIPT

Egocentrism makes it difficult for the individual to differentiate between...how things ought to be and...how things are.
—Rolf E. Muuss (1988, p. 271)

If a more pressing issue than egocentrism exists in adolescent psychology it has eluded me. Although I am not as extreme as Piaget, who according to W. R. Looft (1972), claimed that "egocentricity of thought...has perhaps been the central problem in the history of human existence," I am convinced that the consequences of egocentrism are profound in every aspect of adolescent life: in private thinking, in peer evaluations, in confrontations with parents, and most assuredly in the adolescent's fascination with pop culture.

Egocentrism can be seen as a Great Wall of China designed to keep impartial reason out while self-interest and self-absorption flourish within. Breaching this Great Wall is part of the adolescent adventure; but all adolescents are not the same, some dash headlong through the slightest opening while others (like the great Dynastic Emperors) are content to remain behind the security of their Great Wall. The consequences of using one's egocentrism (and one's narcissism) as barriers to the outside world is the object of our concern in upcoming chapters.

To assist those readers who seek a brief overview of the major ideas put forth in this chapter, the following summary is provided.

- Egocentrism is an *embeddedness* in one's own point of view. Its "pure" form is expressed in the natural selfishness of children, who reduce all experience to their own point of view and therefore distort without awareness.
- Late adolescents are less egocentric in thought, manners and morals than early adolescents. They are more accepting of both positive and negative aspects of their nature, they possess greater ego identity and see more clearly the individuality of parents and relatives, they experience a deepening of interests, and a greater certainty about what is meaningful in the long run. All in all, late adolescents are so comprehensively more mature than early adolescents that it is easy to think of them as in separate developmental stages.
- The "conquest" of egocentrism means that one perceives in increasingly accurate terms the thoughts, moods, and emotions of others.
- We assume that egocentrism is in a state of decline:

  - When the adolescent begins to perceive adults as individuals with their own private individuality.
  - When the adolescent accepts that it is impossible for another person to completely understand what it is like "to be me."

- When the adolescent ceases to demand that others always accept his (her) point of view.
- When the fable of total singularity begins to lose power.

What we do not fully understand in all this is why most youngsters become less egocentric during their adolescent tenure, yet some become more egocentric; why most youngsters become increasingly clear in their thinking, yet others become increasingly clouded; why most youngsters become more accurate in their social perceptions, yet others become more distortional; and, finally, why some youth expand in sharing and cooperation, yet others harden into a narcissistic selfishness.

With these unknowns beckoning, we are now ready to embark upon a deeper look at how egocentrism shapes the adolescent character.

3

Fables and Fabled Thinking

Every powerful emotion has its own myth-making tendency.
—Bertrand Russell

Fables are not unique to adolescents. Adults and children are also inclined
to fabled thinking, and their capacity for it is well documented in the literature
of personality psychology. But here we are concerned with the fables of
adolescents because they are, in structure and genesis, different from the fables
created either by children or by adults. My intent, therefore, is to try to explain
how age-based, developmental processes (both intellectual and emotional)
encourage fabled thinking during adolescence.

In the previous chapter I spoke in general terms about egocentrism and how,
as a rule, it lessens during late-adolescence and how this lessening contributes
to the adult-like features we associate with late-adolescence. In this chapter
I will take a look at how egocentrism encourages adolescents to misperceive
the actions of others, to misunderstand the motives of others, and to misread
their own individuality.

To fully appreciate the adolescent, like the seven-layered cake, we must slice
all the way through, from top to bottom, and take the bitter with the sweet.
What psychologists have discovered in sifting through the many layers of
adolescent life, is that the intelligence which shapes morality and guides
behavior is not a single, unified force, but that it is made up of rational and
irrational imperatives, right and wrong reasoning, facts and fables, positive
and negative illusions.

With fables we get a bit closer to the edge than we prefer. The risk is that
we will begin to think of adolescent thought as a kind of shamanistic magicalism,

and this is not so, not even close. The adolescent thought process is not governed by fables, but it is predisposed to them, especially when they are socially advantageous or narcissistically comforting. The opposite extreme is the fictitious belief that adolescents are, at bottom, completely rational thinkers who easily produce orderly and coherent thought. This also is not so, and probably never has been. Accepting this inclines us to believe wrongly that adolescent fables come from the outside (i.e., from peer pressure or imitation) or from chance rather than from mental operations inherent to their thought process.

In ordinary parlance, a fable is a brief narrative which makes edifying points through animals that speak and act like human beings, as in *Aesop's Fables*. This is not our usage. In our usage a fable is a self-serving deception, or an irrational conclusion which better allows one to follow one's desires and inclinations. In fables belief supercedes reality, and facts are bent to fit one's ends; they are "bent," not "broken," because fables must have an appearance of truth. A fable that is obviously false or blatantly stupid is not of much use to anyone. A fabulist, therefore, is an inventor and a creator of semi-truths. Fables are not a sign of mental illness; they do not even suggest a fundamental malfunction within the perceptual process—especially as far as adolescents are concerned.

Certain researchers claim that the fables come into existence from lack of education. This is not right. Fables are constructed from the mind's intrinsic creativity and nourished by the predisposition to create narcissistically comforting conclusions; they are the embodiment of self-enhancing intelligence. Good education helps youngsters to double-check and rethink their fables, even to discard some of the most ridiculous ones, but lack of education does not account for their existence. In the simplest possible language, fables are a natural product of the adolescent thought process.[14]

The fables of youth are not barely believable creations of the imagination, or completely fictional contrivances, ideas from the edge of some remote galaxy; when we think of them this way we miss their utility, their truth, and most importantly, their believablity to the fabulist. All fables *must* possess a believable element, otherwise they cannot pass the inspection of even a modest intelligence; fables sometimes shade and darken the truth, and they sometimes inflate the truth, but they never completely destroy it because a fable must be believable otherwise it is just an absurdity. As Piattelli-Palmarini says in his exciting work *Inevitable Illusions*, "There is always some truth in any illusion; there is always some persuasion in a fallacy" (1994, p. 31). And so it is with fables.

The fables described in this chapter are not false and phony portraits of how a small percent of teens think, rather, they indicate how the adolescent thought process bends and shapes reality. Fables, for the most part, are created *reflexively* (without conscious intent), and then they are crafted into a coherent, believable (at least to some) story. Despite the initial plausibility of some fables, they are rarely convincing before a healthy skepticism, and this is one reason adolescents prefer companions who are not likely to dismantle their fables. The fables described in this chapter occur with such regularity in the community of teens that they can be thought of as normal in the statistical sense of that word, but they can also be thought of as abnormal (unhealthy) when they lead to destructive outcomes.

When we talk about the adolescent predispositon to create fables we are not breaking fresh territory. In the 1920s Jean Piaget reported that the adolescent thought process periodically operates as though the world should bend to it rather than it to the world (a remarkable testament to the power of narcissism in the thought process), and that they also sometimes seem to accept that the world should submit to their own idealistic views rather than to the systems of reality upon which they already operate (Piaget, 1928).[15]

But enough of these preliminaries. It is now time to peer into the adolescent thought process to see if we can better grasp how fables come to life. We are drawn to five basic fables: the fable of the audience, the fable of total uniqueness, the fable of invincibility, the pregnancy fable, and the idealism fable.

THE FABLE OF PERFORMING BEFORE AN AUDIENCE

All the world's a stage, And all the men and women merely players, And one man in his time plays many parts.
—William Shakespeare

For, when they come together, each young person is an actor to himself or to herself and a spectator to everyone else.
—David Elkind

Teens sometimes do not know for sure when they have an audience and when they don't, a confusion of no small consequence to their day-to-day lives. For starters, the thinking of many adolescents is stamped with the presumption that people are paying attention to them when they are not, and that they are concerned about them when they are not. Here is one way to think about how this blurs social perceptions.

The adolescent is continually constructing, or reacting to, an imaginary audience. It is an audience because the adolescent believes that he will be the focus of attention; and it is imaginary because, in actual social situations, this is not usually the case.... The construction of imaginary audiences would seem to account, in part at least, for a wide variety of typical adolescent behaviors and experiences.... When the young person is feeling critical of himself, he anticipates that the audience ... will be critical too. The adolescent's wish for privacy and his reluctance to reveal himself may, to some extent, be a reaction to the feelings of being under the constant, critical scrutiny of other people. (Elkind, 1967, p. 1030)

The sense of always being evaluated produces within the adolescent an exaggerated self-consciousness similar to what adults experience during a job interview; a blistering self-consciousness which causes them to mold every sentence just so to elicit the desired reaction from the interviewer. As the adult is on stage in the job interview, so the adolescent is on stage in the presence of peers, parents, and passersby. One 20-year-old, describing his adolescent years, recalled: "I was obsessed with the thought that everyone was always watching me. I was always conscious about what I was doing, just in case someone was watching and would sometimes do things just because someone was watching (or so I thought)."

The imaginary audience excites a sense of being outside and inside the self at exactly the same instant; two selves in the same body, one acting while the other is watching the act. One person recalled of his teen years:

> I was always conscious of how other people saw my reactions. It was as though there were two of me. One part was living my life, feeling happy and sad, excited and disappointed. The other part was outside of me watching and noting my effect on others. The outside part enjoyed getting sympathy, attention, and praise. It could romanticize even the worst situations. It put me in the place of the injured heroine from the movies. It was the part of me that imagined what people would say about me if I were to die, and wished to be involved in tragedies for the effect of it. The inside of me did the feelings. (Garrod, et al., 1992, p. 176)

This mode of thinking invites paranoid beliefs and, secondarily, a fascination with the idea that they themselves are paranoid. Ask an adolecent you know well if he ever thinks he is paranoid. If the conversation flows naturally, without being steered, you will most likely observe that the adolescent does not walk away from this idea, or even view it scornfully; rather, the idea proves intrinsically fascinating because it provides the opportunity for the self to investigate itself and then to talk about itself. If your adolescent friend doesn't know the meaning of the word "paranoid," the same results are obtained by inserting the word "weird."

How the Imaginary Audience Differs from Childhood Fantasy

Children do not have the mental capacity to construct the complex imaginary audiences which adolescents assemble routinely. The imagination of children, although vivid and exciting, simply cannot negotiate the complex demands of an imaginary audience. The imaginary audience, as we are here describing it, cannot come into being until the onset of formal thought and the range of intellectual skills which come with it.

> The main point about the imaginary audience is the fact that it is imaginary, not real. *What young adolescents can do, and what children cannot do, is create such audiences in their head.* Where the young adolescent has difficulty is in recognizing the subjectivity of his or her own mental constructions. The young teenager has trouble in differentiating between the concerns of others he or she has created and concerns which are properly his or her own. So, the fact that children can infer the thoughts or feelings of others given the situational context, does not really speak to the issue of the imaginary audience, which is mental construction and not social reality. (Elkind, 1985, original emphasis)

To further explain how the imaginings of children differ from the imaginary audiences of teens, Elkind offers this:

> A child reconstructs the thought of an existing person or persons. But an adolescent reconstructs the thought of a person or persons *whom they themselves have created or constructed.* The imaginary audience is a second-order, not a first-order symbolic construction. (1985, p. 222-223, original emphasis)

All of which brings us to our final point: The intellectual complexity of the imaginary audience is well beyond the developmental range of children. It cannot blossom until the treasures of formal thought have enriched the adolescent's intellectual capital; it is, ironically, a perceptual regression born of a mental progression.

THE FABLE OF TOTAL UNIQUENESS

> When I say "I" I mean a thing absolutely unique,
> not to be confused with any other.
> —Ugo Betti

The tendency to think of oneself as completely different from everyone else on the planet is called "the fable of total uniqueness." This fable grows out of the narcissistic premise that one's experiences are more profound, one's thoughts are more advanced, and one's fears are more intense than anyone else's. Because of this fabled uniqueness, it is thought that no other person can know the pain of my suffering, can comprehend the profundity of my convictions, or imagine the depths of my love. "I" am a sun unto myself, completely unique and totally singular. Under the influence of this fable it is not a wonder that teens feel hopelessly isolated from the rest of us. And so it is with adolescent love:

> A young woman who falls in love for the first time is enraptured with the experience, which is entirely new and thrilling. But she fails to differentiate between what is new and thrilling for herself and what is new and thrilling to humankind. It is not surprising, therefore, that this young lady says to her mother. "But Mother, you don't know how it feels to be in love." (Elkind, 1978)

From their special perch, youth come to believe that they see what others cannot and experience passions grander than anything known to their friends, teachers, and most assuredly, their parents. This misperception prevents them from recognizing what they share with others and encourages an obsession with the particular at the expense of the universal. The egocentric immersion of this fable prevents youth from seeing how principles which apply to others also to them, and vice-versa. It is through this process that the fable, "I am an island unto myself," gathers force in the adolescent personality.

In summary, the uniqueness fable is based on the presumption that I am so unique that no one could possibly grasp my thoughts, or fathom the depth of my emotions. The first fable we discussed, the imaginary audience, places the adolescent on center stage in direct view of knowing eyes, whereas the second fable, the uniqueness fable, places him in leprous isolation from an audience of strangers who could never understand him even if they tried. These fables disorient the self in relation to others, increase the attraction to heroic individualism, and impede participation in the lives of others.

THE FABLE OF INVINCIBILITY (ALSO KNOWN AS THE FABLE OF INVULNERABILITY)

> The extreme risk taking of certain youths requires neither coercion nor ignorance of the likely consequences.
> —William Gardner (1993)

The issue is not whether teens are risk takers, because we accept as a starting point that they are. Whether we are talking about the 1950's "chicken" players in their hotrods speeding toward each other on a collision course, or the 1990's "surfistas" riding on the top of high-speed commuter train cars in Rio de Janeiro with high-voltage wires inches above their heads, the risk-taking habits of adolescents are no rarity. Indeed, there has never been a culture anywhere, to my knowledge, where adolescence is known as a time of reduced risk taking. In North America, for example, the mortality rate increases by about 200%

from early to late adolescence, the single largest percent increase in any two consecutive age cohorts in the life cycle; injuries account for most of this increase. Death rates from motor vehicle injuries increase by about 390% (in Canada 58% of all traffic accidents involve 16- to 21-year-olds, and in the province of Alberta, Canada, during 1995 one-half of all motocycle deaths involved drivers under the age of 18); homicide by about 590%, and other unintentional injuries by about 75% between early and late adolescence. Other forms of risk-taking are also evident; for example, one in seven adolescents in the U.S. have contracted a sexually transmitted disease, a level twice as high as for people in their 20s. (See Irwin, 1993, for further data on this topic.)

The Puzzle of Educated Risk-Taking

In their ongoing investigations of intravenous drug users in Alberta, Ann Marie Pagliaro and Louis Pagliaro (1993) found that many of their subjects have a relatively high level of knowledge of HIV/AIDS. The authors conclude that among the more than 800 drug users they interviewed, knowledge about how HIV is transmitted is fairly sophisticated. *Nevertheless, users perceive that their own risk of contracting HIV is very low despite the fact that they are participating in high risk drug use and sexual behavior.* According to the Pagliaros, these individuals deny what they know, or believe that what they know somehow does not apply to them; they "harbour illusions of unique invulnerability" (1993, p. 12). These illusions interest us because they exist side by side with objective knowledge which directly contradicts them.

Fables of immunity observed among North American teens

- Pregnancy will never happen to me.[16]
- Car accidents will never happen to me.
- Drug addiction will never happen to me.
- Alcohol addiction will never happen to me.
- Cigarette smoking, tobacco chewing will not harm me.
- The police will never arrest me.
- Marriage problems will never happen to me.
- The usual consequences of behavior do not apply to me.

The research findings of the Pagliaros are not isolated, indeed they support the research findings of Moore and Rosenthal (1993), who investigated adolescent attitudes on the same topic. "This is a common theme among heterosexual adolescents in their responses to the threat of AIDS, the 'not-me' myth. It is clear that most adolescents have not personalized the risk of HIV/AIDS, *perceiving the illness as a threat to others, not themselves.*[17] This is consistent with the belief that adolescents' thinking is characterized, in part, by the 'personal fable'" (1993, p. 128). Then, in further support of how illusions increase risk-taking, Moore and Rosenthal observe:

> Adolescents' belief that it 'can't happen to me' has been shown to influence risk-taking in a variety of health-related situations including smoking and contraceptive use. In a recent study of British adolescents, Abrams et al. (1990) found high levels of concern about the presence of the HIV virus in the community *but little evidence of concern about their own levels of risk.* (1993, p. 129, original emphasis)

Defying the improbable

The attitude of invulnerability is not as irrational or as impulsive as some psychologists make it out to be. For the most part, it involves defying the unlikely, and confronting the improbable; but in most instances the odds are in the adolescent's favor. We all do this kind of thing. When we speed through a just-turned-red light, when we drink too much before driving home, and when we fudge on our income tax, we are risking penalty, but at a level of probability we are willing to chance. Teens follow a parallel line of logic, if we can call it that, in their invulnerability fables, but the difference between adult and adolescent invulnerability fables are twofold. First, the adolescent has a limited ability to estimate the likelihood that negative consequences will follow a particular action. Second, the adolescent's capacity for future analysis is too weak to accurately calculate the price "I" must pay for defying the odds. (Reckless driving, diving into water of undetermined depth, and the use of guns to settle disputes are examples of adolescent behavior clouded by the invulnerability fable).[18]

The fable of invulnerability encourages a continuous defiance of the improbable and, as we know, all unlikely events will eventually take place given enough chances. What we usually discover is that the young defy probable outcome when it relates to narcissistic cravings, to fear, or to peer acceptance. When these three conditions are eliminated teens are remarkably clear thinkers.

PREGNANCY FABLES

Pregnancy doesn't run in my family.
—Sixteen-year-old girl's response to why she doesn't use contraception.

No adolescent fable has more significance to teens (and to society-at-large) than the fable which asserts "I" will not become pregnant. The pregnancy fable is perhaps the most complex adolescent fable, as it requires the acceptance of certain truths and the rejection of others. It is a classic fable in its composition, and a nightmare in its outcome.

The pregnancy fable is bolstered by the invulnerability fable (others become pregnant, but I will not), by the uniqueness fable (my love is so unique that it could not result in an unwanted outcome), by egocentric idealism (if I do have a baby it will be perfect, as will my relationship with it). The pregnancy fable is complicated even further by the fact that it is powerfully reinforced by fidelity (the impulse to bond), and particularization (the belief that one's love is caused solely by the love partner). All of these experiences take place at a time of life when the girl is experiencing her sexuality in a richer and more profound way than ever before, when she is searching for her own sexual identity, and when she is trying to figure out the emotional peculiarities of her boyfriend. Thus, while the fable itself is rather straightforward, the dynamics which create it are not.

One 16-year-old I interviewed was convinced that she would never become pregnant, despite having unprotected sex with her boyfriend "more than several times" per month, because, in her own words, "pregnancy does not run in my family." However, while espousing her invulnerability to the consequences of sexual intercourse, she refused to drink alcohol because of the increased risks it posed while driving, she refused to smoke cigarettes because they increase the risk of disease, and she refused to experiment with drugs because she did not want to risk being arrested. All of these struck me as reasoned, calculated viewpoints, which cohabited with pregnancy beliefs which were ill-reasoned and laced with denial. This uneven reasoning is everyday fare among adolescents. The lesson to be learned in all this is that fabled thinking, like temper tantrums, binge eating, and moodiness, *appear in episodic bursts*. They are not permanent qualities of the adolescent personality—more like uninvited visitors.

Most young people have a friend, or parent, suffering the calamities from which they claim exemption. These human tragedies are not denied in their totality, and to perceive adolescent denial in this way is to miss the overall picture. Rather, the adolescent acknowledges these tragedies as facts of human life, but, as facts which affect me differently than they affect everyone else. Why? Because I live by different rules, different probabilities, and different consequences. And why am "I" different from the others? Because "I" am completely unique. Rules, probabilities and consequences are for others.

The conclusion that presents itself in this matter is that adolescents have considerable difficulty assessing probable outcome in emotionally charged topics. And while this might, on first glance, seem harmless, it is not. The failure to infer *probable* outcome contributes to adolescent mortality, to adolescent unemployment, to adolescent drug use, to adolescent gang membership, to adolescent runaways, and of course, to adolescent pregnancy. *Nothing is more relevant to adolescent life than to predict accurately the outcome of one's actions.*

Consider that almost all pregnant teens report being surprised at finding themselves pregnant. (A. Phoenix (1991), in her investigation of young mothers, reports that 82 percent of pregnant adolescent girls had not planned to get pregnant.) When adolescent girls are asked how they planned to avoid pregnancy a stunning range of fables emerge.[19a] For example:

- the belief that they did not have sex often enough to become pregnant;
- the belief that they did not experience an orgasm, and therefore, could not conceive;
- the belief they were "too young" to become pregnant;
- the belief that they would not be "caught" during high risk days (even when they understood the ovulation cycle);
- the belief that it couldn't happen to "me."[19b]

In a superbly documented investigation of adolescent sexual behavior, which Maccoby described as "by far the best thing that's been written on the subject," Moore and Rosenthal (1993) make pertinent observations on the adolescent thought process. They report:

> In some ways, these young women are reminiscent of the 'invulnerable' adolescents.... These are young people who believe that they are unlikely to suffer the negative consequences of their actions, and hence take risks that others would not. (p. 149)

Upon close inspection one usually discovers that these beliefs are not acquired from friends, from parents, or from TV; they are neither copied nor stolen. Rather, these beliefs are the creation of a mental process which reflexively manufactures protective fables and comforting illusions when emotionally charged topics are first investigated.[20]

Can Teens Reason Clearly When it Comes to Sex?

> Teenagers are not able, as a rule, to be mature
> and responsible about sexual relating.
> —Lauren Ayers (1994)

All thinking about pregnancy is not fabled. But this does not mean that it is reasoned and objective, nor does it mean that one can talk about it openly with one's boyfriend. Thinking about pregnancy does not necessarily convert to action, or even to discussion. One sexually active girl said:

> I didn't ask him about it and he didn't ask me about it. It was really strange because I was terrified that I was going to get pregnant. I always thought about

it, worried about it, *but I couldn't do any thing about it.* Although we didn't use contraception, and we didn't talk about it, I thought about it constantly, and I was scared. I even wrote a paper about teenage pregnancy for a psychology class. I remember working on it thinking, "This could be you, you have to do something about this." I remember having this feeling that I HAD to talk to him about it, but I couldn't. It seemed easier not to say anything and put it out of my mind, to try to forget about it. (Garrod et al., 1992, p. 252)

Perhaps things are not really this complicated. Perhaps girls become pregnant simply because they cannot restrain themselves when they are sexually aroused. Perhaps their thinking is not fabled, merely overruled by lust. Among early- and middle-adolescent girls this explanation seems lacking because, according to youngsters themselves, the sexual act is not emotionally overpowering. During the early years of adolescence, intercourse almost always has to do with something beyond the sexual. It is expressed sexually, but sexual desire is not the dominant cause.

Pleasure does not appear to be a driving force in a teen girl's decision to become sexually involved with a boy; rather girls seem to enter into the relationship as a rite of passage that they must undergo. When a girl says that she feels it's time that she had sex with a boy her decision does not stem from unrestrainable passion. (Ayers, 1994, p. 163)

If not from passion, from what? That is the question to which we have not as yet discovered an acceptable answer. Our ignorance is based on the fact that youth themselves do not know with certainty *why* they engage in sexual intercourse, and equally perplexing, they usually don't know with much certainty why they *abstain* from sexual intercourse.[21]

THE FABLE OF A PURE AND LOFTY IDEALISM

> A fantasy is always more satisfying and credible if someone else can be
> made to believe it.
> —Karl Meninger

Like their elders, adolescents dream of greater things and better days. These dreams spring from their intelligence, their idealism and their egocentrism, but the relative mix is never easy to determine. Wadsworth claimed that much of what passes for adolescent idealism is "false" and "incomplete" because the thinking process which produces idealism is routinely swamped by its own egocentricity. "The reasoning of adolescents...seems to be idealistic. The idealism can be viewed as false, or incomplete, idealism. What looks like idealism frequently, in reality, is reasoning based on egocentric use of formal thought" (1989, p. 138). Hence, the idealism of youth is real but not pure. A small matter if you recognize that self-enhancement plays at least some role in every idealistic system, but a great matter if you are one of those adults who naively accepts that all youthful idealism is grounded in innocent detachment and open-eyed objectivity.

Perhaps nowhere is this seen more clearly than in the idealism of youth who Inhelder and Piaget (1958) called *idealistic reformers*. Idealistic reformers claim that they want to transform society in order to make it better, but the real motivation behind their desire is to better satisfy their own needs, desires and cravings.

> The adolescent not only tries to adapt his ego to the social environment but, just as emphatically, *tries to adjust the environment to his ego*. In other words, when he begins to think about the society in which he is looking for a place, he has to think about his own future activity and about how he himself might transform this society. The result is a failure to distinguish between his point of view as an individual called upon to organize a life program and the point of view of the group which he hopes to reform. (p. 146, original emphasis)

Idealistic reformers are obsessed with talking about their reforms, how they will initiate them, how dissenters will be punished, how these changes are destined by history, by race, by gender. One investigator described a similar tendency among troubled adults which may be worth a moment of our time:

> A sure symptom of this neurosis is the effort such individuals make to be certain that other people know about their unorthodox views as soon as possible on making their acquaintance. They are prone to whipping out their opinions, apropos of nothing at all, merely to flaunt them publicly. Because they value the unpopularity of their ideas, they are unlikely to do much to further general acceptance of these views, regardless of their protestations. They are more interested in shocking than communicating. (Putney & Putney, 1964, p. 61)

Ideology and Idealistic Reform

Ideology is the system of ideas, beliefs, and attitudes that make up a world view; it is the doctrine that guides political plans, and provides the strategy for putting them into operation. An ideologue is one who adheres to, believes in, and advocates the truth of a particular system of thought. The power of ideology (as far as the adolescent is concerned) is in its power to explain mystery and to resolve contradiction and, in this regard, it holds the same attraction as myth and illusion.

Idealistic reformers are attracted to ideology that justifies their desired reforms. Something of a dependency circuit exists here because reform cannot take place without an ideology to guide it, and ideology cannot guide without reformers to put it into action. And here the connection is forged: Youth are drawn to the coherence of ideologues and ideologues are attracted to the energy of youth. Youthful reformers and older ideologues exist symbiotically, each filling a need of the other. In today's society, it is pretty much axiomatic that wherever one appears so does the other.

From what we have thus far discussed it appears that idealistic reformers are a somewhat unpredictable mixture of devotion to self and to humanity, and the onlooker is never completely sure when the devotion is to one or to the other. How is such a potion brewed? How can the idealistic reformer be compassionate toward humankind and yet be driven by selfish needs and private fears? David Elkind provides us with an especially fruitful insight:

> The young person can conceive of ideal families, religions, and societies and when he compares these with his own family, religion, and society he often finds the latter wanting. Much of adolescent rebellion against adult society derives, in part at least, from this new capacity to construct ideal situations. The ideals, however, are almost entirely intellectual and the young person has little conception of how they might be made into realities and even less interest in working toward their fulfillment. (1974, p. 103)

The current divined in every fable is pretty much the same, not in content, but in consequence, and that is that they make self large and non-self small. *How* youth clasp these fables to their bosom is a mystery, but *why* they do isn't.

FINAL OBSERVATIONS ON THE FABLES OF ADOLESCENCE

> We don't see things as they are. We see them as we are.
> —*The Talmud*

It has been emphasized throughout that fables are not mere *diverimenti* in the adolescent's mental ecology, and that they carry profound implications in day-to-day behavior—especially the pregnancy fable ("I will not become pregnant"), and the immunity fable ("I will not experience the negative consequences associated with this behavior"). Fables cause youth to underestimate or overestimate the probability that certain events will (or will not) occur; they distort reality and, therefore, they twist one's relationship with it.

We are still very naive, of course. We really do not have a very polished understanding of the adolescent thought process and we are not terribly enlightened about either their brightness or their dullness. But we do know that adolescents are predisposed to manufacture fables, and this, all things considered, contributes more to their dullness than to their brightness. Fables, like all myth and fantastic legend, embroil the natural with the supernatural, the real with the greater-than-real, and in this mixture we discover their truth and their purpose.

A fable is not a superstition as much as a subliminal inflation. Fables stand halfway between wishful thinking and the simple assumption of good fortune. I do not want to convey the impression that the realignment of thought necessary to produce fables occurs only in deviant or disturbed youth; the mental shuffling required of fable creation is part and parcel of the adolescent thought process. All adolescents, quite obviously, do not subscribe to all of the fables described in this chapter and some adolescents don't subscribe to any of them; but all adolescents, at one time or another, pay homage to fables.

In this chapter I overviewed several fables, including:[22]

- the fable that one is being watched, evaluated, scrutinized and, in general, the object of everyone's attention when this is not the case—the fable of the imaginary audience.
- the fable of uniqueness where the adolescent fails to recognize the commonalities he (she) shares with others, and views himself (herself) as a solitary island in an indifferent sea—the fable of total uniqueness.
- the fable of personal invulnerabilty (sometimes called "the invincibility fable" or "the immunity fable") leads the individual to believe that the laws of probability do not apply to "me." This fable gains momentum when the individual is emotionally charged, and when narcissistic gratification is on the line. This fable is situation-grounded and emotion-driven rather than free-floating. Fables, afterall, are exceptions to the adolescent's general tendency toward rational thinking and objective analysis; they are abberations in an otherwise powerful thought process.
- the fable that negative consequences will not accrue from sexual activity. I called this the "pregnancy fable," but it could as easily have been called "the AIDS fable," or "the STD fable," or "the immunity to natural consequences fable."
- the fable of a pure and lofty idealism imbues the young person with the belief that his (her) ideals are better than anyone else's, and that the reforms suggested by them are in *everyone's* best interest.
- the fable that those who believe in "me" and "my" reforms are noble and worthy.

I have tried to indicate how a feeling of unease cloaks these fables because the objective portion of the adolescent's thought process usually recognizes that they are, at bottom, fiction, but this awareness is not enough to reason (or muscle) them out of existence. It is encouraging to learn that fables do not remain convincing to the adolescent forever, and that most of them are discarded or outgrown, but they are convincing in their moment.

Finally, we return one last time to Rolf Muuss. "Egocentrism...makes it difficult for the individual to differentiate between...how things ought to be and...how things are" (1988, p. 271). The implications of this statement, assuming its general truthfulness, are momentous and affect profoundly our view of how and why youth create fables. For what could possibly be more important to a young person than difficulty differentiating between how things ought to be and how things are? Yet, when all is said and done, this is at the heart of every adolescent fable.

4

The Emotionalization
of Thought

> The head is always fooled by the heart.
> —Francois, duc de La Rochefoucauld

Writers who claim to know how adolescents think have their hands full; but an extra burden is placed on those of us who are so bold as to claim to know how they *fail to think*. In a nutshell, however, that is exactly what this chapter is about—why teens sometimes fail to think effectively, and why they sometimes fail to think, period. My aim is to show how clear, coherent thought is periodically sabotaged by emotionality and by affective logic.[23]

AFFECTIVE LOGIC

> All of us, in our several ways, are illogical, irrational.
> —H. L. Mencken

Youth is a time of intellectual industry and intellectual laziness, of critical analysis and critical lapses, of penetrating insight and dopey platitudes; understanding how these mental opposites work in the same person at the same time is the business of adolescent psychology. But, like so many mysteries of the second decade of life, they have not yielded much to progress. What is clear is that the thought process of teens does not stay on one track; rather, it skips back-and-forth between impartial reason and emotion-charged logic, and in skipping back-and-forth it is prone to errors and inaccuracy.

Jean Piaget was among the first to observe that even though formal reasoning is available to teens they often do not use it because they lack familarity with the tasks they are required to reason about. He also observed that the ability to reason does not exist on a one-to-one relationship with its expression; that is, to have reason is not necessarily to use it. "Individuals who have developed, and who thus have this type of reasoning available in their cognitive repertoire, may, in fact, prefer to reason on a concrete level, *or not to reason at all in many situations.*" Furthermore: "It may be the case that although an individual has developed the competence to reason formally, the individual may not have developed the appropriate strategies or procedures to best access and apply this competence" (Overton, 1991, p. 741).

Cool logic is of two types, *inductive* and *deductive.* Inductive logic is a method of reasoning by which a general law or principle is inferred from observed particular instances. It is the process by which we conclude that what is true of certain individuals is true of a class, that what is true of part is true of the whole, or what is true at certain times will be true in similar circumstances at all times. Deductive logic begins with a general premise and from it inferences are drawn; it is a reasoning that flows from general to particular statements. Deductive logic is the only form of reasoning in which the premises provide conclusive evidence for the truth of the conclusions. Reasoning would be: "If computers are used for business, then the cost of such a computer merits a tax deduction." However, "This computer is used for business," therefore, "The cost of this computer merits a tax deduction," is deductive reasoning. If the premises are true, they provide certainty that the conclusion is true.

Inductive and deductive logic require calm reasoning and comparative objectivity to produce an unfettered line of reasoning. This is by no means "pure reason," but it is a form of thinking that focuses on the object of inquiry, which assesses by specified criteria, and which emphasizes objectivity. And in all these ways represents formal thought at its best.

Warm logic is known as *affective logic,* and it is another matter altogether. Affective logic is a style of thinking in which the connection between judgments is not rational but emotional. "Susan is nice to me; she is good." Or, "I received a 'D' in Mr. Wilson's class; he hates me." Affective logic speaks to cravings, desires, and fears: "There are too many students in the university; therefore, we should keep all minorities out." Affective logic blends rational thinking with personal desires under the pretense of objective thought, fostering in the thinker's mind the illusion that impartial logic is the only force at work. Affective logic works most efficiently when the thinker is emotionally aroused, is narcissistically invested in the topic, and convinced that he (she) is thinking objectiviely when this is not the case. Wishes, fears, cravings, and narcissistic yearnings are the forces that shape and give meaning to affective logic.

Affective logic is swayed by arguments which flatter, which employ theatric pleading, and which claim that the opponent is prejudiced, biased, or evil; it is the fusion of rationality and emotion. When thinkers are charged, affective logic flows freely and easily.

The affective logic of adolescence is sandwiched between two extremes: its primitive manifestation as expressed in children, and its pathological manifestation as expressed in narcissists. Being in the proximity of one by age and the other by egocentric predisposition, it is easy to understand why adolescent thought so easily drifts into affective logic and other forms of emotionalized intellecualism. When "you feel it in your bones," it certainly must be true:

> Teenage girls engage in emotional reasoning, which is the belief that if you feel someting is true, it must be true. If a teenager feels like nerd, she is a nerd. If she feels her parents are unfair, they are unfair. If she feels she'll get invited to homecoming, then she will be invited. There is limited ability to sort facts from feelings. Thinking is still magical in the sense that thinking something makes it so. (Pipher, 1994, p. 60)

EMOTIONALIZING ARGUMENTS

> In all matters of opinion, our adversaries are insane.
> —Mark Twain

Understanding how adolescents argue is a bit of a challenge because intellectual etiquette has few hard and fast rules during adolescence; arguments are sometimes orderly and civil, but usually not. One educator said of high school students: "Their notion of debating is to say things louder and louder, rather than searching for some evidence...Kids usually see things right away as either right or wrong, or look for instant answers and tend mot to go much further than that" (Lyons, 1990). Turning up the volume, right/wrong perceptions, data denial, and infuriating the opponent are only a few of the impediments to clear thinking.

An argument is a discussion in which reasons are put forward in support of, or against, an opinion; in other words, an informal debate. In reasoned arguments the participants attempt to demonstrate the truth or falsehood of a proposition. An argument is a *fair* consideration or a reflection upon a problem that involves providing reasons for or against a matter of dispute. This may sound more orderly than it is in real life. Arguments can be "won" and they can be "lost," but in real life rarely does a judge arbitrate; participants themselves decide the winners and the losers by standards having to do with the argument itself. Sometimes, especially among early adolescents, the victor is determined merely by stamina.

To emotionalize an argument is to inject it with so much feeling and passion that the real object of discussion is lost. To emotionalize defeats the purpose of a reasoned argument, which persuades by evidence, coherence, and common sense. Arguments are supposed to be logical, fair, and honest, but when they are emotionalized reason takes a back seat. In the course of emotionalizing their arguments adolescents are drawn into an organic irrationalism reminiscent of D. H. Lawrence's epitaph against reason: "We can go wrong in our minds. But what our blood feels and believes and says, is always true. The intellect is only a bit and a bridle. What do I care about knowledge? All I want is to answer to my blood, direct, without fribbling intervention of mind or moral, or what not." Answering "to my blood" is the right mixture of narcissism and responsibility to catch the adolescent's attention, but when all is said and done, adolescents glorify the irrational because they fear the rational.

An interesting aside to this is how some adults wrongly perceive the adolescent's fascination with the irrational as an expression of their romanticism. Nothing could be further from the truth. Teens are too fearful and too protectionistic for romanticism. (Although they like to think of themselves as "romantic" because this affirmative term grants a certain maturity to their emotivism.) But they are bright enough to see its possibilities. Egocentrism and narcissism, the dominant currents in adolescent phenomenology, are inherently antagonistic toward romanticism because they are self-absorbed whereas romanticism is life-absorbed. Teens are romantic when to be romantic is opportune, and this, of course, means they are not romantics at all.

STRATEGIES DESIGNED TO EMOTIONALIZE
AN ARGUMENT

The strategies which teens invent to keep at bay the swarm of critics which buzz their every thought are creative in expression and virtually infinite in number. These strategies all serve the same purposes—to emotionalize the topic, to aggravate the person with whom one is arguing, and to steamroll the fairness on which honest arguments depend. If you are a parent, a teacher, or an adolescent, you have seen them all before.

1. **Angering an opponent so that he (or she) will argue badly.** "Of course you think I should be home before midnight, you are a woman-hating male." "You wouldn't understand being in love; you never really loved Dad." "What do you know about homework. You're just a construction worker who didn't graduate from high school."
   Angering an opponent is made easier by the use of antagonizing definitions

of everyday words. For example, an arguing adolescent may define a teacher as someone who lets the student do whatever he (she) wants, or a parent as someone who slavishly looks after the child's every need. Or, conversely, they might define a teacher as a lackey of administrative oppression and a parent as a police officer. Using words in such a narrow, antagonizing way prevents the real topic from being investigated. The energy of debate is redirected to fighting unfair terminology. (Many teens, in fact, consider this a points victory. "She really blew her cool.")

Adolescent arguments are often more about tension reduction and energy release than anything else, and when teens argue calmly and dispassionately they sometimes lose not only their tenacity, but sometimes lose their convictions. Anger heightens energy and lowers reason, and this is one of its advantages to an emotional thinker. Teens, as a rule, have not mastered reason as fully as adults, and to compensate for this inferiority, they strategically infuse emotion in their arguments to lessen the persuasive power of reason. When they argue by reason alone they all too often lose the argument, and in this way reason becomes, to them, counter productive.

2.   **Accepting or rejecting an idea because of its popularity with the audience.** This tendency carries great weight in group discussions and "bull-sessions." Its value is that it shifts the focus from the points of the debate, to what is accepted or rejected by the listeners. In sum, audience reaction is more important than the merits of the actual argument. Pandering to audience reaction is considered by most teens to be a legitimate weapon in argumentative battles.

Rejection and disapproval carry such force during adolescence that to twist arguments in order to avoid them is simply a matter of course. Often it is not until hours later, when replaying the day's activities, that the individual realizes what he (she) has done. Sometimes this realization enlightens the thought process, but not necessarily as during early and middle adolescence social approval sits higher on the need hierarchy.

3.   **Using affect to reduce the listener's concentration on the object of disagreement.** "Dad, I know you always want me to be happy and to do what is best for me, well, quitting school and getting a job are best for me and will make me happy."

The manipulation of feeling as an intellectual strategy comes into play when the adolescent recognizes how emotionality influences the thoughts of others. (Teens know from personal experience how much their own thinking is influenced by fear and anxiety; it takes time, perspective-taking and formal thought to see the same principles at work in others.) Hence, middle- and late-adolescents are rather adept at it while early-adolescents, who have not as yet developed a very sophisticated understanding of their own thinking habits, are less so.

4. **Disarming the opponent with charm.** This is really a subset of tactic 3, but it is so widely used that it earns a place of its own. Albert Camus, the great existential thinker asked: "You know what charm is?" Answering himself: "A way of getting the answer yes without having asked any clear question." Charm is an attractive strategy to those who have trouble getting the answer "yes" by reason, muscle or obstinance; it is the "fourth-force" in mental persuasion.

5. **Attributing undesirable motives to one's opponent.** Emphasizing the unworthy qualities of the opponent is a proven way to wreck an argument. "You hate Jason because he is white." "Why should I work? Your generation screwed up the world." This strategy is especially effective against individuals who feel that they must defend themselves against every attack on their character; it also works well against individuals low in security and high in inferiority—which means all youth some of the time and some youth all of the time.

   Attributing undesireable motives to one's opponent is most likely to occur when the attributor is fearful, anxious or both. Because teens hold an anxious vigilence against dark and dangerous forces, they see evil where it does not exist, especially in argumentive opponents.

6. **Using emotion-laden words to deflect the topic.** "It is hard for me to talk about responsibility when it was you who *divorced* my Dad and *ruined our family.*" "Historians are all male chauvinist pigs who leave women out of their 'brave men and their heroic deeds' stories. It makes me sick." Or after parents discover drugs in the bedroom: "I can't believe you *invaded* my privacy. I feel like I have been *violated.*"

   Incendiary language keeps conversation hot. Teenagers, although predisposed to this style of argumentation, are not its masters. This honor goes to daytime TV talk show hosts and political propagandists; not coincidentally, both of whom have great success attracting adolescent audiences.

WHY TEENS EMOTIONALIZE

> The defining character of thought is its product.
> —Jerome Bruner

Why do adolescents emotionalize their arguments? Like so many questions in adolescent psychology, this one is easier to ask than to answer. But a few comments may be in order. First, anything important enough to argue over often relates to self-esteem, self-worth or self-importance, narcissistically charged topics which lend themselves to emotionalization. Second, during adolescence emotion has a raw forcefulness that abstract thought lacks. Third, the ability to assemble a good argument, and then to defend it against hostile questions (and questioners) takes years to develop. Even members of the high school debate team don't necessarily argue effectively with peers or parents. (Many individuals remain weak at this skill even after four years of university education.) The ability to present an argument, to impartially analyze the data on which it is based, and to consistently draw accurate inferences from these data is a late-adolescent, young-adult phenomenon. It is seen only sparingly during the earlier years of adolescence.

POSTSCRIPT

Not being clued-in to reality.
—The response of a 21-year-old university student to the question:
"What was the greatest single problem you faced as an adolescent?"

The themes put forth in this chapter do not represent a completely new set of ideas; rather, they are a speculative response to the adolescent inclination to faulty reasoning, and, in turn, to faulty decision-making. The task we have set out for ourselves is an inherently frustrating one because the more we reflect on the subject the greater appears the distance between the abilities of young people and the dangers they are routinely required to negotiate. We wishfully think of adolescents as junior rationalists but very few of them are; we seem reluctant to admit that each day they make life and death decisions through an incomplete and immature intelligence.

In addition to the impressive advances which elevate and dignify adolescent thought discussed in chapter one, we also observe regressions which distort and darken it.[24] The intent of this chapter has been to show how youth are *predisposed* to think emotionally rather than rationally, and how this tendency undercuts intelligence and undermines wisdom.

We remain close to the heartbeat when we remember that the signature of adolescent intellectualism is neither clear rationalism nor murky emotionalism; rather, it is the ebb and flow between concrete thinking and formal reasoning, the intermittent shifts between cold-blooded and warm-blooded reason, and the periodic fluctuations between healthy skepticism and crippling cynicism. Not until we acknoweldge these uneven features of the intellect can we fathom how difficult it is for them to embrace objectivity and impartiality as guiding principles in their day-to-day lives, and how easy it is for them to lose their determination to work for a dignified understanding of life's mysteries.[25]

5

The Manipulation of Arguments

Half our mistakes in life arise from feeling where we ought to think,
and thinking where we ought to feel.
—John Churton Collins

One of the first things I try to impress upon anyone interested in learning about how adolescents think is that their thought process is infused with a nervous self-consciousnes and a fearful protectionism which deprives them of the full strength and wisdom of their own intelligence. These features of their phenomenology do not ruin their thought, but they do hamper it and undercut its proficiency. As I have already mentioned, adolescents are *capable* of sophisticated reasoning, but not all the time and not on all topics.

The disposition to be guided by the light of reason is not a strong one in the day-to-day mental operations of most teens. This is not to say that they are predisposed to shade or concealment; rather, it is to say that nothing is built into their intellect which, on its own, impels them to search out the real, the genuine, the authentic. Every individual possesses a natural intelligence (which, of course, is not the same in every person), but rigor and objectivity are not inherent to adolescent intelligence. Rather, they are acquired through imitation, through education, through coaching and coaxing. The acquisition of intellectual rigor and objectivity (when it occurs) is one of the great advances of the adolescent years.

Some scholars claim that to focus on the mental inefficiency of adolescents trivializes not only their thinking process, it trivializes them; I totally oppose this claim and I have actively fought against it in my career as an educator and as an author. The honest reporting of limitations never trivializes anything, but it does force us to reconsider many of our unexamined prejudices. Great nations, great leaders, great artists all have their own limitations and weaknesses, but this in no way implies they do not also have great strengths and admirable qualities. So it is with youth.

Before I proceed, a brief cautionary note is in order. In what I am about to say, I am not claiming that adolescent thinking is universally emotional; neither am I following the lead set long ago by G. Stanley Hall (1916) and Anna Freud (1948) when they claimed that adolescents are persistently irrational. My intent here is merely to show how the adolescent thought process is prone to lethargy, emotionality, and ineptitude.

At the risk of appearing apologetic about investigating these limitations of the adolescent thought process, I want to, once again, remind the reader that most adolescents possess tremendous intellectual potential, including the potential to think comprehensively and propositionally, to connect remote abstractions, to anticipate the future, and to double-check their own mental operations for errors and lapses. The "formal" thought which adolescents have at their avail is awesome in its speed and power, but it helps us when we remember that even a Ferrari is in trouble when the brakes or the cooling systems don't work properly.[26]

THE TENDENCY TO ARGUE UNFAIRLY

> Ah! Don't say that you agree with me. When people agree with me I always
> feel I must be wrong.
> —Oscar Wilde

In the normal course of events adolescents have a somewhat mercenary attitude toward arguments in general, and the act of arguing in particular. Many factors contribute to their "win-at-all-costs" mentality, some of which I will try to spell out in this chapter.

In the next few pages I will describe, in no specific order of importance, some of the more common strategies adolescents use to present an argument that is not worthy but has the appearance of being so. These strategies serve different ends but their main purposes are to deflect reason, to deny unwanted data, and to infuriate the opponent. They are not designed to seek out the truth as much as to valorize one particular version of it. These strategies specialize in wrong-reasoning, in solving problems with inadequate data, in coming up with an answer when a satisfactory one does not exist. Encouragingly, in the intimacy of their reason, teens seem to have an intuitive awareness that these strategies are unfair and, given the opportunity to see them for what they are, they are surprisingly willing to give them up for fairer ones. But getting them to see them for what they are is no small achievement because, for many teens, frustrating the will of others is more meaningful than a coherent argument.

STRATEGIES OF UNFAIR ARGUMENTATION: TECHNIQUES DESIGNED TO WIN ARGUMENTS RATHER THAN TO GET TO THE HEART OF THE MATTER

> I think there is only one quality worse than hardness of heart and that is softness of head.
> —Theodore Roosevelt

Let me make one thing clear before I go any further, because I don't want there to be any misunderstanding about the remarks that follow. What we have here is a compilation of mental habits which short-circuit the reasoning process. They are not universal to adolescent thought, but they do show up with remarkable consistency in their argumentative exchanges.[27] Indeed, debates among adolescents without them are rare. Most of the reason-degrading habits I describe in this section are most prevalent among early adolescents (11 to 14-year-olds) but, regardless of age, they surface whenever individuals are intellectually frustrated, emotionally uptight, or narcissistically threatened. Unfortunately, adolescents are intellectually frustrated, emotionally uptight and narcissistically threatened a great deal of the time, a fact that predisposes them to manipulate arguments rather than to use them to investigate the truth.

Without consciously intending it, adolescents are pragmatic, even Machiavellian, in their thinking. They tend to view arguments as a form of battle in which they attack, defend, counterattack, change their positions, engage in espionage, propaganda, and dirty tricks. Generally speaking—and there are many exceptions—adolescents use arguments not as a way to tell right from wrong, but as a method of convincing others of the correctness of their position. Adolescent argumentation involves much more than promoting a clearer understanding of an issue; indeed, some arguments have nothing whatsoever to do with either clarity or accuracy. Most adolescent arguments hide a narcissistic agenda where self-protection and self-aggrandizement are as important as the issue argued; rarely can the argument be meaningfully understood until the narcissistic motivation behind it has been taken into account.

With these preliminary comments behind us, let us take a quick look at some of the most common errors teens stumble upon in their efforts to win their disputes.

1. **Making statements in which "all" is implied but "some" is true.** Arguing by universality when the question at hand is specific and local. "Everyone does it," when only some are doint it; "I'll be the only one who doesn't have one," when many do not. "Mr. Smith always picks on me," when Mr. Smith did so only once. This tendency is the product of either/or, right/wrong thinking, which is so prevalent in the concrete thought of children and in the protectionist thinking of early adolescents. Mary Pipher described the habit of unfair generalization among adolescent girls this way:

   > The tendency to overgeneralize makes it difficult to reason with adolescent girls. Because they know of one example, they'll argue "Everyone else gets to stay out till two," or "Everyone I know gets a new car for their sixteenth birthday." They'll believe that because the girl next door gets a ride to school, every girl in the universe gets a ride to school. They aren't being manipulative as much as they earnestly believe that one case represents the whole. (1994, p. 60)

2. **Using proof by selected instances.** "Jane's parents let her use their car and she never crashes it"; "Doing drugs doesn't hurt your grades: I have a friend who smokes pot, and he's an honor student." The youngster who thinks, "I didn't make the team, I'm a real loser" is using proof by selected instances. So is one who argues: "Our principal has a tattoo and people respect *him*!" The advantage to this line of thinking is that it creates the illusion that one specific example of one real-life event is adequate grounds for justifying a larger issue. "If people like me don't get part-time jobs, how will the economy ever turn around?" This strategy is especially prevalent when youngsters are hard pressed to "prove" their point, or when they need a larger principle to confirm something specific to themselves.

3. **Opposing a proposition by misrepresenting it.** "I am opposed to kids having to do household chores and to all forms of child slavery." "I don't listen to feminists because they are lesbians."
   A favorite misrepresentation is to disagree with what doesn't exist, or with what barely exists. "Abortionists hate babies; babies are our future." This strategy misrepresents an idea to better attack it. It most frequently occurs when the opposed idea is too strong to attack as it is; by misrepresenting and simplifying the idea it becomes an easier target.

4. **Diverting to a side issue when one is losing a point.** "You always treat me like a kid." "You said I was old enough to make my own decisions," are examples of attacking the person rather than the issue in dispute. Arguing with her mother over whether she should be dating an older man, the daughter accuses: "At least I have a steady boyfriend. You go out

with a different guy every week." All of this is in accord with the tendency to divert the argument away from the main topic in order to gain the upper hand.

5. **Promoting a conclusion simply because it is the mean between two extremes; claiming that compromise is always reasonable.** Mother tells her daughter to be home at midnight; the daughter replies that she wants to return home at 4 a.m. An argument ensues. The child says: "OK, let's compromise, 2 o'clock." Notably missing from the reasoning process is that compromise involves more than merely halving the difference between two contested viewpoints. Enhancing one's position through compromise is appealing because it gives the impression of fair play even when it isn't fair at all.

6. **Arguing so that no other conclusion is deemed plausible.**

> He admits that there are two sides to every question—his own
> and the wrong side.
> —Channing Pollock, drama critic

"Only an idiot would believe that disputes can be settled in the United Nations." "Every moral person knows that abortion is murder." Begging the question: "Why should I try to get people to like me; you can't be popular unless you're a cheerleader." The extreme nature of these pronouncements is lessened by the adolescent tendency to perceive emotionally charged topics in black/white, all-or-nothing perspectives. This tendency is an even more potent resistance to reason when the individual is frightened, defensive, or narcissistic.[28] And, at the risk of repeating myself, this means some youth all of the time, and all youth some of the time.

7. **Stating one's position over and over without defending the merit of the position.** This involves the repetition of the same idea in different words, as if by stating it over and over somehow makes it correct; it is the classic example of entrenchment through repetition. What we have is merely the throwing of words at an argument instead of an examination of it. "Tremaine quit school and he makes $50,000 a year." "Yes, but he's a drug dealer." "Yes, but he makes $50,000 a year." "He might get sent to prison, or get killed." "Yes, but he makes $50,000 a year." "Yes, but what he does is wrong." "Yes, but he makes $50,000 a year." Arguing in this way is an unwelcome exaggeration of the egocentric speech of childhood; it is grounded in the phenomenological deception that makes one feel that the *act* of saying is more important than what actually is said.

> A bare assertion is not necessarily the naked truth.
> —George Prentice, American journalist

This might be an appropriate time to introduce a parallel point. Much adolescent arguing is really about testing the spoken-out-loud coherence of ideas, and for scouting the reactions they elicit from one's own rational functions. In other words, what one says is not necessarily an indicator of how one thinks as much as it is a sampling of fragments related to it. After numerous repetitions the target idea becomes progressively refined. Consequently, many so-called "arguments" are not arguments at all as much as a mixture of reason and release, and it is virtually impossible to ascertain which is which in the heat of battle.

To do justice to their own ideas, adolescents require an enormous amount of bull-session time, freewheeling philosophizing and unguarded meandering simply to get their ideas out into the open so they can inspect them for what they are. One significant function of peers in this process is to serve as honest critics of the ideas their friends create.

8. **Arguing by forced analogy.** An analogy is drawing a link between things otherwise dissimilar; an inference based on the assumption that if two things are alike in some respects they will be alike in others. With adolescents, reasoning errors about known alikes are daily routine. "Jane's Mom's letting her have a party, so I should be able to have one too." "Teachers are allowed to smoke at school so students should be allowed to smoke at school." Arguing by forced analogy, like so many forms of emotionalized argumentation, is used when "winning" the argument is more important than honestly evaluating the merits of the argument. The more an individual's thinking is controlled by the "winning is everything" mentality, fair argumentation is out of the question.

9. **Failure to say exactly what it is that one is proposing.**

> I am most fond of talking and thinking; that is to say, talking first
> and thinking afterward.
> —Osbert Sitwell, English playwright

"School is stupid;" "Teachers are unfair." "I'm tired of being exploited." Employing vagueness in an argumentative exchange is helpful to the unfair arguer because it prevents the real topic from being investigated freely and openly. (In response to the parent's demand to know where the teen was until 2 a.m.: "Out." In response to what was he(she) doing: "Nothing." In response to what a teen hates about school: "Everything.") The refusal to use precise language protects one against a precise rebuttal, a fact of debate (and life) that most kids learn by grade 6.

10. **Speaking as if prestige words are more powerful than ordinary words.** "It's not my fault I drink too much. I come from a *dysfunctional family*,

my parents *emotionally abuse* me, I suffer from *unrecovered memories.*" A parallel tendency tries to gain the upper hand through pseudotechnical jargon. Both of these habits make it difficult to distinguish erudition from pretentiousness. Indeed, in some youth subcultures there is no attempt whatsoever to differentiate information from showmanship. The point made with the most style prevails; argumentation is inseparable from theatrics.

11. **Arguing by "straw-man."** A "straw-man" argument is a bogus set up knocked down to produce an easy victory. Usually they have emotional, anxiety-provoking aspects which persuade by diffusing logical thought, by preventing focus on the central issues in question. "Scientists make bombs because they don't care about the people they kill." "Straw-man" arguments are common fare for propagandists; their deception is in presenting points as "logical" when they are, in fact, artificial or false. It is an especially effective strategy with emotionally charged audiences who make no effort to establish the truth of the initial point being knocked down.

"Straw-man" is similar in certain regards to what is known as "red herring," a name which goes back to the seventeenth century when strong-smelling red herring were used by escaping criminals to cause bloodhounds to lose the human scent they had been following. This practice inspired the expression "to drag a red herring across the trail" which has been shortened to "red herring." Although adolescents may not know what a red herring, is they do know how to evade an issue by dragging in something irrelevant. "Straw-man" and "red herring" degrade discourse by their tendency to claim that which is important isn't and that which isn't is. Under the protective umbrella of this strategy, fair argumentation is impossible.

In all of these strategies there is at work an elementary principle. You or I or an adolescent can honestly tackle an argument only when we are earnestly committed to adapting our mental energy *to the actual points being debated.* This is precisely what adolescents fail to do. Instead of adapting their mind to the issue, they adapt the issue to their needs and fears. As long as this approach prevails, the arguments which follow from it are not real. What we have is not an argument, but an artificial exchange where participants merely throw words at the argument's shadow.

The tendency to impose oneself on an argument *is a natural reflex of the adolescent intellect.* Overcoming this reflex requires patient repetition of the same sequence of thought. "What is being investigated here?" "Am I dealing with the real issue?" "Am I merely protecting my own agenda?" "What are the criteria which validate the argument?"[29] M. Piattelli-Palmarini drives home the same point.

Full-blown, self-checking rationality...does not act in us spontaneously or without effort. Rational judgment brings many different forces into play, and some of them are in conflict with each other. Rationality is not, therefore, even an immediate, psychological given; it is a complex exercise that is first won, and then maintained, at a certain psychological cost. (1994, p. 160)

Rationality must be practiced but it cannot be hurried or forced; it takes virtually the entirety of adolescence to cultivate an automatic, unconscious tendency to focus one's mind on the real object of discussion and, once focused, to rally the necessary strength of will to commit to reality-based thinking.

It is wrong to think of adolescents as intellectual contrarians, and please do not assume, even for a moment, that this is how I want to paint them. But to claim that their thinking is unbiased and unprejudiced is equally absurd. Like all of us, teens defend their ideas, but they have not as yet learned how to do it openly and honestly. Their reflex is to defend before they have evaluated the integrity of their defense and then to defend the defense. In this instance, adolescent thought is little more than protectionistic narcissism.

The strategies which I have presented in the past few pages operate without much calculation and with minimal premeditation. They are, quite literally, part of the thought process itself, and this naturalness contributes immeasurably to the adolescent's struggle with intellectual integrity.

A considerable element of practice is involved in presenting a reasoned argument. Reason, like muscle, must be exercised, and arguments, like speech, must be rehearsed. To argue unfairly and narcissistically are inevitable first steps in the adolescent's journey to mature intellectual discourse.

HELPING TEENS BECOME BETTER THINKERS

Since all young adolescents ... are ill-prepared to make fateful decisions with lifelong consequences...it is valuable for them to learn how to make informed, deliberate decisions rather than ignorant and impulsive ones.
—David Hamburg

What can we do to make adolescents better thinkers? This is a practical question to which many answers have been brought forward, some better than others, but none infallible. I find a good deal of common sense in an observation made by Raymond Nickerson: "It is not reasonable to expect that we shall discover any time soon how to turn our students into perfectly logical, consistent, thorough, sensitive thinkers... What is reasonable to expect is a gradually better understanding of what it means to think well and how to promote good thinking" (1991, p. 7). To think well and to promote good thinking is the issue. But how to go about it?

A necessary starting point is to openly admit that adolescents are not *naturally* rational thinkers. Which is to say that they are not by instinct, by hard-wire programming, by heredity, by predisposition, or by inclination rational beings. This is not to say that they are irrational, or antirational, even though some are; it is merely to say that disciplined reason, clear thinking, and reasoned discourse are not *built into* their intellectual operations. Each of these valued traits is acquired, and whereas the acquisition process is easier for some than others, it is nevertheless exactly that—an acquisition process. And in the absence of the acquisition process you have a thinker predisposed to self-serving intelligence with little concern for whether thought is rational or irrational as long as it is self-serving.

Most of you, especially parents and educators, prefer more practical, "hands-on" suggestions on how to advance and elevate the thinking process of adolescents. I suggest the following as worthy starting points:

- Helping teens to foster the habit of listening carefully to what other people have to say.
- Helping teens to increase their willingness to consider points of view which differ from their own.
- Helping teens to restrain their tendencies to act impulsively.
- Helping teens to use analogies effectively and appropriately.
- Helping teens to improve the skills by which they evaluate the merits of an argument.
- Helping teens to reward objectivity when analyzing evidence.
- Helping teens to recognize when peers are acting as narcissistic gratifiers more than as objective evaluators.
- Helping teens to recognize the difference between defending an idea and defending themselves.
- Helping teens to recognize the differences between affective logic and impartial logic.

POSTSCRIPT

> Sometimes reason is enslaved; it is forced to collaborate—to protect our illusions, to render them immune to verification.
> —Massimo Piattelli-Palmarini

The purposes of arguments are many, and to discover the truth is only one. During adolescence, intelligence has many responsibilities, among the foremost is to protect the feelings, needs, desires, ambitions, and insecurities of the person whose intelligence is being exercised. When we recognize this collusion we are better equipped to understand why adolescent reasoning and arguing are often flawed.

Massimo Piattelli-Palmarini's splendid work, *Inevitable Illusions* (1994), is subtitled "How mistakes of reason rule our minds." This I find unfortunate because mistakes of reason do not *rule* our minds, but they do exert considerable influence on it; and it is this negative influence on reason, as it expresses itself in adolescence, that here concerns us. The adolescent thought process is not fundamentally irrational, but it can be when it has to be. The human thought process operates in tandem with the emotional unconscious, with the ground of insecurity, and with the hopes and aspirations which give purpose to our lives, and each of them influence the thought process to different degrees at different times. In our tired moments it may appear that the adolescent thought process is so burdened with emotional freight that it sometimes turns into a black hole from which light can no longer emerge. This is not so. But it sometimes does appear that way!

Sancho, Don Quixote's faithful (and slightly more clear-headed) companion, once said of his master: "He's a muddled fool, full of lucid intervals." This is not the picture I want to paint of adolescence, but it is a portrait where the contours and outlines bear some resemblance. The "lucid intervals," everyone agrees, tend to become more frequent as age increases, and this accounts for the late-adolescent's improved success with philosophy and the early-adolescent's almost complete failure with it; the "muddled fool" part, everyone agrees, is quite unpredictable. Part of my motivation in writing this chapter has been to document the mental habits which muddle adolescent thought. And although it is true that the adventures of Don Quixote inspire an appreciation for our foibles, intellectual and otherwise, Cervantes' great genius was for human nature—not adolescent nature. The differences between the two are profound, as I have tried to make clear throughout the course of this text.

6

Why Adolescents Have Trouble Thinking Clearly

The light of mature reason does not suddenly shed its clarity upon the young adolescent as by a magic wand.
—E. A. Peel (1971)

I spent more time than anticipated choosing the title of this chapter because it is important not to say "Why adolescents *can't* think clearly," as this contradicts the fact that they can, and do, think clearly. Neither did I want to say "Why adolescents have trouble *thinking*," because they rarely have trouble thinking, if by this we mean creating thoughts; but they often have trouble thinking clearly and coherently and that is what I want to look at.

I have already discussed several characteristics of the adolescent thought process which encourage ineffective thinking, including the tendency to distort data, the tendency *to create* (not the same as "to imitate,") fables, the tendency to use affective logic, the tendency to manipulate arguments, the tendency to twist assumptions to fit one's needs and desires and, finally, the tendency to pretend that one has made a solid argument when one hasn't. Here in the final chapter of this section dealing with adolescent intelligence, I would like to introduce a new line of speculation which, hopefully, will provide further insight into the frailties and the limitations of adolescent intelligence.

But first a brisk condensation of ideas previously discussed.

THE RISE OF INTELLIGENCE: A QUICK OVERVIEW OF
THE ADOLESCENT'S REMARKABLE POTENTIAL FOR
CLEAR THINKING

To understand how youth seek the trugh we must first understand the intelligence that guides their search. For the past several decades this intelligence has been known as "formal thought." The advances in intellectual power associated with it emerge during early adolescence, and it brings with it the ability, as David Elkind put it, "to think in a new key." But it is not merely a new key, it is also a higher, richer, and purer key. Formal thought creates the mental infrastructure for philosophy and science, theology and poetry; it is the bridge that connects the concrete practical intelligence of the child with the structured, formal intelligence of the adult. Formal thought is to the philosopher as the athletic body is to the athlete, and as the finely tuned body makes *possible* (but does not guarantee) the skills of the NHL goalie, so formal thought makes possible (but does not guarantee) philosophical inquiry. So important is formal thought that aside from puberty it is the most profound transformation of the entire adolescent period.

As I tried to spell out in chapter one, a cluster of intellectual skills come into being with the attainment of formal thought. Here, in abbreviated form, are some of the more important ones.

- **Formal thought increases the adolescent's power of abstraction and opens new conceptual worlds.** Adolescents are in the process of exchanging the rigid intellectual apparatus of concrete thought for a more flexible and far-reaching way of thinking which will allow them to negotiate abstract intellectualism. As abstract thought grows the thinker shifts in gradual increments away from the here-and-now to the there-and-then. R. S. Siegler, one of the foremost Piagetian scholars, expressed it this way:

  Adolescents begin to see the particular reality in which they live as one of only several imaginable realities. This leads at least some of them to think about alternative organizations of the world and about deep questions concerning the nature of existence, truth, justice and morality. (1986, p. 41)

- **Formal thought stimulates intellectual comprehensiveness.** Not only do adolescents learn to focus on the "larger picture," they also embrace a larger range of data when trying to solve a problem; their thought, as a result, is much less susceptible to oversights, and to errors of omission. This increased scope allows them to "plan in considerable detail what they are going to do, and to interpret whatever they do within the total context" (Siegler, 1986, p. 41).

- **Formal thought opens to critical investigation one's own thought process.** Adolescent intelligence shines inward illuminating itself. To children a thought is a thought is a thought; adolescents discover that a thought may be born to rich or poor parentage, that it can be weakly constructed or strongly presented. Children possess few standards by which to judge whether one thought is more coherent than another; adolescents know that the quality of a thought is measured by standards beyond the thought itself. They learn to tell a good idea from a lousy one by standards other than the authoritarian or the autocratic.

- **Formal thought increases the capacity for propositional thought.** A proposition is any statement capable of being believed, doubted, denied, or argued; propositional thought allows the thinker to investigate ideas beyond reality as it is presently understood, and to reason about hypotheses—true, false, or unknown. Basically, propositional thought allows one to reason about anything and everything; under its influence "off-limits" ideas are brought into closer scrutiny.

    Children are not gifted propositional thinkers; they focus on the perceptible elements of a problem and tend not to speculate much about possibilities that do not bear directly on the matter at hand. They solve problems with few systematic strategies; they rarely have an organized gameplan. When they solve a problem correctly they often do not know how they solved it, or when faced with a similar problem, they may not be able to beckon the strategies that only a few minutes before were effective. Adolescents are not necessarily gifted propositional thinkers, but they are vastly superior at it when compared with children.

- **Formal thought fosters future analysis.** Children are not chained to the present, but neither are they free to take flight from it; their concern is with "here and now." Formal thinkers, on the other hand, are liberated from the clock, even the calendar; they glide through light years, infinity, timelessness in ways that concrete thinkers cannot even contemplate. Immediate time is recognized as a flickering instant of eternal time; clock time is differentiated from experiential time. The adolescent's awareness of the future is profound for many reasons, but most important is that thought is primitive until it transcends present time.

- **Formal thought beckons scientific thought.** Formal thinkers form hypotheses, conduct experiments, control variables, describe and record outcomes and, from these steps, they draw conclusions in a disciplined, formal manner. Formal thinkers come to recognize that patient observation and systematic experimentation are the meat of science, whereas disciplined reason and coherent speculation are the heart of philosophy. This is the age when the reality of probability begins to replace the magic of possibility; when "it *could* happen," is replaced with "it *probably* will [or will not] happen."

When everything goes right, formal thought gives the adolescent the ability to go beyond the real to investigate the ideal, to peer beyond the physical to investigate the hypothetical, to see beyond fragments to investigate wholes, to think beyond "what is" to "what if," and to wander beyond the present into the future. All in all, these are impressive intellectual credentials that elevate the adolescent to a plateau where he (she) now holds the *potential* to think clearly and concisely, rationally and objectively, philosophically and scientifically.

Transforming the potentiality of intelligence into actuality is the greatest challenge of the adolescent years. When young people meet this challenge they blossom and grow in line with the developmental blueprints that guide our species; but when they fail this challenge they downgrade not only their intelligence but their humanity. The squandering of intelligence and the wasting of potential are no small matters, but for many youth, that is what adolescence in North American culture amounts to.

THE DECLINE OF INTELLIGENCE: A QUICK OVERVIEW OF THE ADOLESCENT'S REMARKABLE POTENTIAL FOR CLOUDED THINKING

> The fact that a human brain of high amperage, otherwise highly efficient, may have a hole in it is surely not a secret.
> —H.L. Mencken

It is inevitable that in the investigation of youth you turn up things that you wish you hadn't, and that is exactly our situation here with the study of adolescent intelligence. One of our first discoveries is that adolescents think best about what they know and worst about what they fear; the implications of this are momentous when we consider the climate of fear that prevails during adolescence.[30]

A fair generalization holds that as adolescents get older their egocentrism decreases. In normal development this is policy. Hence, late adolescents are less egocentric than early adolescents, and middle adolescents, as we would expect, lie between the two extremes. However, as we have seen from our investigations of adolescent narcissism, some youth become *increasingly egocentric* and *increasingly self-serving* throughout their adolescent years. This observation has led us to hypothsize that under certain circumstances the normal egocentricity of youth erodes into a selfishness which stifles intelligence and stunts the normal growth of the personality.

Despite its great forward surge, adolescent thinking is not always clear, coherent, or accurate; at one moment it may be tight and logical, while at another, clouded and confused. Upon close inspection we usually find that clouded moments occur under the following conditions:[31]

- when the thinker abandons the system of checks and balances inherent to formal thought and regresses to the concrete, authoritarian thought typical of children;
- when the thinker accepts fables as though they were facts;
- when the thinker emotionalizes an argument;
- when the thinker rejects objective reasoning in favor of affective reasoning;
- when the thinker shifts attention from the real issue to how the issue affects "me."

As a result of these clouding tendencies, the product of adolescent intelligence is sometimes not what it could be, and as Jerome Bruner (1986, p. 106) aptly noted, "The defining character of thought is its product." Bruner's observation also brings home the point that every adolescent needs an impartial companion to serve as a brake on the natural propensity to choose ideas that favor oneself. An ideal person for this job is a compassionate adult who can think clearly and who has the best interests of the young person at heart. The least ideal person for this necessary job is a peer who cannot think clearly and whose main job is to serve as a flattering mirror.

FINAL OBSERVATIONS ON ADOLESCENT INTELLIGENCE

Here I would like to leave you with some final observations on adolescent intelligence which have not thus far been treated with sufficient care. These observations center around three overlooked and neglected principles of adolescent intelligence: the fear of reason, the need for self-protection, and the power of narcissism in the thought process. My comments on these topics are too brief to be convincing before a healthy skepticism, so I present them to you as thought probes more than anything else. Some of these ideas I have defended elsewhere, whereas others I am presenting here for the first time. At any rate, here are a few and, I hope, worthy speculations about the forces that cloud adolescent thinking.

YOUTH ARE INHERENTLY FEARFUL ABOUT THE REASONING PROCESS

> To conquer fear is the beginning of wisdom.
> —Bertrand Russell

Despite the claims of Seneca and the stoics, Descartes and the rationalists, and Voltaire and the enlightenment philosophers that reason is man's true and essential nature, reason, it seems to me, is neither a natural nor an inevitable fact of our species. Bertrand Russell was more perceptive, or perhaps merely more honest, than the hardline rationalist philosophers when he claimed: "Man is a rational animal—so at least I have been told. Throughout a long life, I have looked diligently for evidence in favour of this statement, but I have not had the good fortune to come across it, though I have searched in many countries spread over three continents" (Dennon, 1961, p. 73,). Like Russell, I believe that the evidence indicates that developed reason, when we find it in ourselves and others, invariably has been arrived at slowly, methodically, and painfully. We all have some capacity for reason, much as we all have the capacity for a second, third, or fourth language. But potentiality and actuality are different sides of the same reality, and "the difference makes a difference," as William James was fond of saying.

From a developmentalist's view of things, adolescence is the time of life when the potential for disciplined reason runs head on into the practical demands of actualizing this potential. In no way is the actualization of intelligence automatic or guaranteed; adolescents, like the rest of us, resist having their prejudices undermined by reason or by anything else.

Before youth are willing to commit to reason they first must be convinced that something is in it for them; fortunately, this demand is easy to appease because the benefits to reason are abundantly clear to anyone with even a morsel of it. The practical temptation of reason is that it offers the young person the possibility of creating a correspondence between inner thought and the outer world, and the prospect of apprehending the world as it is. Another allure of reason is that it helps us to contextualize our own private experience into a mental scheme more coherent than experience itself. Reason permits a structure of reality which intelligence can grasp. Reason is attractive to youth because it is functional and productive. In all of these ways reason appeals to the practicality, to the common sense, and to the integrity of youth. But the *benefits* to reason are only part of the story.

Adolescents doubt the reasoning process not only as it expresses itself in others, but as it expresses itself in themselves. Reason, although valuable in theory, is as yet an unproven commodity in practice. Adolescents know that reason is essential to knowledge and that to reason clearly is a virtue, yet they are apprehensive because they have no real mastery of it. The greatest obstacle to reason is not the lack of it, but the fear of it. Fear puts frightening masks over the unknown, and reason, to the novice, is unknown.

Reason requires courage, and not merely the courage of defiance, which youth possess in great abundance, but the courage to see the world as it is. Required of a disciplined and persistent intelligence is the courage to affirm *the necessity of reason* in spite of those elements in life that contradict it. Attaining this courage is one of the great challenges of adolescence, and one that meets with only modest success because teens in our culture are not much trained to this kind courage, and on their own they tend not to see the importance of it.

Certain other features of the adolescent personality also conspire against the ascent of reason.

- Adolescents do not always know when the product of reason reflects their prejudices and when it is real, bonafide, genuine. They are suspicious of reasoned conclusions because they don't know for sure when they are bogus. To overcome their natural suspicion of reason they require a good deal of practice with the reasoning process, they need to see that reason works to their own ends, and more than anything, they need the guidance of someone who possesses more of it than they do.

- Reason does not inherently favor one idea over another and this threatens the young person's need to be favored. Reason is impartial and youth are narcissistic, and these opposites compete for psychic territory; neither easily concedes to the other.

- Reason is one way that the mind discovers things as they are. Reason cannot show favoritism or bias without losing integrity; this even-handedness violates the young person's desire for priority. In a phrase, youth resent the *neutrality* of reason. If you grasp this you will also see that youth fear reason because it can rob them of precious fables and protective illusions. Reason, in its raw form, is a threat to the stability of life as it is presently known.

- Teens fear that reason will somehow convince them of what they don't want to be convinced of; and it often does. Because the outcome of reason is not totally predictable, it takes you where you don't always want to go. And who needs that?

- Reason is valued in proportion to its utility, and when it lacks utility it is abandoned. The periodic abandonment of reason is at the heart of the "empty zones" that plague adolescent intelligence. And although the abandonment of reason is a common reaction to the fear of it, it is a reaction which can produce devastating consequences.

- Teens (especially early adolescents) are confused about why they can sometimes follow the flow of reason and sometimes they cannot. Reason has an alien and bewildering texture. Attaining the courage to handle reason's unanticipated twists is a necessary first step in mature intelligence.

- Reason is abstract, emotion is concrete; reason is remote, emotion is now. Creating a workable alliance between reason and emotion is one of the crowning achievements of adolescence but, like so many advances during the second decade of life, it is several years in the making, and during those years we see periods when reason prevails and periods when emotion prevails.

- Emotions are involuntary, but how we respond to them is not. Learning to reason in the midst of pulsing emotion is a necessity of adolescent intelligence, but the solution is not found in reason alone nor in emotion alone, but in the mingling of them in proportion and measure.
- With increasing maturity reason attains a more persistent presence, but during the early years of adolescence (ages 12-14) it easily recedes into the background of daily routine; when needed, it must be consciously beckoned. It doesn't arrive on its own like some Guardian Angel whenever problems present themselves. Reason does not become an automatic part of mental operations until late adolescence; under normal developmental conditions, however, it gathers increasing proficiency with each successive adolescent year.

Amid all this insecurity and fear, an attitude of reason tries to take hold in the adolescent personality. By "an attitude of reason," I simply mean a mental posture where the object of analysis is considered as an entity in itself, and not merely an extension of one's own needs or desires. This attitude of reason is mandatory if intelligence is to actualize itself during adolescence. In some youngsters an attitude of reason takes hold and in some it doesn't, but the taking hold is no mere random processs. Reason is learned; reason is imitated; reason is acquired; reason is nurtured; reason is cultivated; but most importantly, reason grows from the courage to face reality as it is. Without courage reason goes nowhere.

The *potential* for reason is nature's gift to the adolescent; the *actualization* of reason is the adolescent's gift to himself and to his community.

THE ADOLESCENT INTELLECT IS PROTECTIONISTIC AND SELF-PRESERVING

> A youth lives in a condition of perpetual self-defence against everything
> new that he cannot love.
> —Friedrich Nietzsche

Islands of Competence in a Protectionist Sea

The forces that cause youth to defend themselves at the expense of truth are not clearly understood. No one can fathom their causes confidently. What is known is that everyone is characterized to a certain degree by intellectual protectionism; therefore, it is by no means exclusive to youth. Mature thinkers, however, try to minimize its influence. Adolescents are learning this vital skill, but their system of mental checks-and-balances is inefficient, and this makes it difficult for them to evaluate ideas that touch upon their self-worth, their self-esteem, indeed, anything at all to do with self-interest.

I come now to my main theme, which is that protectionism blocks the mind from learning new truths. And whereas it is necessary to defend and protect one's beliefs, there is a considerable downside when it is done defensively and with a closed mind. Protectionism and open-mindedness serve different functions and, generally speaking, the advance of one signals the retreat of the other. Taking this into account, here are a few observations on how protectionism impedes adolescent thought.

- Adolescent intelligence is driven by the need to prove the worth of its owner. This is not its only function, but it is taken seriously; among youth characteristed by "the narcissistic style" it is their number-one priority.
- The adolescent is engaged in an ongoing struggle between self-preservation and intellectual objectivity, and when the two collide the former prevails. Growing beyond this is a developmental task of the first order during adolescence; its satisfactory completion is a necessary step toward philosophy and wisdom. On the other hand, when the adolescent fails to transcend this reflex and continues to defend the self at the cost of truth, he has made a regressive stride away from reason and toward the intellectualism we see in "the narcissistic style."
- The anti-intellectualism of youth originates in intelligence itself because the exercise of intelligence inevitably results in the creation of demeaning hypotheses about self, family, peers, and society. Adolescents try to protect themselves from the full force of their own intelligence through cynicism. In sum, the raw force of intelligence necessitates defensive barriers against its own creations. The tremendous force of adolescent intelligence gives rise to the need for a protective anti-intellectualism.
- The self-conscious emotions of jealousy, envy, rage, embarrassment, shame, and pride impede formal thought, which is to say they get in the way of comprehensiveness, propositional analysis, and future focus. This would not be such an important matter except for the fact that some adolescents are continuously under the influence of self-conscious emotions, and as a result they must solve life's puzzles without access to the upper reaches of their own intelligence. When inflamed by self-conscious emotions, one is temporarily learning disabled.[32]
- Adolescents experience great confusion knowing when their ideas are being attacked and when they themselves are being attacked. This confusion leads them to the erroneous belief that an attack on one is the same as an attack the other. From this basic confusion a harmless exchange of ideas triggers a "protect-and-defend" thinking. The inability to distinguish an attack upon one's ideas from an attack upon one's person is a perceptual limitation youth share with narcissists. As narcissism heightens, one is less able to distinguish an attack on "my" ideas from an attack on "me," and as narcissism decreases one

increasingly makes this distinction. "Normally a person does not become angry when something he has done or said is criticized, provided the criticism is fair and not made with hostile intent. The narcissistic person, on the other hand, reacts with intense anger when he is criticized. He tends to feel that the criticism is a hostile attack, since by the very nature of his narcissism he can not imagine that it is justified" (Fromm, 1964, p. 74).

• During early adolescence all hypotheses which flatter the self are *initially* thought noble, therefore defended; hypotheses which criticize the self are *initially* thought ignoble, therefore rejected. When the adolescent fails to re-examine this mental reflex, self-serving hypotheses crystallize into irrational beliefs and, with the passage of time, they become integrated into the identity project, which is to say they become part of one's identity.[33] The end result is an identity inspired by fables and sustained by illusions.

• Adolescents are drawn to the veto power of cynicism, but they are, generally speaking, frightened by the open-mindedness of healthy skepticism. Cynicism and skepticism are completely different mental attitudes which carry completely different consequences to adolescent intelligence. Let me briefly explain what I mean by this.

Skepticism is an attitude of questioning and doubting based upon uncertainty and the finiteness of human knowledge; it is the matured echo of childish negation. As a philosophical doctrine, skepticism claims that truth must always be questioned, hence, to the skeptic intellectual inquiry is an ongoing process of doubt and examination. (Among the ancient Greeks skeptics believed that humans are incapable of attaining ultimate knowledge.) Skepticism treats doubt and uncertainty as legitimate facts, and this means that one need not fear the unknown or the different.

Cynics disbelieve the sincerity of human actions and doubt that motivations can be altruistic or idealistic; they even question the value of living. A cynic believes people are motivated only by selfishness, and that the values we aspire to are no better than the ones we discard. Adolescent cynicism is the prelude to adult nihilism.

Perhaps the steepest price youngsters pay for their cynicism is that it cuts away the trust necessary to believe in themselves and in their social community.

ADOLESCENT THOUGHT IS AROUSED, SHAPED, AND DISTORTED BY THE NARCISSISM INHERENT TO THE DEVELOPING PERSONALITY

Adolescent intelligence is, in great measure, a narcissistic enterprise. By this I mean that its primary reflexes are protectionistic and self-serving, as are all successful biological adaptations. This does not mean that it will always remain this way (indeed much of the business of normal adolescent growth has to do with maturing beyond the intellectual narrowness natural to youth in general and to concrete thought in particular). But this journey into expanded and enriched thought is impeded by an elementary maxim: When intelligence is not trained outward to investigate the world on its terms, it is deflected inwards to protect the self on its terms. In other words, when not trained to higher purposes, the thought process reflexively becomes narcissistic.

Narcissism inclines one to see the world in simplistic terms. The starting point of every investigation becomes: "How does this help me. How does this hurt me?" Erich Fromm's insight is especially instructive: "The narcissistic person ends up with an enormous distortion. He and his are overevaluated. Everything outside is underevaluated. The damage to reason and objectivity is obvious" (1964, p. 74).

In youth, as in the rest of us, robust common sense requires a sense of fair play and an honest look at the evidence; therefore, to achieve intellectual honesty one must first overcome the narcissistic bent inherent to every thought process.

Here are a few additional ideas about how narcissism frustrates clear thinking.

> When a man is wrapped up in himself he makes a pretty small package.
> —John Ruskin

- The narcissism inherent to the personality inclines one to accept as true that which merely is flattering. Formal thought (when it is operating at full capacity) monitors this predisposition and tries to hold it in check. When it succeeds the adolescent has taken a giant stride toward establishing reason and objective impartiality as dominant mental traits; when it fails, the adolescent has taken a giant stride toward the selfish intellectualism we associate with "the narcissistic style."
- The initial predispositions of intelligence are narcissistic in character in that they protect self-interest as convincingly as possible. It is not until adolescence that these predispositions lose some of their force, and it is at this age when most individuals are first able to intentionally direct their intelligence. This moves intelligence into a world where reason exists as an independent force and not merely as an ally of the self.
- The narcissistic element within the thought process punishes ideas which make one less than someone else.
- As is true for the egocentrism of children, the narcissism of adolescence shapes thought without the thinker's awareness. Narcissistic intellectualism does not require conscious effort. (This is one reason why narcissistic thinkers are the last to recognize how completely self-priority dominates their thoughts and their judgments.)

- Narcissistic thinkers (all adolescents some of the time, some adolescents all of the time) insist that their intuitive strategies and their spontaneous deductions are always truthful because, at bottom, they are not concerned with truth as much as with affirming the legitimacy of the thinker who produced the thought—"me." To the narcissistic thinker an idea is true unto itself when it is "mine," but when the idea is "yours," it must be defended by reason, evidence, and experience.

- Youth believe in miracles, and they are fascinated with miraculous events. They have a strong need to believe, but they have not as yet completely accepted that you cannot believe only what you want to believe. Few adolescents have taken to heart the rationalist's admonition to beware of theories unsupported by observation or experience. Consequently, miracle workers, doomsday prophets, and purveyors of supernatural mysteries never suffer for followers when they practice their art in the community of teens; in teen society the hunger for comforting platitudes is much stronger than the craving for verifiable truths.[34]

- Adolescents are mesmerized by the self-enhancing possibilities of propaganda and chauvinism because they speak to their need for importance. Youth do not believe every flattering message but they are intrinsically fascinated by an idea that exalts their importance, acknowledges their relevance, and advances their worth.

- Intelligence and reason regress in proportion to the narcissistic benefits their regression produces.

POSTSCRIPT

> To avoid the various foolish opinions to which mankind are prone, no superhuman genius is required. A few simple rules will keep you, not from all error, but from silly error. If the matter is one that can be settled by observation, make the observation yourself.
> —Bertrand Russell

My purpose in this chapter has been to give you the desire to make further voyages into the turbulent waters of adolescent intelligence. In pointing out how youth live in a state of conflict with their own rationality, I seek nothing more than to encourage clarity and honesty about a topic which, at this moment in our understanding, has little of either. I feel a bit like what the psychologists of the 1920s and 1930s must have felt when they tried to describe the intelligence of children in terms of what it actually could or could not do, rather than in terms of what the popular wisdom of that time demanded it *should* be able to do.

The popular wisdom of our era ascribes to adolescents a rationality they rarely possess. It is my belief, and one which I hope that I have well-demonstrated, that the adolescent thought process is prone toward irrationality and error. The vast reserves of reason which bless adolescent intelligence do not take hold on their own; they must be nurtured, cultivated, and practiced repeatedly to work effectively. Neither reason nor intelligence is automatic; they are learned and they are earned. These facts of the adolescent's mental ecology impose upon adults a more profound responsibility for nurturing the adolescent thought process than any of the current experts has heretofore acknowledged.[35]

II

Adolescent Selfishness

7

The Dynamics of
Self-Absorption

It is a curious state of affairs when an academic discipline dedicated to the study of a particular age group (adolescence) makes almost no attempt to investigate the most profound emotional states of that age group. Yet that is exactly what we have in the modern study of adolescent psychology. The human experiences which dominate adolescent existence are virtually nowhere to be found in the research or in the literature. (Indeed, take it as a challenge to find *any* human emotion analyzed in depth in a current adolescent psychology textbooks.) The literature on the subject is little more than what H. L. Mencken called "hollow word-chopping." The contemporary schools of adolescent psychology are barren to anyone who wants to learn about the feelings, the determination, the vitality, the tenacity, the altruism, or the spirit of youth.

A mini-correction to this sorry state of affairs will begin humbly with our look at adolescent self-absorption. At first glance one might think that the topic of self-absorption would already have been exhaustively researched as every parent on record seems to have claimed that their teenage child is self-absorbed, self-centered, lost in her own world, etc. But this is not the case. Indeed, in the nearly one hundred adolescent textbooks in my library, the term "self-absorption," is not listed even once. To learn about self-absorption we must leave behind the field of adolescent psychology as we know it; the most fruitful area of research, as near as I am able to determine, is what we might call "the psychology of narcissism."

For those of you already versed in narcissistic theory, this chapter will be a repeat of ideas with which you are already familiar. For those of you who know very little about narcissism, this chapter may serve as a general introduction to the topic.

Narcissism is not an easy topic. Like existentialism and phenomenology, it is grounded in the polarities of human consciousness, but unlike existentialism and phenomenolgy, it draws upon mother-infant connections, unconscious cravings, and the primal emotional states of grandiosity, omnipotence and fear to explain self-absorption. The various schools of narcissism are rich sources of information about two groups: narcissists and adolescents. They, of course, are not the same, but they do share important commonalities, and a close analysis of one tells us quite a bit about the other. And that is what we are up to here: trying to learn something about youth by looking at the narcissism of adults. One way to do this is by investigating the parallels between the adolescent personality and the narcissistic personality.

Narcissism, of course, is not a new concept. Its ancient origins are found in Ovid's myth of an adolescent boy, Narcissus, so totally absorbed in himself that he could love no one else; he was so self-enamored that the feelings of others meant nothing to him. He was a sun unto himself, and his radiance drew to him those in need of light and heat; but despite their desire to bask in his glow, his suitors received no real love as Narcissus could not give himself. Lovers gave to him, but not he to them. Of all those who pursued Narcissus, none suffered more deeply than Echo.

NARCISSUS AND ECHO

Narcissus, the son of the river-god Cephissus, was a physically perfect young man who was the object of desire among the nymphs, in whom he showed no interest. When he reached the age of sixteen his path was strewn with heartlessly rejected lovers, for he had a stubborn pride in his own beauty and a ceaseless fascination with himself. One nymph, Echo, who could no longer use her voice except in foolish repetition of another's voice, loved Narcissus deeply and one day she approached him only to be rudely rejected. In her shame and grief she perished, fading away, leaving behind only her responsive voice. The gods, in deciding to grant the nymph's wish for vengeance, decided that Narcissus must also experience the pain of an unreciprocated love. One day, while looking into a clear mountain pool, Narcissus viewed his own image and immediately fell in love, thinking that he was looking at a beautiful water spirit. Unable to tear himself away from his own image, and unable to evoke any response from the reflection, which disappeared when he attempted to embrace it, he grieved until death. When the nymphs came to bury him, he too had disappeared, leaving in his place a flower.

In this myth we see Echo, who had no self to speak of, trying desperately to fuse with Narcissus, who had no self to share; both ultimately withered away to nothing, Narcissus from an all-consuming self-absorption, Echo from the melancholic failure to bond with the selfish one. (Because there is so much to be learned from the pathological fixations of these mythological creatures, we will look more deeply into how the self-deficient (Echo) are drawn to the self-absorbed (Narcissus) in chapter fifteen.

Many centuries passed before Ovid's myth attained a niche in psychological theory. Ellis introduced the term "narcissism" to modern psychology (in 1898) when he referred to it as a normal state which is prone toward morbid exaggerations. In his paper "Auto-Erotism: A Psychological Study," he described a "Narcissus-like tendency" for the sexual emotions to be absorbed into self-admiration. Ellis viewed this phenomenon as an extreme form of auto-eroticism, in essence, a sexual perversion where the individual treated his (or her) own body as a sexual object. Later Paul Nacke, a German psychiatrist, after reading Ellis' paper coined the term *Narcismus* for the "Narcissus-like tendency." And while Ellis was the first to ascribe a specific psychiatric significance to the term we today call "narcissism," it was Sigmund Freud who gave it wings, and it was he who formulated the premises from which virtually all 20th century writing on the topic has evolved.

Whether Freud explicitly chose the adolescent hero of this myth to articulate what we now call narcissism, we do not know. What we do know is that Narcissus is the epitome of everything which we now call "narcissistic:" he was selfish, arrogant, obsessed with the visual, lacking in empathy, and consumed by an attitude of entitlement.

Let us begin, then, with a look at narcissism to see what possibilities it opens for us.

THE GENERAL MEANING OF NARCISSISM

In ordinary language narcissism refers to vanity, illusory love, and *hyper* self-absorption. Narcissism is an infatuation with self "so extreme that the interests of others are ignored, others serving merely as mirrors of one's own grandiosity" (Alford, 1988, p. 2). Its selfish nucleus, however, is not perceived by all scholars in a completely negative light, indeed, some scholars even make the case that narcissism is a positive trait of human nature—a case given only brief review here.

THE POSITIVE SIDE OF NARCISSISM

> Self love, my liege, is not so vile a sin as self-neglecting.
> —Shakespeare, *King Henry V*

That narcissism *can* be a positive force in the human personality is generally accepted in the psychological literature, that it *is* a positive force is not. Typically, the positive side of narcissism is designated "healthy narcissism," "normal narcissism," or, "favorable narcissism." "Favorable narcissism mobilizes behavior to beneficial purposes and is represented by normal self-concern and an adequate level of self-esteem: productive pride, we might call it" (Barrett, 1991, p. 34). Furthermore: "The mighty engine that drives the self in all interaction is abetted by the individual's inimitable stock of narcissistic energy" (p. 64).[36]

Narcissism's healthy and productive side inspired Carl Goldberg to write: "I view *healthy* narcissism as enhancing to the fulfillment of human existence.... Narcissistic strivings coexist with mature object love, both confounding and enriching its development... Narcissism, in its positive sense, is ...an enrichment of human experience" (1980, p. 13, original emphasis).

After all, a healthy self-concept without some narcissism is really quite unthinkable. What person could honorably exist without self-love, self-esteem, and self-admiration? We all are characterized by a selfish core which is a vital, worthy part of our being. Erich Fromm (1964), one of the first Neo-Freudians to envision the tremendous implications of Freud's theory of narcissism, claimed: "Even in the average individual ... there remains a narcissistic core which appears to be almost indestructible." And further, "In the case of normal development, man remains to some extent narcissistic throughout his life." Finally, and perhaps most significantly: "We can say that nature had to endow man with a great amount of narcissism to enable him to do what is necessary for survival" (1964, p. 72).

The positive elements of narcissism are only one side of the story, and a side not fully developed in this discussion. The reasons for this are rather straightforward: As narcissism gains strength it becomes progressively more hostile to the rights of others, it heightens selfish behavior, and it inflames the demand for entitlements. In *moderation* narcissism is part of our natural egoism, in *excess* it is pathological. Somewhere between healthy narcissism and its pathological extremes lives adolescence as it is known in North America.

NARCISSISM AS A DESTRUCTIVE FORCE IN THE HUMAN PERSONALITY: THE PSYCHOANALYTIC UNDERSTANDING OF NARCISSISM

> One of the most far-reaching of Freud's discoveries
> is his concept of narcissism.
> —Erich Fromm

Virtually all 20th century formulations of narcissism have as their starting point Freud's landmark essay "On Narcissism," first published in 1914. Scholars do not agree with all of Freud's formulations, but they do agree that he was the modern pioneer of this rich concept. Alfred Alford matter-of-factly observed: "Not surprisingly, Freud's 'On Narcissism' is the basis of almost all subsequent discussion of the topic." The heuristic richness of this original essay is even more impressive when we consider that it was not written for the purpose of formulating either a narcissistic personality type or a narcissistic character structure, but rather to explore variations in the development of libidinal cathexis—that is, *where the energy of the primitive self is invested.* Most experts agree that Freud's essay "On Narcissism" remains, after three-quarters of a century, indispensable reading for anyone interested in the subject.

Freud saw narcissism as the turning of love away from the world and inward upon the self, making the self the object of its own investment. In his own words, "The libido withdrawn from the outer world has been directed on to the ego, giving rise to a state which we may call *narcissism*" (1914, original emphasis). Freud claimed that each of us begins life in a blissful state of "primary narcissism" where no distinction exists between self and world, hence no painful tensions from unfulfilled desires, no experience of frustration; a stage of development where the infant has not as yet established any ego boundaries, and thus experiences itself and its environment as one. *Primary narcissism is the most primitive of all emotional states*: The infant is bestowed with a grandiose inflation, with feelings of perfection and power. From Freud's original ideas emerged the belief, still held in some quarters today, that the infant is fused with the mother and the world in a condition of wholeness and harmony. This fusion is a blissful, short-lived state, yet one that registers so forcefully on the evolving psyche that all of us, in certain measure, *spend our adolescent [an adult] years trying to recapture its splendor and glory.*[37]

Primary narcissism[38] is neither a perversion nor a defect; it is the stage of psychosexual development where the child's pleasures are concentrated within the self and the body. It is a developmental stage between autoeroticism and object love when distinct autoerotic sensations become fused into one's body, which then, together, become a single, unified love object. This "narcissistic condition" is the libidinal storehouse from which the love of self, and love in general, emerges. Eventually, much of the child's primary narcissism is abandoned in favor of ego development, and in time, the child replaces self-love with love for others. But the love received from others cannot yield the primal satisfaction of one's original self-love. (The significance of this point cannot be over-stated: It implies that shared love is a reduced, less fulfilling than self-love; primacy of self-love, at the expense of other-love, is the defining feature of narcissism.)

Central to Freud's theorizing about narcissism is the assumption that, in the earliest stages, the infant is at one with the mother and not yet able to distinguish objects or relate to the world.[39] Freud recognized that the developing infant eventually separates self from surroundings, and from this separation a primitive sense of tension differentiates *into the experience of need for others*. As the infant grows, its separation from itself allows the merger with other selves—a necessary starting point in the journey toward loving others, toward community, indeed, toward all sharing behavior.

> Needs put pressure on the developing ego to acquire the skills necessary to fulfill the need, and so the ego adapts to object-reality. *All the energy that in infancy was bound exclusively to the subject in this way slowly extends out and becomes bound up in the subject's pursuit of objects.* The process is essential to normal development. (Satinover, 1987, p. 87, original emphasis)

The Freudian position, despite its web of unverifiable starting points, is actually rather straightforward. During childhood, emotional development is dependent upon "giving up" one's basic narcissism; the selfish love we each have for ourselves eventually is shared with others. This extending of self-love creates only partial satisfaction within the evolving personality; cravings persist for the total self-absorption of primary narcissism.

> Freud never altered the basic idea that the original state of man, in early infancy, is that of ... primary narcissism in which there are not yet any relations to the outside world, that then in the course of normal development the child begins to increase in scope and intensity his (libidinal) relationships to the outside world, but that in many instances ... he withdraws his libidinal attachment from objects and directs it back to his ego ("secondary narcissism"). But even in the case of normal development, man remains to some extent narcissistic throughout his life. (Fromm, 1964, p. 63)

Furthermore:

> Indeed, the development of the individual can be defined in Freud's term as *the evolution from absolute narcissism to a capacity for objective reasoning and object love....* The "normal," "mature" person is one whose narcissism has been reduced to the socially accepted minimum without ever disappearing completely. Freud's observation is confirmed by everyday experience. It seems that *in most people one can find a narcissistic core which is not accessible and which defies any attempt at complete dissolution.* (Fromm, 1964, p. 64, emphasis added)

Narcissism expresses itself *through the struggle to re-experience* the infant's "oceanic oneness." As Freud conjectured in his famous essay: "The development of the ego consists in a departure from primary narcissism and *gives rise to a vigorous attempt to recover that state*" (1914, p. 95, emphasis added). The desire to recover the state of narcissism is an unsatisfied craving within the adolescent personality. But, unfortunately, there is a rub: Archaic emotional states cannot be recovered—like infancy, they are forever gone. The most any of us can recover of our previous narcissistic glory are fleeting episodes of euphoric self-immersion, periodic flashes of primal grandiosity. The narcissist and the adolescent share a common craving—the euphoria of the primitive self.

Although perhaps an untimely note here at the end of this brief overview, no known way exists to prove or disprove the vital assumptions which serve as the building blocks for Freud's theory of narcissism. Freud, in his favor, was completely aware of this, as he candidly reports in his 1926 treatise on inhibitions, symptoms, and anxiety: "Unfortunately, far too little is known about the mental constitution of the new-born child to make a direct answer possible. I cannot even vouch for the validity of the description I have just given."

The problem is that no way exists to verify that the infant exists in blissful, perfect harmony with "mother and the world." To reject this assumption, which Christopher Lasch mistakenly called a discovery, is to reject the psychoanalytic foundation of narcissistic theory. Even so, some experts have done precisely that. Fine states: "The whole Freudian notion of primary narcissism has come under severe attack from the infant researchers, and properly so. The image of the infant as 'narcissistic' or living in a state of 'narcissistic bliss' has to be abandoned" (1986, p. 57). Fine also reports the conclusions of C. Chiland, who claims: "The concept of a purely dyadic relationship between infant and mother is now as unacceptable as the concept of a stage of normal autism" (p. 58). All of these criticisms make clear that the theoretical foundations upon which the theory of narcissism rests, are open to question. However, the focus of this book is upon adolescent behavior not the weaknesses in psychoanalytic theory; therefore, these criticisms of Freud's thinking will infuse caution into, but will not halt, our investigation of narcissism and its relationship to the adolescent community. In this regard our situation is similar to that of the teacher who tries to teach the child to read without having any clear understanding of how the brain processes symbols.[40]

KAREN HORNEY'S UNDERSTANDING OF NARCISSISM

Karen Horney originally trained as a psychoanalyst in Berlin, then moved to America to become a member of the New York Psychoanalytic Institute. In 1941 she was dismissed from the Institute because of ideological differences with Freudian orthodoxy; she subsequently founded the American Institute for Psychoanalysis. Horney emphasized social factors in the human personality far more than Freud, and she held a considerably more open and optimistic view of human nature. Her theories relied heavily on several psychoanalytic concepts, such as repression, but her differences with Freud were genuine and significant, especially in her belief that neurosis originated in basic anxiety and disturbed human relationships. And even though most of her writings were devoted to psychotherapy, neurosis, and female sexuality, her insights concerning narcissism were considerable.

She was an effective theoretician but not a system-builder in the same way as Freud. She explained her theory of narcissism without concepts such as libido or internalized self objects and representations, all of which she believed were clinically unverifiable. Horney's clinical observations did not support Freud's libido theory, which claimed that self-esteem is a desexualized form of self-love, and that persons tending toward overvaluation must be expressing self-love. In a technical sense, Horney believed that narcissism is the identification with the idealized image of the self, a loving of the unrealistically glorified attributes of the self. In a practical sense, she believed that narcissism is *an unjustified egocentric self-inflation, an overdone self-absorption.* This belief, as it turns out, is one of her most important contributions to this topic because it is predicated on the idea that the self-esteem of the healthy person and the self-inflation of the narcissist are mutually exclusive. She viewed healthy self-esteem as based on authentic attributes, on positive and pleasurable feelings of pride and worth. Narcissistic self-inflation, on the other hand, pretends to possess capabilities that do not exist.

In *New Ways in Psychoanalysis* (1939, p. 47) she advanced ideas which speak both to narcissism and to adolescence. In narcissism "the person loves and admires himself for values for which there is no adequate foundation. Similarly, it means that he expects love and admiration from others for qualities that he does not possess, or does not possess to as large an extent as he supposes." She placed great emphasis on an honest portrayal of oneself and one's abilities and, by implication, upon the distortions and fables which subvert an honest understanding of self and others. It is from this line of reasoning that she made inroads into our understanding of adolescent behavior and its commonalities with narcissism.

In her line of speculation, the narcissist is someone whose emotional links are brittle, and who, in over-protecting the self, suffers a loss of the capacity to love. Perhaps more than any feature this is the defining feature of narcissism: the loss of the ability to love.

The overvalued self sees the world selfishly (just as we might suspect) because it values itself more highly than it values the outside world. Narcissists see only through the lens of self-interest and because of the failure inherent to such perceptions, narcissists are, in a profound way, learning disabled.

To make clear her divergence from Freud, Horney wrote: "The correlation between love of self and love of others is not valid in the sense that Freud intends it. Nevertheless, the dualism which Freud assumes ... contains an odd and significant truth. This is, briefly, that *any kind of egocentricity detracts from a real interest in others, that it impairs the capacity to love others*" (1939, p. 100, original emphasis). This idea goes a long way toward summarizing the basic conficts of adolescent life—egocentricity does, indeed, detract from a real interest in others. As we will see in future chapters, it impairs the adolescent's capacity for shared intimacy and mature love, just as Karen Horney predicted.

POSTSCRIPT

> He that falls in love with himself will have no rivals.
> —*Poor Richard's Almanac*

I have assembled these ideas on narcissism in the hope that they would help us to draw fresh conclusions about the adolescent experience. In the present discussion I am putting forth nothing new; the ideas brought to your attention have been as much for review as for any other purpose. However, even in this form, they enable us to conceive ideas important to adolescent psychology.

To Freud, narcissism is a turning of love away from the world and inward upon the self. During the formative months the infant is fused with the mother in wholeness, harmony, and bliss: a fusion so perfect that each of us strive to regain its euphoric splendor. Primary narcissism, therefore, is the first stage of psychosexual development, a time when the child's pleasures are concentrated within the body. This narcissism weakens as the child replaces self-love with love for others; but every person, to greater or lesser degree, craves to return to the grandiosity of self-love. This driving passion to return to primal self-love is one of Freud's great contributions to our understanding of human nature, and as well, to our understanding of adolescent self-absorption. (An idea I will develop in upcoming chapters is that the adolescent personality is engaged in an ongoing struggle to lessen self-absorption in order to better pursue reciprocal friendship. As one pretty much precludes the other it becomes a struggle of self-love versus other-love, just as Freud predicted.)

Karen Horney's portrayal of narcissism is less eloquent than Freud's, but perhaps because of its simplicity and common sense, it more closely approximates how most people think of it. Horney believed that the narcissist admires and loves the self for reasons "for which there is no adequate foundation." Self-absorption is a fear-driven substitute for legitimate esteem which thrives in individuals so insecure that they dare not share themselves for fear that they will be rejected, ridiculed or scorned. Narcissists are self-absorbed not because of self-love but because they fear everything beyond the self.

Horney, to her credit and our benefit, stressed the behavioral consequences of narcissism whereas Freud was concerned primarily with its infantile origins, and the psychic conflicts which produce it. As a result of this fundamental difference in their orientations, Horney was more attuned to the socially destructive aspects of narcissism, especially to the stream of entitlement demands which flow from the narcissistic core. Her person-oriented research, coupled with Freud's foundation in theory, provides us with some starting points in unraveling the mystery of adolescent self-absorption.

8

Adolescence and Narcissism

> Narcissistic traits may be particularly common in adolescents and do not necessarily indicate that the individual will go on to have Narcissistic Personality Disorder.
>
> —*DSM IV*

Several years ago I began to investigate the classic theories of narcissism to see if they had something to offer someone with an interest in adolescent psychology. The findings have been rather encouraging, especially as they relate to self-absorption and self-centerdness. And although rarely is anything *completely* new under the sun, there are moments, as Noam Chomsky once wrote, "when traditional ideas are reshaped... and the opportunities that lie ahead appear in a new light" (1989, p. 45). Hopefully, by taking a look into the basic themes of narcissism we can generate fresh insights into the psychology of youth; insights which allow us to see adolescence, if not in new light perhaps in a brighter one.[41]

THE CONNECTIVE LINKS BETWEEN NARCISSISM AND ADOLESCENCE

From chapter seven we recall that narcissism refers to vanity, to excessive self-centeredness, to illusory love, and to protective self-absorption, the totality of which produces a self-infatuation so complete that others are ignored unless they feed or flatter the self. As narcissism gains strength in the personality it is increasingly inconsiderate of the rights and needs of others. Narcissistic individuals, therefore, do not grant to others what they demand for themselves, and they do not see themselves as members of a community, but rather as individuals surrounded by a community. For all of these reasons, narcissism is of interest to those of us who study adolescence.

Freud understood narcissism as the turning of love away from the world and inward upon the self, making the self the object of its own investment. Freud also believed that every person begins life in a blissful state of "primary narcissism" where no distinction exists between self and world; this is a stage of development where the infant has not as yet established any ego boundaries, and thus experiences itself and its environment as one. Primary narcissism bestows the child with feelings of perfection and power, wholeness and harmony. It is a blissful fusion so profound that youth spend their adolescent years trying to recapture its glory.

Primary narcissism is the stage of psychosexual development where the child's pleasures are concentrated within the self and the body—a developmental stage between autoeroticism and object love when autoerotic sensations become fused into one's body, which then together become a single, unified love object. This "narcissistic condition" is the libidinal storehouse from which the love of self, and love in general, emerges. Eventually, much of the child's primary narcissism is abandoned in favor of ego development, and in time, the child replaces self-love with love for others. *But the love received from others cannot equal the primal grandiosity of self-love.* In narcissistic theory, this final point is vital and its acceptance or rejection shapes how we view the adolescent's approach to love, sharing and cooperation.

Theories of Narcissism Highlight the Data of Self-Experience

Theories of narcissism are concerned with the contradictions of human existence, including how the self can feel powerful and inflated, and yet at the same time vulnerable and deflated. Recognizing these contradictions as inherent properties of the self helps us to understand the polarities of mood so prevalent among young people. This, I think is what Wexler was getting at when he observed:

> *Adolescence is a period of intensely heightened narcissism and self-preoccupation* .... The self-esteem swings typical of narcissistic syndromes ... are plainly visible. (1991, p. 29, original emphasis)

Feeling powerful and at the same time vulnerable, feeling worthwhile and at the same time worthless are experiences adolescents share with narcissists.

When we take into account the adolescent's "intensely heightened narcissism and self-preoccupation" we see why self-absorption dominates youth culture.

The contradictory and oppositional nature of the adolescent personality helps us to recognize how incomplete the concept of self-esteem is in understanding adolescent behavior. Youth do not have positive self-esteem or negative self-esteem; *they have both at the same time*. Self-evaluation and self-esteem are not static features of the adolescent character; they ebb and flow with the situation, with affective arousal, with success and with failure. The adolescent lives in a world of dualities and contradictions, and to expect a uniform pulse is to misread their basic rhythm.[42a]

Theories of Narcissism Help Us to Understand the Adolescent Predisposition to Shrink (Rather Than to Expand) Life's Opportunities

If we have learned anything over the past several decades of personality research, it is that narcissists are cowards. Narcissists hide from the world because they fear it will shatter their eggshell-thin sense of worth. Like every frightened soul, they avoid fear by hiding from its source. But how can one hide from life? Through self-induced narrowness. And what we see in narcissists we see almost identically in frightened adolescents. Why? The answer is simple mathematics: The narrower the borders of one's life, the greater is the self which lives within these borders. Hence, narrowing one's life is a strategy to expand one's significance.

The benefits of narrowness are inherently attractive to the fearful. Here are a few to think about:

- Narrowness lessens the pain of interacting with others who do not think of us as grand and glorious. Narcissists (and adolescents) abhor interactions where they are thought of as *just another person.*
- Narrowness and isolation are perceived by adolescents as statements of independence even when they are motivated by a fear of participation.
- Narrowness, even when racked with pain or failure, is more narcissistically rewarding than a world which does not spotlight "me."
- Narrowness flatters the self by excluding everything unflattering to it.
- Narrowness is the adolescent's first flirtation with heroic isolation; that is, perceiving oneself as heroic by hiding from the embrace of others.
- Narrowness manipulates intimacy by declaring that it must be achieved in "my" territory and on "my" terms. And although this may appear self-defeating, in the adolescent world it often is not. Many more adolescent friendships than we care to acknowledge begin from self-enhancing narrowness.
- Narrowness, at bottom, is a narcissistic response to the demands for social expansion which come to play during the adolescent years.

Theories of Narcissism Help Us to Better Understand the Alternating Qualities of Self-Love and Self-Hate So Frequently Observed During Adolescence

For some time now educators, parents, and psychologists have been fascinated with self-esteem. To them almost everything positive comes from it and almost everything negative from the lack of it. And I don't want to say too much about this except that as a concept, self-esteem lacks the range to do justice to the adolescent experience. Much of what we see in the adolescent arena is not adequately explained by "low" or "high" self-esteem because it is grounded in the far more profound experiences of love and hate. Narcissism offers important insights, one of which is that during adolescence love and hate intermingle so fluidly that one easily transforms into the other.

While interviewing a 15-year-old as part of my ongoing research, she unexpectedly offered: "You know, I really am my own best friend." She said it with such convincing sincerity that I immediately believed her. However, after consulting my notes, I calmly reminded her that in our interview of the previous day she had said, after a lengthy discussion, "I guess you could say that I am my own worst enemy." I brought these conflicting statements to her attention and then asked her if they involved a contradiction. She replied: "No way! Everyone is their own best friend *and* their own worst enemy." Putting aside the implicit sophistication from an otherwise startlingly immature 15-year-old, her comment contains interesting points worth looking into. Of course, being one's own best friend is not the same as self-love, and being one's own worst enemy is not the same as self-hate, but some overlap is easily observed, especially when focusing, as we are, on the narcissistic elements within the developing personality.[42b]

Theories of Narcissism Help Us to Better Understand Why Children Raised in North American Culture Are So Intensely Self-Invested

When adolescents cannot invest their energy outward they invest it inward. This reflex, preserved from infancy, is no small matter in the psychology of youth. Our culture provides young people with few opportunities for worthy outward investment; instead, we offer them carnival showmanship, street corner theatrics, and juvenile self-stim which pulls them down the developmental ladder and alienates them from the worthwhile machinery of society. Our consumerist mentality encourages youth to define themselves by appearance, by status, by gender, but almost never by honest, meaningful contribution.

The conclusion which presents itself is that we as a society are lacking in the human endorsements needed to transport youth beyond their natural narcissism. One outcome of this failure is that many youth become self-obsessed; but, as psychologists have known for decades, the young self cannot grow and mature until it invests itself in beyond-the-self projects. The failure to journey beyond the self is the prison of both narcissists and youth, and the consequences are quite similar for both: a fascination with the visual, a fixation on the superficial, and an obsession with the immediate. Self-obsession as it is expressed in youth, and as it is expressed in adult narcissism, is an inherently diminishing and defeating enterprise. It produces underdeveloped selves which grow into underdeveloped citizens.

Cooper (1986) had some interesting comments about the persona of a society deformed by consumerism and warped by egotism:

> The high divorce rate, the loss of religion, the inability to maintain an extended family, the abandonment of the home by women who join the work force, the lack of traditional pursuits, which are valued for their own sakes rather than for the material rewards they bring—all of this and more have been cited as causes for, and evidence of, the so-called narcissistic generation. From this perspective, individuals are more than ever self-centred, incapable of self-sacrifice for another person, without deeper moral, spiritual, or emotional values, and capable of experiencing only shallow transference relationships—all of which ultimately subjects them to the perils of alienation, boredom, and insecure relationships. (1986, p. 125)

Is it likely that the youth of our society lack the narcissism of their elders?[43] Probably not: "A culture which valorizes narcissism...will be registered psychically and reproduced intergenerationally" (Frosh, 1991, p. 113). "American culture can't lead people to narcissistic waters and expect them not to drink in their reflections on its surface. American culture can't spend billions on advertising that tries to cultivate glittering images, and then snatch away the mirror" (Olgivy, 1995, p. 88). Less eloquently, but to the same end, Cervantes long ago wrote: "It is nature's law that everything shall beget its like." Frosh, Olgivy, and Cervantes speak to the same question: "How can childen overcome the narcissism of their parent society?" It is one of the most profound moral questions of our era.

Some Final Connective Links Between The Phenomenology Of Narcissism And The Phenomenology Of Youth[44]

Here I would like to briefly overview some of the emotional predispositions and behavioral tendencies shared by adolescents and narcissists.

Concerning criticism

Teens share with narcissists a confusion between criticism and aggression. The bottom line is that narcissists and adolescents share an almost paranoid fear of criticism, and from this fear sprouts an anxious aversion to anyone who in any way criticizes. The adolescent's universe cannot be grasped in its totality without taking into account the fear of criticism.

Concerning rights and benefits

Teens share with narcissists the presumption that they are *entitled* to receive extra benefits and special rights. Adolescents do not have to be taught an attitude of entitlement because they are emotionally predisposed to it. This predisposition, as I tried to make clear in previous chapters, is grounded in their egocentrism, in their lack of perspective-taking, in their need to affirm the self, and in their tendency to perceive adults merely as providers and suppliers. These predispositions can be overcome by effective teaching, by seeing from another's perspective, by having a safe and secure environment, by working on worthwhile projects, and by participating meaningfully in the lives of others. In their absence, the selfish side of the adolescent personality becomes dominant.

Concerning the receipt of favors

Teens and narcissists share the tendency to presume that they receive favors *because of something special within them,* not because of anything special within the one who provides. This tendency, so natural to the child, contributes to an indifference to their providers and this indifference heightens the tension between them. As a rule, adolescents begin more fully to appreciate the qualities of their teachers, parents, and other providers near the end of middle adolescence (ages 16-17). Narcissists, on the other hand, never get around to it. Hence, at 40 their attitudes concerning the receipt of favors are remarkably similar to those of 12-, 13-, and 14-year-olds. In a very real sense, the psychology of the early adolescent parallels the psychology of the narcissist, and vice versa.

Concerning humiliation

Teens and narcissists harbor a fear of humiliation in any way, shape, or form; this fear leads to their refusal to participate in activities where humiliation might possibly occur. Both groups are overly infatuated with perfection and both share the belief that any less-than-perfect performance will shower shame or ridicule upon them. Both groups hold self-images they cannot possibly defend. Polansky (1991) observed: "Obsession with an image of yourself can make you so sensitive to criticism that ordinary give and take is humiliating and you avoid people.... Teenagers trapped with this defense certainly cannot be loose and spontaneous." With regard to shame: "An overconcern with your image exacerbates feelings of shame. Some cannot even ask a question, for not to know is to admit being less than perfect. Others cannot acquire skills. To practice a sport means living through a period of looking bad" (Polansky, 1991, p. 74).

Louise Kaplan was equally impressed with the adolescent's fear of humiliation: "Another reason for the increased self-centerdness of an adolescent is her susceptibility to humiliation. This brazen, defiant creature is also something tender, raw, thin-skinned, poignantly vulnerable. Her entire sense of personal worth can be shattered by a frown. An innocuous clarification of facts can be heard as a monumental criticism" (1984, p. 189).[45]

Bleiberg (1994, p. 116) claimed: "Perhaps like no other phase of life, the passage through adolescence bears the hallmarks of narcissistic vulnerability: a proneness to embarrassment and shame, acute self-consciousness and shyness, and painful questions about self-esteem and self-worth." He could easily have added another link connecting adolescents and narcissisists: the fear of humiliation.

Concerning "good" people and "bad" people

Teens and narcissists share a tendency to divide their social world into "good" people and "bad" people, "good" groups and "bad" groups. The basis for this classification is fairly simple: Good people are those who nourish "me" and bad people are those who don't. From this primitive partitioning of the social order springs a remarkable willingness to love, honor, and obey the "good," and to hate, slander, and disobey the "bad." Teens and narcissists are both prepared "to do battle against whatever or whomever does not reinforce his fragile construction of reality" (Schmookler, 1988 p. 103).

Adolescents and narcissists break the outside world into "good" and "bad" to render their allies great and their foes unworthy. Indeed, the real function of what they describe as "good" or "bad" is to deflate everything which does not support "me" and to inflate everything that does.

POSTSCRIPT

Current theories fail to adequately encompass the paradoxes of adolescence. The study of narcissistic regulation and narcissistic vulnerability does, however, provide a window onto the paradoxes marking normal and pathological development in adolescence.
—Efrain Bleiberg

To encourage new perceptions about the adolescent experience, I am here suggesting that some of the core concepts of narcissism, seen in the proper light, can enrich our understanding of adolescent psychology.

I have embarked on this venture because it seems to me that we have not made much progress in understanding why adolescents so easily choose self-destructive paths.[46] It is not an exaggeration to say that we simply do not understand why they so easily become involved in relationships destructive to their emotional, economic, and human welfare. We have a long journey to travel before we understand why teens, as Musick phrased it, "turn their back on opportunities, deliberately sabotaging their prospects for success" (1993, p. 4).

What we need, and cannot lay our finger on, is a worthy explanation as to why some adolescents move in self-destructive directions when others do not. Hopefully, our investigation of narcissism will shed some light on this mystery.

The following ideas were given a brief introduction in this chapter:

- The theory of narcissism helps us to understand the self-fixation so typical of adolescence;
- The theory of narcissism helps us to recognize that young people inflate themselves in order to neutralize their fear that they are nothing;
- The theory of narcissism helps us understand how a consumer culture promotes self-obsession;
- The theory of narcissism tells us that love blossoms in youth only after they have received large doses of it from the important people in their lives.

Two conclusions cannot be escaped in all this. First, through constructive participation in real events young people grow beyond their primitive narcissism. Second, in the absence of meaningful participation in the lives of others, narcissism colonializes the adolescent personality eventually to become the dominant force within it.

9

Developmental Selfishness

Adolescent selfishness has both healthy and unhealthy expressions, and in this chapter I will try to explain something of its healthy side. It is my belief that developmental selfishness is as natural to adolescents as egocentrism is to children, and like egocentrism, it shrouds their character with an enveloping egoism and a pressing, nervous self-awareness. It is not a greedy, fearful form of selfishness as we see in *narcissistic selfishness* (the focus of the next chapter). Rather, developmental selfishness is a normal, natural, inevitable fact of adolescent development.

THE NORMAL CONDITION OF
DEVELOPMENTAL SELFISHNESS

> The ego needs to be loved, requires attention, and wants exposure.
> This part of its nature.
> —Thomas Moore

Here I want to lay the preliminary groundwork for the idea that adolescents are infused with a developmentally driven selfishness which, while not as innocent as that which graces children, is equally grounded in their particular stage of life. Developmental selfishness, as I am here describing it, is a relentless awareness of one's own feelings, fears, and desires, and this awareness, in turn, fosters a burning self-consciousness and a network of self-protective morals and manners. This omnipresent self-consciousness is the trademark of healthy youth. We want to learn more about it because it is natural, because it is universal, and because under the wrong conditions it deteriorates into an unwelcome, unhealthy selfishness.[47]

Let's begin by refreshing our understanding of egocentrism because it is the heart and soul of the kind of selfishness we are now considering. To be egocentric is to be preoccupied with one's own concerns and insensitive to the concerns of others. Piaget understood it as an *embeddedness* in one's own point of view. Very young children cannot distinguish their own point of view from the point of view of others; they may not even know what "a point of view" is. Most developmentalists assume that young children (toddlers and preschoolers) do not seem to know that other perceptions of reality exist, but older children and adolescents do. And this is one of the differences between children and adolescents—the awareness of alternate viewpoints. Margaret Donaldson put it this way: "The child does not appreciate that what he sees is relative to his own position; he takes it to represent absolute truth or reality— *the world as it really is*" (1978, p. 20, original emphasis). Egocentrism is the starting point for developmental selfishness.

Developmental selfishness contributes to a preoccupation with everything pertaining to "me." Not only with that which praises, validates, and affirms, but also that which criticizes, weakens, and deflates. This incessant preoccupation with self heats the oratory of youth.[48]

That youth are selfishly preoccupied and wrapped up in themselves is certainly not a new observation. Aristotle, the most meticulous and methodical of the early observers, knew that lava flowed in the blood of Athenian youth, and he said as much in documenting their habits and inclinations:

> They are passionate, irascible, and apt to be carried away by their impulses. They are the slave, too, of their passion, as their ambition prevents their ever brooking a slight and renders them indignant at the mere idea of enduring an injury....
> If the young commit a fault, it is always *on the side of excess and exaggeration* for they carry everything too far, whether it be their love or hatred or anything else. (Kiell, 1964, p. 18-19, original emphasis)

And although it is likely that Aristotle exaggerated both the virtues and the defects of youth, there is little reason to doubt that some basis in fact existed for his observations. Indeed, when he reported that youth were self-centered and impetuous in 300 B.C., there is every reason to believe that he had good reason to do so. Anna Freud, 2300 years after Aristotle, judged that North American teens "are excessively egoistic, regarding themselves as the centre of the universe and the sole objects of interest (1966, p. 124)." Both Aristotle and Anna Freud, in their own way, were trying to tell us about the developmental selfishness inherent to youth.

POSTSCRIPT

I am here trying to convey a simple idea: Adolescents possess a vigilant spirit which invigorates their sense of themselves and creates a sustained egoism. This "sustained egoism" colors their perceptions of the world, it narrows their vision, and it makes them more alive to the realities within their boundaries than to those outside it. The end result is an uneven concoction of self-love, self-centeredness and selfishness, leading Gordon Allport, one of North America's great psychologists, to conclude: "Self-love may be prominent in our natures without necessarily being sovereign" (1955, p. 45). And that pretty much sums it up: Developmental selfishness is prominent in the adolescent's nature without being sovereign. All young people do not experience it with identical intensity or express it with identical vigor, but all healthy youth possess it in rich supply.

The selfishness I am describing here is not grounded in a hostile disregard for others, nor in pushing one's own advantage at the expense of others; it is a friendly, natural self-centeredness which does not degrade others. It is spiced with vanity and self-reference—the universal tattoo of healthy youth. When we love youth, we acknowledge the developmental selfishness inherent to it, for when it is properly acknowledged and lovingly nourished it grows beyond itself into altruism, social interest, and mutuality.

When development proceeds on schedule, developmental selfishness lessens. However, when development is thwarted, when the self expends all of its energy protecting itself, when the young person does not invest in others, then developmental selfishness descends into defeating forms of selfish investment. They are the focus of the next two chapters.

10

Narcissistic
Selfishness

Although an accentuated self-awareness is a normal part of adolescence,
excessive selfishness is dysfunctional.
—Lauren Ayers

In ordinary language, narcissism refers to vanity, illusory love, and chronic self-absorption; an infatuation with self "so extreme that the interests of others are ignored, others serving merely as mirrors of one's own grandiosity" (Alford, 1988, p. 2). Narcissism represents a turning of love away from the world and inward upon the self; hence, the narcissistic self is obsessed with its own gratifications but, in addition, is burdened with a morbid fear of humiliation and an unhealthy fear of losing. In order to make clear how narcissistic selfishness differs from developmental selfishness, let me describe some of its oppressive features.

First, narcissistically selfish persons are always anxiously concerned with themselves, they are always restless, and they are driven by the fear of not getting enough. It doesn't matter too much what it is that they want, they are afraid they won't receive enough of it, and this fear dulls the pleasure of attaining what they crave. Narcissistically selfish individuals do not experience real pleasure when they give but they always experience great pleasure when they receive. They have little genuine mercy, and they show little concern for the needs of others; they judge everyone from the standpoint of usefulness or nonusefulness.[49]

The narcissistically selfish cannot maintain any sense of themselves without massive infusions of attention and admiration, and without these infusions they disintegrate into to a "minimal self." And this is one of the many paradoxes of the narcissistically selfish: While their life is governed by selfishness, they are completely dependent on others to provide attention and admiration—without which they will disintegrate. Thus, they cannot isolate themselves, living a hermit's life within the circumference of their own vanity because they desperately need others as providers. Their ravenous hunger for attention and admiration drives them to solicit acceptance to confirm their worth. Individuals with the right skills may eventually become expert solicitors, and as we will see, some are extremely skilled at cultivating younger youth to their own ends.[50]

Their obsession with grooming, with physical appearance, and with presenting a beautiful body, rather than building confidence within themselves, triggers a chronic envy of these features in others. They crave and hate the same thing at the same time: They love stylish haircuts when they have one, but hate them when they are "flaunted" by someone else; they love to walk with confidence but hate the cocky swagger of those who walk the walk; they love to be the object of admiration but despise it when others are admired.

To this list we must add envy—the feeling of resentment aroused by another's possessions and achievements. Envy causes us to perceive others in terms of our own yearnings and imposes our insecurities on them. Envy characterizes all of us to some degree, but among the narcissistically selfish it is relentless.

> If I have an internal conviction that I am lacking in some way and that my inadequacies are always at risk of exposure, I will be envious toward those who seem content or who have assets that I believe would make up for what I lack. Envy may also be the root of the much-observed judgmental quality of narcissistically organized persons, toward themselves and toward others. *If I feel deficient and I perceive you as having it all, I may try to destroy what you have by deploring, scorning, or criticizing it.* (McWilliams, 1994, p. 172, original emphasis)

Narcissistically selfish individuals cannot handle relationships in which give and take exist in equal portions; therefore, basic needs which require equality for their gratification (intimacy, deep friendship) are never satisfied in these individuals. They displace their feelings of unworthiness onto others, and their contempt for themselves becomes contempt for others, even their friends, their parents, and their lovers.[51]

In a thoughtful discussion of this topic Ben Bursten asked: "Why do these people need to have so high an interest in themselves?" Answering his own query: "They cannot take themselves for granted; *they constantly need to confirm their selves*" (Bursten, 1977, p. 17).[52]

It is definitely a two person relationship in which, however, only one of the partners matters; his wishes and needs are the only ones that count and must be attended to; the other partner, though felt to be immensely powerful, matters only insofar as he is willing to gratify the first partner's needs and desires or decides to frustrate them; beyond this, his personal interests, needs, desires, wishes, etc., simply do not exist. (Bursten, 1977, p. 104)

Narcissistically selfish individuals seek relationships in which they are praised but not challenged. Finding companions to serve this function is their social mission; without "suppliers" (who they call "friends") they have no purpose, no meaning, no direction. Hence, the narcissistically selfish are always on the recruitment trail, always in search of friends to provide them with emotional supplies.

I have here defined narcissistic selfishness, but I am not trying to make the case that it is universal in the adolescent community, because it is not. But, on the other hand, it is an extreme human selfishness which is not rare during adolescence.

POSTSCRIPT

> To take and not to give is an amoral, self-centered, predisposition that
> ultimately no society can tolerate.
> —Amitai Etzioni (1993)

My conclusions on this topic are not particularly profound, but they do have profound implications. It is my belief that the regression from developmental selfishness to narcissistic selfishness is possible during the course of adolescent development. It does not occur with great regularity, but it does occur. The migration from developmental selfishness to the narcissistic style (which I discuss in the next chapter) to narcissistic selfishness is encouraged by our society's isolation of youth from real life, by its exclusion of youth from real responsibility, and by the endless barrage of narcissistic images hurled at youth by our image-driven society. The ability of youth to honor their social obligations is determined not so much by their natural skills, but by how effectively the adults in their lives have *taught* them, by word and by deed, to follow standards greater than those to which they are predisposed by age and inclination.

In view of the differences between developmental selfishness and narcissistic selfishness, a question may be appropriately raised: Is there an in-between ground where a hybrid of these two types of selfishness is found? The answer, in my understanding of adolescence, is yes. I call this midground *the narcissistic style,* and it is the object of investigation in the next chapter.

11

The Narcissistic Style

Between the natural egoism of developmental selfishness and the self-protective cocoon of narcissistic selfishness we find a third kind of self-centeredness which I call *the narcissistic style*. In this chapter I will try to chronicle its essential features, and in doing so I think we will obtain a better feel for the differences between youth who are completely cloaked in self-priority and those who are only partly so.

Before we begin, a brief step backward might help us to better set our sights. Developmental selfishness, we recall, refers to the natural self-centeredness and to the necessary egoism which announces the adolescent personality. Narcissistic selfishness, in contrast, is a pathological selfishness resembling the Narcissistic Personality Disorder. I introduced the concept of narcissistic selfishness not because I believe that it is a significant force in the adolescent community, but because I believe that its subdued version, the narcissistic style, is.

The narcissistic style is an excessive swelling of the selfishness natural to youth (developmental selfishness), with a few additional twists. In addition to an exaggerated and persistent self-focus, the narcissistic style also carries with it a seething resentment which causes one to continually demean and degrade others. Because of this feature the narcissistic style, in its extreme form, resembles narcissistic selfishness; yet, in its subdued form it resembles the normal, developmental selfishness of youth.

My primary concern is with the thought patterns associated with the narcissistic style, not the psychogenic causes which create them. (As I tried to indicate earlier, a clear picture of the origins of narcissism is virtually impossible; it at the least requires one to accept as fact completely unverifiable premises.)[53]

I have no doubt about the pervasive presence of the narcissistic style in the adolescent population, and neither, if my assessment is correct, do teachers, coaches, social workers, clergy, and parents. The narcissistic style acquires its strength during a time of life when normal developmental ground plans move youth away from the egocentric narrowness of childhood toward the more allocentric openness required of adulthood. The narcissistic style thwarts this natural transformation by imbuing the adolescent with an egotistic focus which yields precious little on the affirmative end while extracting dearly in sociability and mutuality. The narcissistic style maximizes self-investment and minimizes other-investment suffocating the attitude of community required of dignified maturity. The narcissistic style is a peculiar mix of egotism, moral selfishness, egocentric narrowness, and an overdeveloped attitude of entitlement.

With these preliminary comments serving as a general guide, let us now take a more detailed look at the habits and reflexes which make up the narcissistic style.

WHAT IS MEANT BY THE NARCISSISTIC STYLE?

The defining feature of the narcissistic style is an egotism which exceeds normal developmental boundaries but does not equal the outrageous excesses of narcissistic selfishness. The narcissistic style inhabits an in-between world with developmental selfishness on one border and narcissistic selfishness on the other, showing itself sometimes as exaggerated developmental selfishness, and at other times as subdued narcissistic selfishness.

The individual immersed in the narcissistic style is a sun unto himself, a beacon in his own harbor. An important aspect of the narcissistic style is that it is demeaning to others, and in this regard it is closer to narcissistic selfishness than to developmental selfishness. It usually is grounded in emotional protectionism and an anxious apprehension that, with progressive maturity, usually lessens into an acceptable adult egotism. However, in the absence of normal progressive maturity, the narcissistic style may erode into the cluster of habits and attitudes we typically associate with adult narcissism. In sum, the narcissistic style holds the potential to become a more serious psychological problem than its adolescent expression.

Fine (1986) claimed, "All people are narcissistic; the difference is only one of degree." To this Alford added: "Although pathological narcissism sounds so sick...healthy narcissism shares many of the same characteristics...This is explained by a presumption...shared by almost all theorists of narcissism that there is a continuum between pathological and normal narcissism" (Alford, 1988, p. 70). If one accepts the idea that narcissism exists on a continuum from healthy to pathological, the narcissistic style would be found somewhere near the midpoint. Its excessive self-centeredness has typified adolescence since the Greeks first described its general manifestations circa 300 B. C.

In this chapter my focus is on the five basic themes which, seen as a totality, make up the psychological profile of the narcissistic style:

- expectations of entitlements;
- deadness to the feelings and rights of others;
- reduced capacity to give love;
- reduced moral circumference; and,
- reduced ability to think objectively.

THE FIRST FEATURE OF THE NARCISSISTIC STYLE: THE EXPECTATION OF ENTITLEMENTS

A presumption of the narcissistic style is that it is the responsibility of others to look after "me" and "my" needs. Individuals who exhibit this attitude expect far more from others than is reasonable, and they demand far more from their school, their government, and their family than can reasonably be delivered. They view their parents, their schools, and their governments as providers, and when they fail to provide they are viewed with contempt. Individuals obsessed with entitlements, as a rule, do not even faintly recognize how utterly objectionable their attitude is to their providers.

Although it is not necessary to our purposes to claim that the adolescent desire for entitlements originates within the same subconscious core that psychoanalysts believe produces narcissism, no doubt as far as demands and self-centered preoccupations are concerned, the behavior of the overly entitled adolescent parallels that of the classic narcissist.[54]

> They operate on the fantastic assumption that their mere desire is justification for possessing whatever they seek.
> —Theodore Millon (1981)

Entitlement expectations lead one to believe that one should be admitted to a theater after it is sold out or should be given permission to take an examination late when such permission is granted to no other students. Boys charged with entitlement believe that they are entitled to the affection, loyalty, or sexual favors of a girl they know, or date, or with whom they simply share a classroom. When these entitlements are not received the boy may pout, hold a grudge, or slander the girl who failed to deliver. However, keep in mind that entitlements need not be spoken aloud, because they are so firmly accepted as true that articulation of them seems unnecessary. Hence, a comfortable smoothness connects expectation with action. After all, why should one feel self-conscious taking that to which one is entitled?

The Origins Of Entitlement Demands

Mead (1986) claimed that an attitude of entitlement is encouraged by the family and the school (the two most important institutions in the lives of the young) both of whom have granted a wide range of benefits but have set few requirements for how the young ought to function in return. Which is to say that benefits are in place, but obligations are not. There is little doubt that in our present society adolescents live under a regime of social values which allows them to make demands on family, school, and society-at-large far more than vice versa. Perhaps from this tradition of being able to make demands without having to accept duties and responsibilities, irrational and exaggerated entitlement springs (Mead, 1986). At least it jibes with Sebald's observation: "In the forefront of the psychology of entitlement ... stand the young" (1984, p. 107).

Sebald contributed to the dialogue which examines the entitlement mentality, and some of his ideas speak to the youth culture and its narcissistic style.

> For generations, Americans have modeled their ideas of success after the Protestant ethic, with occupational status, money, investment, and possessions as focal points. The new generation seems to have shifted its preoccupation to various forms of self-fulfillment, moving psychological demands to the forefront. The new emphasis has effected corresponding changes in their sense of obligation to friends, family, employer, and community. ...Young Americans remain relatively unimpressed by the economic crisis and somehow seem to assume that some satisfactory economic security will materialize for them. This is not so much personal optimism as it is a new *philosophy of entitlement* anchored in the burgeoning American welfare state... a curious conversion of wants and desires into presumed "rights"...The desire "I'd like a secure income" becomes "I am entitled to a secure income." While the tendency to feel righteous about one's desires is natural and has been with us for a long time, *the equation of desire with right has grown significantly in the current generation.* (1984, p. 245)

Not only do the young salute a philosophy of entitlement, it appears to be a common phenomenon among them.

> Large numbers of young Americans expect society to provide a career and lifestyle that is both economically secure and psychologically rewarding. The attitude can be summed up as the "philosophy of entitlement", referring to the development of a pervasive feeling of being entitled to all sorts of material and psychological benefits and that the provision of these benefits is the responsibility of society. Postindustrial ability to cater to liberal consumption patterns and render an abundance of service unheard of during previous generations has resulted in a peculiar mental state among the young, particularly among the middle class.

Called the psychology of entitlement, it not only expects instant gratification but also assumes that society owes one a financially secure and psychologically happy life. (Sebald, 1984, p. 19)

All of which contradicts Muller (1960), who wrote: "Almost all societies, from the most primitive to the most civilized, have emphasized duties much more than rights or liberties, and almost all of their members have accepted these duties without protest" (1960, p. 26). The present discussion is not the proper forum for a thorough analysis of Muller's ideas, but it is a good place to reflect on possible connections, especially if we see merit in his point that in every society (including the society of youth) *dignified survival depends on a sense of duty and responsibility to the group.* An attitude of entitlement reverses this with the claim that it is the responsibility of the group to look after "me."

The Thought Process Which Justifies Entitlement Demands

Are adolescents capable of seeing things from the point of view of others? Can they apply moral principles to their own behavior? If so, how can their thinking be dominated by entitlements? Let me offer a few ideas on this unclear connection.

Children are infused with the assumption that their understanding is the only possible one; because they have limited skills with perspective-taking, it comes easily to them that their expectations will prevail. The adolescent attitude of entitlement extends this egocentric emphasis to the belief that one's desires *should* be satisfied. An attitude of entitlement fosters the belief that when one's desires are thwarted someone else is at fault.

Entitlement thinkers assume that their beliefs are inherently truthful, whereas the beliefs of others must be defended by evidence. They employ a completely unfair system of accountability in which others must defend their ideas as in a court of law, whereas their own ideas are truthful *a priori.* All in all, entitlement thinkers operate on the premise that "I" am automatically right, but "you" must prove beyond a reasonable doubt that you are right. Entitlement thinkers have another deficiency in their thought process which interests us because of its parallel phenomenon in narcissists: They abhor impartiality. Why? Because of its assumption of fairness; impartiality implies no advantage, and this contradicts the entire idea of entitlements. If you want to lose a narcissistic friend show him impartiality, objectivity, and evenhandedness, and soon he will be gone.

THE SECOND FEATURE OF THE NARCISSISTIC STYLE: DEADNESS TO THE FEELINGS OF OTHERS

The worst sin towards our fellow creatures is not to hate them, but to be indifferent to them: that's the essence of inhumanity.
—George Bernard Shaw

Certain psychologists who have a prejudice against facing up to the selfish side of human nature contend that people act selfishly only when they are required to do so, or when the rewards for selfishness greatly exceed its punishment, or when only slight chance exists for being caught. And although I respect the scholars who hold these views, I find no evidence in my experience to support them. Indeed, as far as adolescents are concerned, I find their line of thinking not only naive, but preposterous. Adolescent selfishness is as natural as childhood selfishness, but its expression differs in important ways.

Teachers try to teach youngsters every day who, when confronted with a wrongdoing, claim they didn't do it. Or, yes, they did it, but they couldn't help it; or, yes they did it but they didn't know they were doing it; or yes, they did it, but so what. Sometimes they don't know what they have done, and at other times they simply disown their actions; an unwelcome mixture of alienation and defiance. "The student of today is deeply unaware of the need to be cooperative with others, either students or teachers. He doesn't even seem to be in touch with being cooperative with himself; *some students appear to be unconscious of their very actions*" (Nelson, p. 67, emphasis added).

When confronted by a teacher for rules violations they claim their behavior wasn't bad because they didn't *intend* anything bad. They act as if motives are more important than actions. Such behavior-deadening was conveyed by a sixteen-year-old boy I once interviewed in a youth detention center, incarcerated after he shot another teen with a hand gun concealed in his jacket. To him it was unfair that he had to serve time because he didn't intend to shoot the victim. "He just sort of got in the way." He intended to shoot a member of a rival gang, but "this other dude just started shoving and gettin' involved where he didn't have any right. I shot him but it was no big deal. I didn't even mean to shoot him. If I shot 'D,' like I wanted to, then they would have a case. Just 'cuz some guy gets in the way. It's really more like an accident. I don't think I should do time for that."

These youngsters hide from their own unacceptable behavior with the claim that only their intentions should be judged. Their logic is simple, though bent: "You can't punish me for what I didn't intend to do." Or, "You can't punish me for what I couldn't prevent." (We gain a certain insight into the narcissistic style when we recognize that these youngsters *never* accept this claim when it is made to them by others.)

Deadness to the feelings (and rights) of others is also seen in the tendency to become irritated with a friend who couldn't help out with homework because he was sick that day, or with a parent who drives a friend to the hospital and therefore cannot loan the car. When their relationships turn sour, when exploited friends complain or simply walk out, when parents tell them they are sick of being their servants, they are usually taken by complete surprise. Unbalanced relationships are so compatible with their nature that it does not occur to them that their partners feel exploited. From these youngsters we repeatedly hear: "I can't believe you're telling me this"; "How come you are suddenly saying this?"; "Why didn't you tell me you feel this way?" Why? Because they never see through the eyes of another.

Youngsters enveloped in a narcissistic style evaluate adults by whether they are flattered by them; therefore, they "respect" adults who praise them, but they have no respect whatsoever for those who don't. In their judgments of adults they are incapable of rendering an independent verdict. Basically, they like adults who flatter and praise them, and dislike those who don't.[55] They may ridicule adults who don't show them attention, because such an adult is, to them, ridiculous. Among their peers these adult-rejecting teens may attain a great deal of acclaim because of their ability to make administrators look like buffoons, teachers idiots, police Nazis, psychologists neurotics.

THE THIRD FEATURE OF THE NARCISSISTIC STYLE: THE REDUCED CAPACITY TO *GIVE* LOVE[56]

> The most grievous cost of a narcissistic orientation is a stunted capacity to love.
> —Nancy McWilliams

Narcissism, in every form, impedes the capacity for love, and the narcissism which laces the narcissistic style is no exception to this rule. Teens imbued with a narcissistic style need love but, for reasons we do not completely understand, their expectations are greatly overloaded on the receiving end. Their pressing urge is to *receive* love, and all of their energy is directed to this end. Their main pleasure is in the praise they receive, so they are bored when no new sources feed their egos. And here we see one of their many contradictions: Their *need* for others is deep, but their *love* for them is shallow. They import, but they do not export, love.

How then, taking their selfish qualities into account, do they attract others into their sphere? How do they get their peers to like them? To fall in love with them? These questions are investigated in greater detail in a later chapter, so for the moment, a cursory overview will suffice. Basically, it works like this. Individuals with a narcissistic style idealize, glorify, and glamorize those who provide them with emotional supplies; they court affection by convincing their suppliers that it is *they* who are loved when, in reality, it is what they supply that is loved. Their friends believe that it is they who are loved, but they are wrong.

One might say, "You must love yourself before you can love others," but it is readily apparent that, at least at this moment in their development, their love is more for themselves than for others. The underlying cause of their failure to give love is unclear, but most theorists who investigate the emotional infrastructure of narcissism believe that it derives either from the numbing pain of rejection or from the smoldering resentment from being insufficiently loved. But what these theorists fail to recognize is that during adolescence selfish love relationships can be triggered merely by the desire to consume. "Why give when you can receive?" is the emblem of all egocentrics; it is simply carried to greater extremes by those who embrace the narcissistic style.

Before closing this brief look at the young person's need to receive love, I will leave you with a few final thoughts from the fertile mind of Erich Fromm:

> Freud said that in *all* love there is a strong narcissistic component; that a man in love with a woman makes her the object of his own narcissism and that therefore she becomes wonderful and desirable because she is part of him...Both people retain their narcissism, they have no real, deep interest in each other (not to speak of anyone else), they remain touchy and suspicious, and most likely each of them will be in need of a new person who can give them fresh narcissistic satisfaction. *For the narcissistic person, the partner is never a person in his own right or in his full reality; he exists only as a shadow of the partner's narcissistically inflated ego.* (1939, p. 515, original emphasis)

Narcissistic individuals do not seek human relationships where give and take exist in fair proportion; rather, they seek relationships in which their partners shower endless admiration without demanding much in return.

What we have thus far uncovered about the narcissistic style is that it is an approach to life that is obsessed with entitlements, insensitive to the feelings of others, and driven by the need to receive love without giving much in return.

THE FOURTH FEATURE OF THE NARCISSISTIC STYLE: REDUCED MORAL CIRCUMFERENCE

Moral diminishment is a subject that has not been studied with sufficient care in traditional psychology. And it is with some trepidation that I put forth any ideas on the topic; yet it is so relevant to the narcissistic style that I feel compelled to do so.

Morality, by definition, requires the alignment of one's actions and beliefs *with a principle or a standard greater than oneself*. Such alignment is inherently difficult for individuals for whom morality is determined by their own needs. This does not mean that they do not believe in good or bad; it means that what they think of as "good" and what they think of as "bad" is determined by whether it favors or disfavors them. Narcissistic morality is a brew of pragmatism and egotism rather than a genuine moral system. For these reasons morality is really *moralization*—morality grounded in rationalization. Hence, the narcissist claims that whatever he craves is morally right and whatever he opposes is morally wrong. It parallels in frightening ways the morality of preschoolers who also believe that whatever favors them is right and whatever disfavors them is wrong.

The "Morally Mature" Adolescent

In a special document drafted in 1988 the Association for Supervision and Curriculum Development outlined their understanding of a "morally mature" adolescent. The intent here is not to defend their definition, but to point out how it contrasts with the manners and morals of the narcissistic style. The Association claimed that the morally mature adolescent is characterized by the following:

> *Respect for human dignity,* as expressed in showing regard for the worth and rights of all people, and by avoiding deception and dishonesty;
> *Care for the welfare of others,* as expressed in seeking social justice, taking pleasure in helping others, and by working to help others attain moral maturity;
> *Social responsibilities,* as expressed in becoming involved in community life, in developing self-esteem through constructive relationships with others, and displaying fairness, honesty, and civility;
> *Demonstrates integrity* by knowing when to compromise and when to confront, and by accepting responsibility for one's choices;
> *Reflects on moral choices* by recognizing the moral issues involved in a situation, and by thinking about the consequences of decisions; and, lastly
> *Seeks peaceful resolution of conflict* by striving for the fair resolution of social conflict, listening carefully to others, and by encouraging others to communicate honestly.

It would be difficult to compile a collection of traits less fitting the narcissistic style. Narcissistic adolescents do not much respect human dignity, they do not care about the welfare of others, they do not assume a fair share of social responsibility, they do not demonstrate moral integrity, and they do not seek fair resolution of conflict. In sum, the narcissistic style is a morally diminished orientation toward life which prevents the individual from venturing beyond the circumference of immediate needs and concerns.

Rights and responsibilities and the narcissistic style
The social contracts which bind children to their parent society might seem straightforward, but they are not. Our society is presently locked in debate about the relative weight of rights and obligations. Billions of education and welfare dollars are appropriated, in great measure, by our understanding of

how much we owe youth, and how much they owe us. The debate is heated because some of us believe that the entitlements of youth far outweigh their responsibilities while others of us believe the exact opposite.

We, as a society, do not agree on the actions youth are morally obligated to perform. What duty do they owe their parents? What labor should youth be required to perform? Are youth obligated to show respect or deference to adults? To what extent are youth accountable? Accountable to whom or to what? To what degree can we expect young people to know right from wrong, to be punished for wrongdoing, or rewarded for doing right? Do the responsibilities of youth require them to meet their financial obligations? Can we rightfully expect them to be morally responsible for the consequences of their sexual behavior, financially responsible in their economic transactions, parentally responsible for the children they produce, legally responsible for the people they injure on the highways?

On the other side of the coin: What are the just and fair claims of youth? What are they entitled to by law, by nature, by merit of being young? What claims can they make "in their own right"? Much of the debate reduces to one key question: Should *rights* or *duties* hold greater sway in the conduct of youth?

Rights are difficult to discuss because in many people's thinking they are prefaced by "inalienable," which translates into "guaranteed," and by "my" which translates into "not necessarily yours."[57] Perhaps no concept, philosophical or legal, is as subject to narcissistic contamination as rights; teaching teens their rights is one of the easiest tasks in the books, the rights of others one of the toughest.

Painfully, youth obsessed with their own rights tend to be indifferent to the rights of others. In one of the major understatements of modern social criticism, Mead, in his analysis of social rights and personal responsibilities says: "Many Americans evidently are less able to take care of themselves and respect the rights of others than in earlier decades" (1986, p. 8). Some critics believe this describes youth in modern society: They cannot take care of themselves, yet at the same time, they do not hold any deep respect for those who provide for them. "We were distressed that many Americans are all too eager to spell out what they are entitled to but are all too slow to give something back to others and to the community" (Etzioni, 1993, p. 48). All of which adds up to citizen infantilism.

THE FIFTH FEATURE OF THE NARCISSISTIC STYLE: REDUCED INTELLECTUAL OBJECTIVITY

The narcissistic person then, ends up with an enormous distortion. He and his are overevaluated. Everything outside is underevaluated. The damage to reason and objectivity is obvious.
—Erich Fromm

The narcissistic attitude has a crushing effect on clear thinking. There are, admittedly, difficulties involved in demonstrating how the narcissistic style corrupts the thought chain, but nevertheless that is exactly what it does. Here we will try to better understand how.

Individuals dominated by the narcissistic style perceive events by how the events affect them, a habit they share with children, with neurotics, and with full-blown narcissists, and one which produces a woeful double-standard in their thought and judgment.

> A person, to the extent to which he is narcissistic, has a double standard of perception. Only he himself and what pertains to him has significance, while the rest of the world is more or less weightless or colorless, and because of this double standard *the narcissistic person shows severe defects in judgment and lacks the capacity for objectivity.* (Fromm, 1973, p. 148, original emphasis)

If lack of objectivity is essential to the narcissistic style the question then becomes: "How is objectivity lost?" To answer this question we take a look at how objective thought comes into being in the first place.

Objective Thought During Adolescence

In chapter one I tried to explain how a higher plane of thought known as "formal thought," comes into being during the adolescent years. The intelligence of youth is directly related to their ability to use formal thought efficiently and productively and, conversely, the fables and illusions of youth are directly related to their *failure* to use formal thought effectively and productively.

We recall that formal thought permits the intellect to go beyond the real to investigate the ideal, to go beyond the physical to look at the hypothetical, to go beyond fragments to envision wholes, to go beyond "what is" to speculate about "what if," and to go beyond present time into the future. Formal thought attains its power from several advances, including the following:

- *Formal thought increases the adolescent's power of abstraction.* Adolescents outgrow the rigid intellectual apparatus of concrete thought, replacing it with a more flexible and dexterous intelligence. As abstract thought expands, the thinker shifts in gradual increments away from the concrete to the esoteric.
- *Formal thought stimulates intellectual comprehensiveness.* The increased power of formal thought encourages adolescents to embrace a greater range of data in problem-solving. Hence, in their summations they are less prone to errors of omission.

- *Formal thought opens to investigation one's own thoughts and one's own thought processes.* The force of formal thought is not merely in brilliant outward focus, but it is also in focus shining inward on the thought process itself; it engages itself in constant dialogue to diagnose its own strengths and weaknesses. Formal thought cross-examines its own evidence and double-checks its own conclusions; it is both prosecution and defense, judge and jury. Unlike concrete thought, formal thought has its own built-in system of checks-and-balances.
- *Formal thought utilizes propositional thought.* A proposition is a statement that can be doubted or denied; propositional thought is the act of systematically questioning an idea to see what germinates from the questioning process. It is a means to reason about anything and everything for no purpose other than to see where reason takes itself. Adolescents are not necessarily gifted propositional thinkers, especially in early adolescence, but they are vastly superior to children.
- *Formal thought fosters future analysis.* Individuals possessed of formal thought are able to think about the future with the same intensity, rigor, and passion as in thinking about the present. Indeed, they can commit themelves to a course of action with virtually no immediate returns. This ability to obliterate the present introduces infinity, theology, and cosmology to their domain of concerns.
- *Formal thought is the foundation for scientific thought.* Formal thinkers form hypotheses, conduct experiments, control variables, describe and record outcomes, and draw conclusions in a formal manner.

Against all of these advances the narcissistic style raises defensive barriers.

The narcissistic style shows its true colors when the object of thought pertains to worth, superiority, shame, glory, competence, beauty, acceptance, achievement, or desirability—in other words, whenever thought impinges on self-esteem. The narcissistic style poses no real problem when the thinker is investigating an emotion-free zone such as wheat production in China, the internet, the Dow Jones average, assuming that none of these topics is close to one's emotional center. The function of the narcissistic style is to protect and elevate; when there is no need for them the intellect operates freely and objectively. This is why intellectual performance is so uneven in the teen years; on one topic the intellect is free to use all of its resources, on another it is bogged down in protection and defense. Twist and turn as we may, we cannot escape the fact that the narcissistic style impedes objective thinking because at bottom it is grounded in self-protection and self-inflation.[58]

WHAT DOES ALL OF THIS MEAN?

The question springs immediately to mind: "Are teens *naturally* drawn to the narcissistic style?" Or, for those who resist the idea of natural attraction, the parallel question reads: "Do teens *easily adopt* the narcissistic style?" To both questions my answer is "Yes."

As to the progression from childhood egocentrism to narcissistic selfishness the evidence is ambiguous. But it seems to me that this progression comes so easily that one is tempted to think of it as natural.[59] We know that children do not learn all things with equal ease. If you doubt this, try teaching a group of children to be left-handed, or to choose celery over sweets; then, try to teach a group of children to be right-handed and to choose sweets over celery. These are not equal tasks. The predispositions children bring to their experience shape their preferences and guide their inclinations and, as a result, influence what they *easily* learn. To teach selfish attitudes and self-serving habits to children (and adolescents) is one of the easiest assignments one could possibly have because their personality is laced with a compatible egocentrism.[60]

There is not much doubt about the predispositions of youth. Their egocentrism, their developmental selfishness, and their natural impulses for survival and self-preservation, taken in combined strength, *incline* them to self-priority. The narcissistic style is easily learned when it is glorified in popular culture, when they are given no viable alternative to it, and when they have not been trained to understand the human diminishment which comes with it. Taking all of this into account, no wonder we see so much of it in our adolescent population.

POSTSCRIPT

> To the extent that he is narcissistic he is incapable of loving
> either himself or anyone else.
> —Karen Horney

As might be expected from the course of developments I have outlined, the relationship between the narcissistic style and adolescent behavior is not an encouraging one. The narcissistic style is dehumanizing in its use of other people as self-esteem maintaining functions rather than as separate individuals.

I would like to make clear that all of the problems of youth are not brought into existence by the narcissistic style, but I also want to make clear that all problems of youth are deepened by it. At bottom, it is really nothing more than the young person's attempt to position himself at the center of the emotional universe. And whereas it often proves to be a productive reflex in the adolescent's insulated and contrived universe, it is ultimately counterproductive because it honors nothing beyond the self. This, in a nutshell, is the pathos of all narcissism.[61]

One final comment. All teens live in a community but without much sense of community; in the adolescent world there are few worthwhile projects in which to invest their decency, and few worthy people with whom to share their higher yearnings. A typical outcome of this unhealthy scenario is an obsession with self without much appreciation of self; a sorry turn of events at an age when one enriches the self by participating openly and honestly in other lives. Sadly, we have discovered that youth who do not find a worthy someone in whom to invest their hopes, who do not build, who do not volunteer their energy and their spirit, and who do not contribute to the well-being of others are prime candidates for the regressive slide from developmental selfishness into the narcissistic style.

III

Adolescent Companionship, Friendship, and Love

12

Treaties, Alliances, and the Beginnings of Mature Friendship

> Of all the things which wisdom provides to make life entirely happy, much the greatest is the possession of friendship.
>
> —Epicurus

As far as I am able to judge, after attending to the subject over the past four decades, we have no simple way to address the topic of adolescent friendship. This, in great measure, is due to the fact that we find no comprehensive theories that focus on this worthwhile topic, and what we do find often lacks the economy of explanation and the range of accountability we look for in a good theory. Rolf Muuss (1988), in his authoritative *Theories of Adolescence,* claimed that because no theory of adolescent friendship is available, its understanding requires "several different theoretical perspectives that are compatible and mutually supportive" (p. 300). I completely agree, and in these chapters I follow Muuss' advice by presenting a range of ideas which, when taken in their entirety, will hopefully provide some fresh insights into the nature of adolescent friendship.

The richness of adolescent life is too diverse for universal generalizations; it must be approached with a humble awareness of how little we actually know about it. Compulsory schooling, pop culture, and our society's pseudo-glorification of all things youthful add to the mystery and to the excitement of youth bondings.

An investigation of adolescent friendship cannot be concerned only with how adolescents *feel* about their friends, although this certainly is a necessary concern. Neither can it be concerned only with the pleasures of companionship even though this too is a worthy topic. The study of adolescent friendship must take into account three overlooked aspects of adolescent life, the cravings which *impel* friendship, the motives which *sustain* friendship, and the immaturities which *dissolve* friendship. Much of what follows in the next few chapters is concerned with how they shape friendship during the teen years.

REAL FRIENDSHIP

> Individual development seems to us a product of the interplay of two
> trends, the striving for happiness, generally called "egoistic," and the
> impulse towards merging with others in the community,
> which we call altruistic.
> —Sigmund Freud

Real friendship is no easy thing, and those who see it as a natural outgrowth of the peer group miss the boat. The adolescent peer group owes its existence to psychological forces and social inclinations which have little to do with genuine friendship. Mature friendship takes time, effort, and sacrifice. Simply hanging out and being together don't do it. Friendship is much more than mere affiliation; it is a gradual, smoldering achievement. Most teens know how precious (and elusive) *real* friendship is; perhaps this is why they idealize it, romanticize it, and why it always works its way to the top of their wish list.

In the teen community to be without friends is to be nobody because the adolescent community is not a real community as much as a collection of cliques, peer groups, and accidental affiliations. To be isolated and left out of these vital connections is a big deal in an age-segregated population that has virtually no friendship base beyond age. Viewed sociologically, youngsters unaccepted by their peers are much more likely to drop out of school, to engage in delinquent behavior and criminal acts, and to develop psychopathology later in life. Low levels of friendship are related to depression and other unhealthy symptomatology during adolescence, especially for girls. *Who* one's friends are also is important as friendship with deviant peers is highly correlated with delinquency, fighting, and antisocial attitudes. And, as we will discuss in greater detail later, the attraction to narcissistic peers produces its own cluster of exploitations.

All youngsters need friendship, companionship, and love, and much of their energy is directed to satisfying these basic needs. However, even though teens very much want to experience meaningful relationships they have difficulty with them because of their lack of experience, their meager social skills, and their difficulty with perspective-taking. These developmental deficiencies are an impediment to deep friendship; Louise Kaplan claimed that among adolescents "new loves and friendships...*usually prove to be unstable, transient, and heartbreakingly disappointing*" (1984, p. 151, emphasis added).

Friendship is no easy thing even at the best of times, but it is especially difficult when the partners crave togetherness but are not prepared to manage the emotional demands and the behavioral expectations required of mutuality. Take respect, for example. Respect implies a sensitivity to the unique features of the respected person, and an acknowledgment of his (her) basic integrity. But this represents only its general contours; respect has many faces. Respect for a partner's beliefs implies sensitive listening and sympathetic responses; respect for a partner's talents means encouraging his (her) ambitions and supporting his (her) endeavors and, as well, appreciating his (her) achievements; respect for the partner's rights means recognizing his (her) freedom and liberty; respect for the partner's privacy means not being intrusive, not sulking when the partner requires solitude or isolation (Martin, 1996). Tragically, many youth think of "respect" as nothing more than a ritualized display of reassurance to the "respected" one.

Mutual respect requires an independent intelligence, and a set of judgments about what is worthy of respect. On these counts younger adolescents (and children) almost always come up short.

Adolescent friendships are initiated by the craving to bond and by the desire to share one's inner feelings with another person. When connection has been made the partners then move slowly toward increased respect for one another, and then, finally, to mutual admiration. Adolescent bonding problems come about when this sequence is reversed; that is, when youngsters try to begin their relationship with mutual admiration without going through the necessary trial period to see whether the partner is truly worthy of respect or deserving of admiration.

Along the adolescent friendship path we see many breakups and, all things considered, this is the best outcome in many instances. Adolescence, after all, is an age for experimentation, for exploration, and for the discovery of an entire range of relationships unknown to the protected sanctuary of childhood, deep friendship being only one. Sexual relationships are even more complex as they demand the juggling of volatile passion with friendship, an especially difficult challenge for novices whose knowledge on the topic is restricted to their own experiences and—even more significant in the long run—to their *understanding* of what these experiences mean in the larger scheme of things.

Resistance to the Theory of Real Friendship

In the past, some of my graduate students at the University of Alberta have resisted my ideas on the nature of adolescent companionship. Their resistance,

I believe, is based on their assumption that adolescent friendship is a pure form of friendship where friends give each other room to grow and the freedom to express themselves honestly and openly, where fairness, generosity and compassion rule the day. They see adolescent friendship as Ruth's was to Naomi.[62] In the words of Allan, they think that adolescent friendships are "unfettered by any selfish or instrumental concerns. Each gives what the other needs, without thought to cost or reward, simply because of the fact of their friendship" (1989, p. 13).

Such an idealized portrayal of friendship in the community of teens is not the way it is. The developmental limitations of adolescents, combined with their narcissism, make genuine friendship extremely rare. In this chapter I will try to explain why adolescent friendships tend to be utilitarian more than humanistic, self-centered more than friend-centered, and short-term more than long-term. In the end I think we will come to appreciate that adolescent friendships are sometimes molded from necessity, sometimes from emotional hunger, and sometimes from the dignified core of a sharing self. But, most typically, from a little of each.

HOW FRUSTRATION AND HOSTILITY SHAPE TEEN FRIENDSHIP

Life is made up of sobs, sniffles and smiles, with sniffles predominating.
—O. Henry

Speaking in broad terms, we can say that adolescent friendships tend to be of three general types. The first may be classified as "friendships of pleasure," in which the partners enjoy each other's company, derive joy and pleasure from it, and each partner adds to the happiness of the other. The second is "friendship of utility," in which the association between two individuals benefits each other in a variety of practical ways, and as a result of their friendship, certain goals and ambitions are better satisfied. Utility friendships are based upon consequences, outcomes, and results; they thrive in settings where individuals share duties and responsibilities—the workplace, the school, dormitories, and sports teams. The third type of friendship is the friendship of "reciprocity and mutuality," in which the partners show concern for each other's needs, for their long-term welfare, and share in a genuine mutual admiration. This kind of friendship weathers misfortune rather well because the connections are sturdy, sincere, and not weighted by the narcissism which typifies pleasure and utility friendship. Reciprocity and mutuality friendship is the highest form of adolescent friendship; it serves as the advance guard of intimacy and mature love.

Research into the companionship patterns of early and middle adolescents suggests that their peer connections are primarily of the first two types: pleasure and utility. From a developmentalist's perspective this is perfectly understandable because the deeper expressions of friendship are, generally speaking, beyond the maturational readiness of early- to mid-teens. Part of what I am trying to convey was first introduced to modern adolescent psychology by Friedenberg in his classic work, *The Vanishing Adolescent.* Friedenberg was fully aware that adolescents are not angelic, that they often behave like self-serving junior executives, and that the cement which holds them together is not always mortared by ideal friendship. He helped us to recognize that adolescent friendship usually is situational, need-driven and more often grounded in necessity than in reciprocity. His insights aren't pleasant, but they aren't wrong either:

> Groups of juveniles are not friendly; and strong-felt friendships do not commonly form among them, though there is often constant association between members of juvenile cliques. They are not there to be friendly; they are there to work out a crude social system and to learn the ropes from one another. To some extent they behave like the gang in an office, jockeying for position within a superficially amiable social group. (1959, p. 44)

More condensed, but to the same point, Weiss claimed that "adolescent conformity to the peer group is of necessity, not enjoyment" (1980, p. 254). Friedenberg and Weiss both recognized something about the dynamics of adolescent life which are completely overlooked in the eyes of the experts in recent decades but which, nevertheless, must be taken into account if we are to understand teen friendship deeper than mere platitudes allow. First, there are important differences between "being friendly" and the attainment of genuine friendship, a distinction which is rarely made in current literature; second, among the young sociability may derive as much from the setting as from the relationship itself; third, while sharing time with comrades brings laughter and deep emotion, it does not follow that these shared experiences are the same as real friendship. As Friedenberg recognized, the peer group is a group of peers, but it is not necessarily a microcosm of genuine friendship.

Lees (1986) investigated teen friendships first-hand, interviewing adolescent girls over a five-year period, and in doing so distilled a more personal assessment of adolescent friendship than is usually reported in the psychological literature. (Friedenberg and Weiss, it should be pointed out, did not base their conclusions about adolescent life on data they gathered from teens as much as from their insights into the adolescent personality and how it operates within its social world.) Lees also investigated the adolescent's social world, but she was primarily concerned with how power relations constrict the adolescent experience, especially for girls; her strategy was "to take the girls' own descriptions and raise questions about the way they describe their lives, their experiences, their relationships" (p. 157).

One of Lees' more intriguing findings was how teen friendships are burdened with grinding antagonisms and uneasy alliances. Although the girls in her study very much desired genuine intimacy, mutual admiration, and true love, they faced a day-to-day social world laced with stinging demands on acceptance, popularity, and reputation. Lees reported that all of the girls she interviewed agreed that friendship means loyalty and sticking up for your friend. However, it is never that straightforward: "The other side of the coin is bitching and spreading gossip and rumours. Bitching is constantly referred to as something that girls are particularly adept at and as the source of aggravation and even fights among girls" (p. 65). One girl says: "Sue, one moment she can be really nice but the next moment she can be really bitchy. Sue will use what you say against you." Another girl reports: "There are boys that bitch as well—but on the whole I think girls have more character for bitching." Another says: "Girls get pretty ratty and annoyed with each other and say things about each other. Whereas boys ... don't bitch about each other behind each other's backs so much."

The adolescent community, as described by teens themselves, is one in which the all too human failings of betrayal, gossip, and slander are facts of daily life:

> That's why you have to be careful who you hang around with, who you speak to, because even the slightest thing you tell them, they can change what you said and get you into a lot of trouble. You might say something to them, "Don't tell anyone what I just told you." The next morning the whole school knows it. (Lees, p. 68)

The condemnation which flows so freely in teen groups reduces to an elementary code of social competition: That which cannot be trivialized is demonized. "One reason why so few girls talk even to their closest friends about sexual desire or actual sexual behavior is through fear that their friend might betray them and gossip—spread the rumour that they were a slag [promiscuous]" (Lees, p. 68). Slander is everyday fare: "A more vicious type of devaluing aspects of other girls is to cast doubt on their sexual reputation, which is why much of the bitching characterized by girls involves sexual abuse [slander]" (p. 66). According to one subject in the study, girls who desire a boyfriend but have difficulty attracting boys are the most bitchy. Lees suggests that "bitchiness seems to be a way of devaluing aspects of other girls that you wish to signal as 'not you'. It is a way of marking differences between other girls and yourself." One girl, describing herself says: "I am bitchy. I say 'oh she's so fat'. You say it in front of friends for instance to see if they say 'You can't talk, you're just as fat' or to see if they agree with you." What is at stake here should not be taken lightly. In the teen world reputation is currency, and anything which inflates or deflates it is big business. "An attack on a girl's reputation is an attack on her personal morality and integrity which only she can defend" (Lees, p. 72).

From what we have learned from Lees' research of teen cliques we can better understand why Collins once claimed: "We make more enemies by what we say than friends by what we do." An aphorism to be sure, but one which drives home an important reality in the community of teens.[63]

I do not want to convey an exaggerated impression of the trials and tribulations of teen life; neither, however, do I desire that this book join the stream of sterile treatises which claim to describe the adolescent experience but instead give the reader nothing but a Pollyanna vision of teen society which sees all problems of youth as caused by unloving parents, by incompetent teachers, by oppressive rules, or by unfair regulations. This is not the way it is. Youth have their own frailties and their own limitations and they account for much (but not all) of their storm and stress. None of us benefit from denying this fact.

An ocean and a continent away from Lees in England, Kostash in Alberta conducted her own investigations of friendship among adolescent girls. Interestingly, though not surprisingly, Kostash's observations parallel in striking ways those made by Lees:

> This is not, however, the whole story about the relationships girls strike among themselves. Through much of the language they use in talking about each other runs a streak of unmitigated nastiness, a shrill and cold-hearted aggression designed to wound. At the very least a vague and free-floating anxiety seems to charge the air when more than two or three are gathered together, as though something unpleasant were about to happen, but from which quarter no one is quite sure. One girl described it as not being able to "trust" your friends fully, fearing that, when your back is turned, they will "put you down"; or fearing that something is planned from which you are to be excluded, or that the other two "know" something you do not. More extremely, girls hurl obscene epithets at and about each other—slut, bitch, sleaze—and cruelly disparage each other's bodies—so-and-so's tits hang down to here, and so-and-so's thighs are gross and check that hairdo, a rat's nest, no kidding. They pass along damaging and probably spurious tales about each other's sexual behavior and reputation (who does "it," with whom, and how many times). (Kostash, 1989, p. 37)

The social toughness observed by investigators who actually participate in the lives of youth (rather then merely report the results of paper-pencil tests) harkens to mind Mark Twain's chide: "It takes your enemy and friend, working together, to hurt you to the heart; the one to slander you, and the other to get the news to you." I think that one of the reasons so many adolescents like to read Twain is because he accepted outright the raw realities of human bondings, and he recognized that in every friendship there is a bit of the devil.

HOW FLATTERY, RATIONALIZATION, AND EMOTIONAL SUPPORT SHAPE ADOLESCENT FRIENDSHIP

Reciprocal Rationalization

Let us pursue a little further the question of how adolescent friendships are sustained by the *duty* of each friend to bolster the other. But, before we begin, we first require a word about *rationalization.*

Rationalization is protecting our self-esteem by finding socially accepted reasons for our behavior. Rationalizations, of course, are doubted and disputed. If I claim that attendance in my university class is high because I am an excellent lecturer, and a student points out that "It's high because you grade on attendance," my claim has lost credibility. Because rationalizations must be defended in a somewhat reasonable manner, conceptually organized, articulate individuals tend to execute them more effectively than disorganized, verbally inept individuals. The intellectual dexterity involved in rationalization led McWilliams to claim: "The more intelligent and creative a person is, the more likely it is that he or she is a good rationalizer" (1994, p. 125).

The most common rationalizations are "sweet lemons" and "sour grapes." Sweet lemon is indicated when one claims that "What I've got is what I want." (I have a lemon, but it is a sweet one, or at least, sweet enough.) Sour grapes enter when one concludes: "What I missed wasn't worth getting." (I don't have any grapes but it doesn't matter because they were sour.)

Now back to our original concept of *reciprocal* rationalization—where two people work cooperatively to reinforce each other's rationalizations. In other words, instead of criticizing the rationalizations (or fables, or illusions) of their partner, they reward them by claiming that they are truthful. The cement which holds the partnership together is each partner's willingness to glorify and glamorize the fables of the other. And while adolescents who engage in reciprocal rationalization may passionately defend their friendship as true and authentic, this rarely is the case, a fact they tend to recognize as they attain greater insight into their own need structure, usually during late adolescence or early adulthood.

Self-serving friendships

What I liked most was that he liked me.
—16-year-old's response to the question: "What most attracted you to your first boyfriend?"

He was older and more mature than friends my age—he was like a trophy for me. I found it very flattering for somebody in high school to want to be with somebody in jr. high.

He even gave me his football jacket.
—First-year university student's response to the question: "What most attracted you to your first boyfriend?"

I have discovered in the course of hundreds of interviews that 19- to 22-year-olds freely admit that their early and middle adolescent friendships were self-serving and egoistic, and that reciprocal rationalization is part of the job description for many friendships. Rather than being embarrassed by this fact of their younger social lives, most university students report matter-of-factly that such self-serving protectionism is simply part of growing up. Many of them view reciprocal rationalization as an unacceptable basis to friendship at their present maturity level, but as an inevitable fact of primitive bondings. And, broadly speaking, I find myself in agreement with this because friendship during the early and middle teens tends to be utilitarian and exploratory.

Genuine friendship, intimacy, and love are different from situational friendship; they operate on quite different principles. Higher levels of human connection require common aims, loyalty, reasoned sacrifice for the partner, a willingness to help when needed, a respect for the partner as a person, and a clear awareness of where one stands in relation to the partner. Many adolescent bondings go by the name "friendship" because the partners spend so much time together and because they so desperately want to share in a loyal bond but, at bottom, their bond is need-driven more than partner-driven. This is not to say that it is not friendship, only that it is not *genuine* friendship.

Synchronized Self-Deception

Friendship is almost always a union of a part of one mind with a part of another; people are friends in spots.
—George Santayana

Many friendships have built into them a mutually enhancing hypocrisy where each person tacitly agrees not to notice certain undersirable things about the partner, and to preserve the deceit, the partners also agree not to notice that they do not notice (Goleman, 1986, p. 274). This psychic tap dance comes into being when friends, family members, and lovers learn to protect one another by failing to acknowledge certain buried secrets which, if uncovered, would force everyone in the relationship to face painful facts. Henrik Ibsen, the Norwegian dramatist and poet, called these buried secrets "vital lies" because they keep disturbing realities away from conscious awareness. In teen society it is advantageous not to openly acknowledge the vices, defects, or immaturities of one's friends; orchestrated silence yields many social rewards. Maintaining the silence of synchronized self-deception is the first requirement of utilitarian friendship. In genuine friendship unpleasant truths can be examined honestly and with mutual encouragement, but they pose insurmountable obstacles in utilitarian friendship.

Synchronized self-deceptions permit the partners to develop an intimate web of acceptable intrusions into each other's emotional lives; these intrusions create deep and profound human connections while staying away from entire domains of the friend's personality which are deemed out of bounds. What usually follows in these friendships is an intense closeness with *part* of the person, and from this closeness an alliance of pseudo-intimacy is spun. This led Goleman to observe: "When some aspects of shared reality are troubling, a semblance of cozy calm can be maintained by an unspoken agreement to deny pertinent facts, to ignore key questions" (1986, p. 279).

We recognize the advantages of such an arrangement. Friends who honor "unaskable" questions (that is, who believe that certain questions must never be raised in the presence of the protected person) provide young people with a certain measure of growing room where their real strengths can be paraded while their undeveloped qualities remain quietly in the background. In this regard, adolescent friendship, like national security, requires a blending of honest disclosure with a bureau of hidden secrets and private files.

A certain insight is gained when we observe the behavior of friends who claim that they have made up after a quarrel yet on close inspection we find that no real settlement of the actual disagreement has taken place at all. When reciprocal rationalization and synchronized self-deception permeate a relationship, surviving a disagreement is more important than the disagreement itself, and "surviving" usually means that the partners are reassured that they still like each other, and that they admit to being sorry that they *hurt the feelings of the other*. The feelings of the partner are more important than the content of the disagreement, which is to say that their bond is more important to them than the substance of the quarrel; it is more important to repair the bond than to resolve the disagreement. (All things considered, it is a decent policy as long as the disagreement is over something inconsequential.) What we usually see when young friends claim they have "made up" is word juggling and sentiment coddling rather than the clarifying of any genuine disagreements. This, of course, allows these same disagreements to arise again and again as their causes are never addressed.

When friendship is involved most teens demonstrate limited skills at slicing to the heart of a disagreement (and what is true for friendship is even more true for romance). As a result, when they claim that their disagreements have been worked out, what they usually mean is that their alliance has been resumed. The alliance always takes priority when the real purpose of the friendship is emotional bolstering.

FLATTERING MIRRORS

> I will praise any man that will praise me.
> —William Shakespeare

Adolescents require friends who understand the world accurately and evaluate it honestly; friends who provide candid, sometimes even brutal evaluations, and who can point out and discuss the agreeable and the disagreeable attributes of the friend. All of which is to say that adolescents need reliable and honest friends who serve as *accurate mirrors*. This need, real as it is, does not always carry into action, and for a simple reason. An accurate mirror reflects what is, and this reflection is sometimes cold, uncomfortable, and damaging to one's esteem. On the other hand, a *flattering mirror* reflects things as one wishes them to be, and this reflection is warm, comforting, and uplifting to one's esteem. In the winter of youth youngsters gain companionship by reflecting the pleasant and deflecting the unpleasant. This service is a vital one to every person low in confidence, and it is a service which is gladly provided in exchange for the goodwill of peers.

In the course of time flattering mirrors may become indispensable to the flattered one.[64] Psychologically speaking, praise is absorbed as an affirmation of one's worth and, especially among the young, it is perceived as a duty of friendship. Eventually, praise and flattery become ends in themselves, with their truth secondary to the reassurance they provide. As this collusion continues, each youngster makes an unspoken agreement to do nothing which will hurt or embarrass the other, and most certainly nothing to disaffirm the other person's worth. The unforeseen downside is that honest criticism comes to be regarded as an attack not only on the person to whom it is directed, but as an attack on the alliance as well.[65]

The Flatterer

> Because we believe our opinions are correct, we're not terribly suspicious of the
> motives of people who agree with us.
> —John Sabini

Praise confirms to the self that it is worthy and deserving, and during the early stages of the identity project this confirmation can become addictive when the young person searches for proof that he (she) is talented, interesting, neat, or just OK. Flattery-addicted youngsters may look self-assured, but internally they have a burning need to be told repeatedly that they are valuable, great, wonderful, and perfect. These youngsters may not know what to believe in, or in whom to invest their allegiance, but what they know for certain is that they love being told again and again that they truly matter. This is the vital responsibility of their flattering mirror, and all who excel at it are fully employed in the teen community.

To serve as a flattering mirror is not as easy as one might think. The flatterer must be able to intuit the emotional requirements of the flattered one, and to recognize what is important to him (her) at any given moment. The role of flattering mirror is a supportive one, and if Oscars were awarded in the adolescent theater, flattering mirrors would be in the running for Best Supporting Actor and Best Supporting Actress. Their most prized skills are making the lead actor appear strong, central to the plot and heroic, while remaining in the background, never stealing the scene.

All of this is easier to comprehend when we recognize that the most exhilarating and meaningful experience of adolescence is to feel that someone is wild about you and that they would do anything for you, or make any sacrifice just to share in your presence, to bask in your radiance. This is the dream of every developing self, not only because it nurtures and aggrandizes the narcissistic core which is the heart of every self, but because it is the purest way to confirm our value as a person—having another person who is "crazy over me."

To conclude this brief segment on flattering mirrors, I will leave you with a brief piece of rhetoric from the pen of Toni Morrison (1977): "Could you really love somebody who was absolutely nobody without you? You really want somebody like that? Somebody who falls apart when you walk out the door?" This, of course, is three questions rather than one, but the answer to all three is the same when asked to the flattered one about his flattering mirror. And the answer is "Yes."

POSTSCRIPT

> In psychology power means the ability to affect, to influence, and to change other persons.
> —Rollo May

I am sure that long before the reader has arrived at this point, a crowd of difficulties will have gathered; therefore, it may be worthwhile to review some of the important themes put forth in this chapter.

Adolescent friendships can be a splendid and beautiful experience, but all friendships are not made of such stardust. This chapter has spoken almost exclusively to the less grand and less glorious aspects of adolescent relationships. And although this approach does not romanticize youth in the manner to which we have become unfairly accustomed, we do well to remind ourselves that when discussing something as fine as friendship there is no honor in denying its less noble elements.

Friendships rooted in emotionally protective maneuvers, such as reciprocal rationalization and synchronized self-deception, may eventually mature into relationships where truth and fairness are given greater play. However, they do not when truth and fairness are valued less than approval and acceptance. This is a bitter reality of everyday adolescent life, and one that cannot be overlooked in our understanding of their frailties and limitations.

In this chapter I have tried to make the case that the following principles carry considerable weight in adolescent relationships:

- Young people are too insecure to unreservedly share themselves with another person; hence, their relationships almost always have a conditional, tentative, wait-and-see quality. Adolescents' friendships are self-driven, practical and immediate.
- Even though adolescent friendships have a strong utilitarian component, learning to grow beyond utilitarianism in human connections is a requirement of the adolescent years. When the adolescent matures beyond utilitarian friendship (which narcissists never do) then, and only then, does genuine intimacy becomes possible.
- Teen friendships help young people to learn the ropes of their social system and, at the same time, they prepare them for the more complex connections of intimacy and love. As Balk phrased it: "Caring for someone else enhances the means to develop capacities for intimacy" (1995, p. 296).
- Adolescent friendship requires giving approval in exchange for the favor being returned. Convincing a friend that his (her) defects are virtues is the glue which holds many teen connections together. Reciprocal rationalization is not the pillar which supports adolescent friendship, but it is a buttress without which many collapse.
- Adolescent friendships are ends-in-themselves, but they are also works in progress which may, or may not, mature into deep relationships. To view adolescent friendship as the highest form of human bonding is simply naive, but to view it in the same way that we understand the bondings of children trivializes its spiritual and emotional qualities. As Aristotle said, "Without friends, no one would choose to live."

13

The Psycho-Economics
of Teen Approval

> We have an innate propensity to get ourself noticed,
> and noticed favorably, by our kind.
> —William James

In North American culture the approval-obsessed are, with monotonous
regularity, fools for consumerism; and what is true for the population is general
is even more so for adolescents in particular. Because most teens are too young,
too inexperienced, and too early in their identity formation to define themselves
with conviction, they come to rely upon the approving judgments of others
to sustain their sense of worth and to bolster their wobbly self-esteem. The
growing self seeks recognition, praise, and acknowledgment, but it also very
much needs to be admired, envied, and pursued. Around these needs the
adolescent's social world orbits.

For many youngsters the patchwork self, in search of confirmation, becomes
bonded to material goods or to the image they hope these goods will create,
and for these youth the right commodities, the right labels, and the right people
become not only their most prized possession, they are, emotionally speaking,
their most *real* possessions. Contemporary teen life is profoundly shaped by
a simple equation: The right "things" bring approval, the wrong "things" bring
rejection. Its grim simplicity is tailor-made for the insecure temperament, the
slippery social slope, and the concrete thinking of 12- to 16-year-olds—not to
mention the narcissism which propels their nature.

THE PURCHASE OF ACCEPTANCE

The consumer lives surrounded not so much by things as by fantasies.
—Christopher Lasch

The fable that the right people will notice every new purchase is the shared theme of all advertising. Youngsters who accept this illusion, even if they accept it only in part, soon find themselves locked into dependence on consumer goods—not only for the approval these goods elicit from others, but for the approval they elicit from themselves. They are so hooked on material goods that without them self-approval is nearly impossible. The patchwork of reactions which make up the self-esteem network of early and middle adolescents is no match for the illusion industry. These young and frightened souls, trying their best to reason their way to stability and acceptance, are simply no match for the professional image makers. They are so hungry for approval that they willingly purchase whatever will bring it. But, in consuming for emotional gain, the adolescent unknowingly makes himself a consumable object as well.[66]

The Canadian Advisory Council on the Status of Women (Holmes & Silverman, 1992) reported that only 13 percent of adolescent girls are satisfied with their appearance. This does not seem surprising for young women living in a society "which stresses the ideals of feminine beauty and thinness, places a higher value on beauty for females than for males, and minimizes the value of women's other qualities" (p. 18). Among the young is a tendency for image to register more powerfully than substance, and for the *presentation* of self to carry as much weight as the real self. Self-presentation is perhaps the biggest single issue in teen society, partly because so few youth hold a genuine sense of themselves in the first place. In the early years the self must be validated by others because it cannot validate itself.

> I constantly cared about how I looked—especially my clothes. Everything I owned had to be name brand: If it wasn't, I wouldn't wear it. It all had to do with what others thought of me. I always wanted to be the best and others to think of me as that and I often was. (18-year-old university student describing her preoccupation with appearance during her early adolescent years)

In reality, of course, the picture is more complicated than I have presented it. I am here suggesting one contradiction of teen social life: Youngsters who try to bolster their self-concept (and their social status) with trendy goods soon discover that image does not strengthen their self-concept, but instead weakens it through the fear that the goods they now own are no longer image-enhancing and must be replaced with newer, more glittering goods. By putting oneself on display, one begs for approval, a gesture of dependency and subordination which, even though productive in the short-term, impedes the adolescent's need for worthy self-definition.

An all-too-frequent outcome of the purchase of approval is not an increase in self-esteem, but merely an increase in envy for those whose image is more beautiful when decorated with the same possessions. Ultimately, what we see among so many youthful consumers is the same lack of regard for their possessions as they hold for themselves; teens, like the rest of us, cannot respect what they own when they do not first respect themselves.

Two Further Ideas on the Purchase of Acceptance

First, young people are not gifted at complimenting others, at offering congratulations to someone who has achieved an impressive goal, or even striking up a casual conversation to pass the time of day; in essence, they have trouble negotiating what clinicians call "moving toward others." Because the force of their personality is weighted toward the egocentric, adolescents are *predisposed* to receive overtures rather than to offer them. (This inability to venture into the emotional sphere of others is what makes social interchange among the young so awkward and stilted and filled with grinding empty pauses. It also contributes to their use of cliche, insult, slogan, shock language, and images from pop culture to move their conversation.)

The heat which melts the barriers is the *visual symbol.* Purchased goods, as long as they are the right ones, invite others into our sphere. A new sweater, a stylish haircut, a designer label which fails to produce this desired reaction is essentially worthless. In teen society the real purpose is to solicit, to entice, to awe, to invite; they serve as substitutes for open and honest speech at an age when these skills are in scarce supply. Eventually most of us learn how to make honest and direct overtures in order to better satisfy our needs, but during the adolescent years this life skill unfolds slowly and awkwardly—a fact of human development the illusion industry understands far more clearly than most parents.

Second, youth flow to visual symbols because they are voiceless, a deficiency which provides them with the freedom to initiate their own speech and to express their own opinions. The visual rescues them from the paralysis of their own self-consciousness by creating an opportunity to respond to others, and by giving others the opportunity to respond to them. In this way voiceless Echoes can display without speaking, and self-absorbed Narcissuses can respond without sharing. The visual is valued because it is an object, and when it fails in its function it is discarded. The relationship between consumer and consumed is completely utilitarian.

The spirit of what I am trying to communicate has also been the object of investigation of Cote:

> Youth culture constitutes a special type of consumer culture. Young people are
> hungry to have their emotions, identity, and tastes defined and redefined for them

by the massive industries that market fashion, music, art, and other consumer items. These goods all have in common an identity-conferring quality. To be "someone," to be "in," one has to consume a particular item. Young consumers are the perfect target for such manipulation because the fact that they have been sequestered into groups at school based on grade levels makes them hunger for an identity. Because young people's identity is so precarious, the industries we have mentioned can make their products obsolete or constantly change them year after year, requiring consumers to follow the trends they arbitrarily set and announce through the media. (1996, p. 29)

Although I must confess to being dubious about whether most teens are as easily manipulated as Cote claims they are, no doubt exists that many, many of them are; and it is they, in their vast numbers, who are the focus of our present concern. Denby (1996) expressed it just right when he lamented that North American youth "are shaped by the media as consumers before they have had a chance to develop their souls" (p. 84). The net effect is that many teens are not only defenseless against the instinct of acquisition which fetters human nature; they are programmed to glorify it before they have the intellectual maturity to examine it.[67]

HOW WORK FOR PAY SHAPES TEEN SOCIETY

The state of mind promoted by consumerism is better described as a state of
uneasiness and chronic anxiety. The promotion of commodities depends on
discouraging the individual from reliance
on his own resources and judgments
—Christopher Lasch

The impulse to consume propels the adolescent work force. That adolescents do not understand their own motivation in this matter is understandable given that this is a new experience in their developmental unfolding, but for psychologists to be impervious to it is downright negligence.

A Brief Historical Overview

During the 1970s and 1980s an attitude prevailed among educators, youth watchers, and most teens themselves that young people would benefit from greater participation in the world of work-for-pay. (By "work for pay" I mean work for which one receives an hourly wage, in contrast to volunteer work, community service, or any activities for which labor receives no cash compensation.) This attitude was encouraged by parents who resented the anti-establishment attitudes of youth in the 1960s, and who were fearful that a similar lack of motivation might strike their own children. Thus, the call to teenage employment was encouraged by parents, and welcomed by youth tired of a school-only menu. On the practical side, this movement was encouraged by the avalanche of employment opportunities presented by the fast food industry and a wide range of minimal competence "clerk" jobs provided by the growing service industry. The President's Science Advisory Committee (1973) endorsed youth employment as sound in principle because it encouraged adolescents to venture out of age-segregated schools into the world of adult roles, habits, and expectations.

A massive number of adolescents entered the part-time labor force while remaining full-time students in the school system. One researcher reported that about 60 percent of grade 12 students, and about 40 percent of grade 10 students are working at any given time during the school year. This contrasts with 1940 where only about 2 percent of similar aged youngsters were enrolled simultaneously in the school place and the work force. This historically unique phenomenon was given impetus by four critically important sets of forces:

- the profound set of economic and occupational changes that swept Postindustrial societies;
- an ideology about the meaning and value of work in American culture;
- the encouragement of youth gratification;
- the increased emphasis on consumerism and materialism in our society, which is stimulated by television and directed to all youth populations. (Greenberger & Steinberg, 1986, xv)

Interestingly, few social scientists investigated the practical consequences of youth entering the work force on such a massive scale. Greenberger and Steinberg (1986) were among the first to research these topics, and their findings jolted an inattentive public. In the past decade (1988-1998) no real progress has been made in our understanding of the motives which impel youth to join the workplace.

The beliefs held by adults who support youth-employment are consistent and earnest. They include the belief that work-for-pay is good for youngsters and that it helps them "to get their feet wet in the real world"; the belief that work helps kids assume responsibility; the notion that working youth contribute to the financial welfare of their household; that income permits young people to pay their own way; that learning about work smooths the transition to the harsher, less personal world of adult work.

The research findings did not (and do not now) support their hopeful expectations. Most data pointed to the conclusion that employment undermines the quality of young people's education; that employment leads to increased spending, especially on luxury items; that employment actually promotes certain kinds of delinquent behavior; that youth employment often leads to increased alcohol, tobacco, and marijuana consumption; and employment generates cynicism and scorn for "lower-level" work.

Findings such as these have led most researchers to conclude that the benefits of adolescent work-for-pay are overestimated while its costs are underestimated.

The mathematics of employment do not fit the 168-hour week. Working teens spend about 34 hours a week in school, about 30 hours per week at their job (including travel time), about 49 hours per week in sleep, about 8 hours in homework, and 10 hours eating. With this schedule they have only 37 hours per week for *everything else in their lives.*

For most teenagers it takes only one semester for their schedule to create symptoms; but some youth are so sturdy that it takes a year or more before they deteriorate into the typical syndrome of chronic fatigue. During that one-year period a fateful event occurs which is of greater significance even than exhaustion: the purchase of a car.

The automobile allows young workers to provide their own transportation to work and to school and thus lessens time demands on parents. At least that is the hook that parents bite. The *real* reason for the car, despite claims of practicality and necessity, is the teen's craving for esteem and popularity. The real outcome is a bank loan. Most youngsters who own cars work to overcome indebtedness even though the word is not in their vocabulary. It is hard to believe that neither adolescents nor their parents see the inherent contradiction in this sequence of events. They eventually feel it, pay for it, sometimes even fall apart from it, but they rarely see it for what it is.

Parents, educators, and youth themselves believed that work for pay would enhance self-cultivation, that it would provide an economic head start, that it would resemble an "apprenticeship" in the best sense of that word. No such luck.

> Today, fast-food chains and other such places of work (record shops, bowling alleys) keep costs down by having teens supervise teens, often with no adult on the premises. *There is no mature adult figure to identify with, to emulate, or to provide a role model or mature moral guidance.* The work culture varies from one store to another.... Rarely is there a "master" to learn from; rarely is there much worth learning. Indeed, far from being places where solid work values are being transmitted, these are places where all too often teen values dominate. (Etzioni, 1993, p. 111, original emphasis)

Youngsters and adults were so wrong because the workplace is different than it used to be and different in ways that conspire against meaningful work. Teen work environments are filled with other youth (just like school); their exposure to adults is limited to those who, for whatever reasons, are still working in the dead-end, low-paying jobs monopolized by kids. The skills rarely transfer to better paying jobs.

Work and Youth Work

Work is purposeful activity performed in producing goods or services whether for remuneration or not. It may or may not contribute to personal meaning, and it may or may not enhance self-esteem. No matter how we slice it, youth work rarely stacks up as meaningful, and young workers are fully cognizant of this even before they enter the work force. They knowingly sell their labor for cash. There is little self-deception about the nature of work, except perhaps among grade 10 students who are inclined to misperceive everything for which they have no first-hand experience. Adolescents know the difference between what philosophers call meaningful work and what Marx called exploitive work, and they enter willingly into work devoid of meaning because they recognize it for what it is: short-term effort for short-term gain. They do not think of work as meaningful in its own right, or as an activity which engenders meaning; therefore, selling their labor is not emotionally deflating. The research finds that adolescent workers view their labor as a commodity to be sold on the open market, that it has no intrinsic value, and that its real purpose is merely to increase consumption. These young workers think they know why they are working, but they don't. They know what they want to buy, and this inclines them to think that they know why they are working. The tragedy, of course, is that they do not understand, in any meaningful way, *why* they desire what they desire. Sadly, many of them never get much of a clue. In the absence of solid adult guidance, it is a difficult puzzle for young people to solve.

Youth know that they are engaged in futureless work for immediate wages and, to their way of thinking, this is a fair exchange. What they do not understand is that the goods they purchase with their earned capital tend to be over-priced, over-hyped paraphernalia which they hope (sometimes correctly) will enhance their desirability and their status. Their failure to understand is not due only to developmental immaturity, although this contributes in serious measure. With remarkable consistency their parents are equally noncomprehending, equally impelled by an ideology of acquisition, and similarly incompetent at distinguishing the real from the contrived. These are the parents who make up what Postman (1986) called "the culture of trivia," where social life is a perpetual round of entertainments, and public conversation is little more than baby-talk. According to Postman and those who think along similar lines, our culture has produced a youth culture dominated by the same consumerist illusions that permeate our entire society.

Judging by their spending habits, Postman is right. Virtually all research confirms that the majority of adolescent earnings are spent on junk food, tobacco, the pop music industry, and youth industry products. Only rarely do we find a family where the adolescent's earnings enhance, in any meaningful way, the family's welfare.[68]

Research conducted in the 1990s confirms that most youth money is spent on automobiles, music, clothing, and fast-food. Greenberger and Steinberg (1986) determined that half of grade 12 students do not save for their future education, and only 1 in 10 youngsters save half of their earnings. Among males, automobiles are the biggest burden. Over half of teenage earners report that they make no financial contribution of any kind to family expenses.

Consumerism and the Media

The mass media are the cornerstone of consumerism and perhaps more than any other force have embedded in our collective conscious the belief that acceptance and desirability can be purchased.

> It is no coincidence that youths in North America are enthusiastic consumers of mass media products, such as magazines, movies, television, advertising, and music… "teenzines" (teen magazines directed at young women) report the latest news about fashion and music trends, and they link these with other youth-oriented, leisure industries through advertising. A recent study examined three leading American teenzines published in 1988 and 1989 and found that almost one-half of the total magazine space was taken up by ads and that about one-half of these ads were selling beauty-care products, fashion, clothing, and other items designed to enhance young women's appearance and popularity. (Cote 1996, pp. 89-90)

Money can be disposed of on luxury items (designer clothing) rather than necessary items (food, rent) because so many young workers come from families situated in the top third of the income distribution. And, as one commentator put it, perhaps this is "only fair and square: the youngsters are just being good … consumers, working and spending their money on what turns them on." Yet, "an educator might bemoan that these young, as-yet-unformed individuals are driven to buy objects of no intrinsic educational, cultural, or social merit" (Etzioni, 1993, p. 111).

The picture painted here is too splashy, but the image is essentially correct, especially for middle- and upper-middle-class youth who hold the majority of work-for-pay jobs. The net effect is that we need to look soberly at how youth employment relates to societal contribution and to personal dignity. If we have learned anything from our investigation of teen employment it is that young people work not to attain necessities, but to purchase what they hope will, in one form or another, bring approval, esteem, or status.

At first glance today's youth may not seem to yield a reasonable harvest to their parent society; but, increasingly, more of us are asking whether the parent society is merely reaping what it has sown.

POSTSCRIPT

A real understanding of the behavior of any human being is impossible without
a clear comprehension of the secret goal which he is pursuing.
—Alfred Adler

Very few parents understand why their teens so desperately need money and
they never will until they comprehend the secret goals their children are
pursuing. Teens need money to balance their social accounts, to increase their
popularity ratings, and to bolster their desirability. It has other purposes, to
be sure, but these are the ones that matter. It has not always been that way,
but that is the way it is now.

The belief held by virtually all teens that they *must* spend and *must* consume
to make it in their social world is in serious need of reanalysis by both teens
and adults. At this moment it appears that neither youngsters nor their parents
are of a clear mind as to *why* the young should work. As well, neither parents
nor their adolescent children seem to know why they are hooked into buying
approval and esteem when more dignified (and cheaper) ways to achieve it
are readily available.

The ideas which have been the object of our attention in this chapter do
not lend themselves to quick and tidy summary. The larger themes are not
new to adolescent psychology (the need for approval has been investigated
empirically since the 1950s), but the sub-themes—how the need for approval
deteriorates into an obsessive fear of rejection, and how the need for approval
is corrupted by market forces—are neglected in mainstream analysis. In
introducing these ideas I have no intention of taking a step backward in our
understanding of young people and the dilemmas which trouble their lives;
rather, my hope is that this crab-like progress, in which an idea advances while
seeming to go backward, will ultimately enrich our understanding of the
adolescent experience.

It helps to stand back for a moment if from the distance gained by such
a retreat we attain improved perspective. Approval for the teen (and for the
child as well) is more than mere approval in the generic sense of the word.
The assembly-line inspector approves the quality of work which passes before
him; he says this is OK, this is faulty, this requires touching up, this is rejected,
and so on. The approval which teens pursue is often of this technical, surface
variety, notably in matters of clothing, hair styles, etc. A deeper craving also
calls—a craving for validation of the self-under-construction, a craving for
acknowledgement of the "me" who cries and sings, the grandiose "me," the
majestic "me." This is the heart of the adolescent's deeper self and it clamors
for praise and affirmation.

When we take the deeper "me" into account we see that the quest for approval
is a struggle where stakes are higher than eyes trained only on the gadgets

youngsters manipulate to receive approval can see. Kids disintegrate when they perceive lack of approval as a rejection of their deeper self. The teen's impulse to consume and to display is nothing more than a cry for recognition, a plea for affirmation. That we as a society have not created dignified ways for our youth to achieve recognition and affirmation is to our shame and to their denigration.

14

Primitive and Mature Intimacy During Adolescence

> In order to establish intimate relations with others,
> one must first know who and what one is.
> —Jerome Dusek

Remarkable as it may seem, very little research has been directed to intimacy; and even today, almost after a century after Hall (1916) wrote: "As to the sentiment of love in the adolescent, we still know too little," we remain in the dark concerning its causes, its origins, and how it expresses itself in adolescent love and romance.

Despite this lack of research, intimacy is a necessary area of inquiry if we are to grasp the emotional lives of youth; intimacy, afterall, is the transition experience between juvenile friendship and adult love. Intimacy differs from ordinary friendship by the depth of its feeling, by the power of its conviction, and by its concern for the real needs of the partner.

Sullivan set the stage for our understanding of this topic when he claimed that intimacy requires "a clearly formulated adjustment of one's behavior *to the expressed needs of the other person* in the pursuit of increasingly identical— *that is more and more nearly mutual satisfations*" (1953, p. 246, emphasis added). I have emphasized two phrases in this well known quote to draw attention to *genuine* needs and *mutual* satisfactions. Intimacy requires care, respect, and responsiveness to the partner's growth and happiness; and, by implication, it requires the *maturity of selfhood* to recognize the partner's real needs, and the *maturity of thought* to think evenly about the partner's long-term best interests.

Intimacy is grounded in a genuine and wholesome concern for the partner, demonstrated in mutual admiration and genuine reciprocity. The mix of affection, eroticism, sentimentalism, loyalty, and losing oneself in the partner is not the same as love, but it is as close as most adolescents get. Intimacy is easily confused with a variety of superficial attractions, and part of the sorting out process we call adolescence is learning to distinguish mature intimacy from its primitive impersonations.[69]

ADOLESCENT IDENTITY—SOME IMPLICATIONS FOR ADOLESCENT INTIMACY

The question for which we do not have an agreed upon answer is this: "Is the attainment of a mature identity necessary before one can experience genuine intimacy?" Before this question can be answered we must first look at what we mean by identity.

Adolescent identity has been the object of systematic investigation for more than fifty years, having been introduced by Erikson in his landmark essay "Ego development and historical change" in 1946. Since his pioneer efforts, most psychologists, and virtually all developmentalists, have come to accept that young people achieve identity as they invest themselves in a relatively stable set of values and beliefs, and as they formulate a set of career goals and occupational options.

Healthy identity has an adaptive and flexible character. "Adolescence is...a period in which past, present, and future are rewoven and strung together on the threads of fantasies and wishes that do not necessarily follow the laws of linear chronology" (Kaplan, 1984, p. 16). Identity also includes the shameful and punitive elements of one's nature "composed of what he has been shamed for, what he has been punished for, and what he feels guilty about...Identity means integration of all previous identifications and self images, including the negative ones" (Erikson, 1959, p. 67). Therefore, when we discuss identity we are recognizing the continuity of identity despite changes which take place within it; we are recognizing a unique totality leading to a differentiation from all other people; we are recognizing the sameness of essential character which resides within a given individual; and we are recognizing that its attainment requires effort and purposeful direction.

Hewitt claimed that to have an identity means:

> to maintain a balance between similarity and difference in the face of individual development and changing social conditions, so that one can assimilate to the

self demands for change or adjustment, but also fulfill an inner desire for constancy. It is to be a whole and complete person, and not fragmented into roles and ruled by scripts. It is to be connected with others and yet true to oneself. It is to participate in a variegated and often fragmented social life and yet to maintain continuity and integrity. Persons with identity know who they are, what they are doing, and where they are going. (1989, p. 152)

Identity is not finalized during adolescence, nor does any valid reason indicate that it should be. Adolescence, however, is the age when identity assumes its adult outlines, when it becomes noticeably less childlike, and when it attains the strength and autonomy we associate with adult character.

In sum, the key ingredients to a healthy identity include an honest recognition of one's strengths and weaknesses, a fairly solid sense of family and community, a stable set of beliefs by which to make important decisions, and a belief in one's ability to cope with adversity. A mature identity is a major life accomplishment, and while a good share of its is constructed during adolescence, it continues to grow and evolve throughout the adult years.

INTIMACY AND IDENTITY DURING ADOLESCENCE

Now to the question at hand: "Are adolescents mature enough in their identity for genuine intimacy?"[70]

Since the prolific writings of Erikson took hold in North America it has been widely accepted that a fairly solid sense of identity is a requirement for intimacy; after all, it is one's identity which is shared in intimacy, and one cannot share what one does not have. "Without an active form of identity, the individual...is unable to make commitments to others or to abide ethically by commitments made. *Put another way, fulfillment of intimacy requires a sense of shared identities*" (Adams & Archer, 1994, p. 194, emphasis added).

As Erikson himself phrased it: "It is only when identity formation is well on its way that true intimacy ... is possible" (1968, p. 135). In other words, intimacy cannot come into being until certain developmental preconditions have been met.

In order to establish intimate relations with others, one must first know who and what one is.... If one is to reveal the inner self to others, one must know what the inner self is and have self-acceptance; for if one cannot accept the self, how can one ask others to accept it? Those who have not resolved the identity crisis ... have trouble developing intimate relationships for they continually fear that they will reveal they have no firm sense of self. (Dusek, 1991, p. 152)

The question then becomes: "How is intimacy experienced by teens lacking identity?" This is an important question because very few teens have sculpted a mature identity, yet they may be intensely driven to forge intimate relationships as best they can. Indeed, for many teens (especially girls) the intimacy project is more important than the identity project, a phenomenon which holds staggering implications for sexual behavior in the teen community.

The conventional picture is that teens embrace, bond, give their loyalty, pledge their fidelity, and share their emotions. These intimate behaviors are perceived by adolescents as love. Love, however, is rarely what they are. Powerful feelings and profound emotions are essential to love, but they are not the same as love. As Sullivan helped us to understand, love requires respect for the real needs of the partner. No matter how intense, no matter how erotic, and no matter how sincere the connecting bond may be, without an awareness of the partner as person, it is not love that blooms. It is rich, it is real, it is more profound than anything before it. But is it love? Not really. What then is it? *Adolescent love.*

The point to be grasped is elementary, but its implications are immense: Because their identities are in process, and because their self-knowledge is in flux, adolescents have difficulty with relationships where the rightful needs of the self must be balanced with the rightful needs of the partner. This, quite obviously, makes intimacy a special problem.

PRIMITIVE INTIMACY

> In grade 9 (14 years old) I went out with two people. I liked the first guy's looks and athletic status. The fact that he found me attractive was really nice too. I liked the happy-go-lucky personality and the smile of the second guy. At 15 (grade 10), I liked Trevor's eyes and view of the world the most.
> —19-year-old describing her "first attractions."

In our endeavor to grasp adolescent intimacy we find ourselves grappling with its legitimate, but lesser, expressions—bondings which include some but not all of the conditions of genuine intimacy. In these relationships feelings are intense, attractions powerful, and desire pressing, yet awareness of the partner-as-person, and sensitivity to the partner's real needs are underdeveloped. Primitive intimacy usually does not evolve into mature intimacy, although we see many instances in the adolescent community where it does. Primitive intimacy is about possession and receiving; in mature intimacy you want the other person's good; in primitive intimacy you want the other person.[71]

It has been my observation that researchers often make a mistake similar to the one that adolescents themselves make when it comes to intimacy: They fail to recognize the differences between primitive and mature intimacy. Teens and teen experts share the myth that mature intimacy is *natural* to the adolescent experience when, in fact, it is not. Bright and alive as youthful intimacy is, it is not alive to the world in the same way it will be after it grows and matures.

As part of my research with adolescents I have interviewed many 12- to 15-year-olds who are pregnant, or who have recently given birth.[72] Many of these girls (I have trouble calling them "young women" even though their life-experience justifies it) tell stories of special relevance to the questions we are looking at. It is not unusual to meet a young mother who refuses to talk to the man (boy) who fathered her child because she feels betrayed.[73] The stories these girls tell hold a surprising consistency. The boy is often three or four years older (during early or middle adolescence this amounts to a tremendous psycho-emotional advantage). At the beginning of the relationship the boy praises, pursues, and woos the girl with an earnest aggressiveness. The girls perceive the boy's actions as proof that he is in "love" (sometimes these girls believe that the actions, unto themselves, *are* love). The girl accepts the boy's persistence as a singular interest in her, and as proof of her desirability, even when she has been forewarned by her girlfriends, her mother and, sometimes, even the boy's friends. Their involvement becomes sexual, she becomes pregnant, he becomes gone. She feels betrayed; she trusted him, and he turned out to be fraudulent. Her betrayal transforms into shame, then anger, then on-going resentment. Yet an open condemnation of the boyfriend destroys her value as the object of his love; to lessen him is to lessen herself. A tough call for a youngster struggling to hold on to even a minimal sense of her own worth. "He liked me; he paid attention to me; he was cool; he was a show off; he was cute." (15-year-old girl's response to the question: What most attracted you to the first guy you had sexual intercourse with?).

The deception does not exist solely within the boy. The girl does not (or cannot, depending on your assessment of adolescent aptitude) distance herself from the chase, the eroticism. These girls discredit their own reality checks (a common practice among early adolescents). At a certain level they know that love is not what is happening, but knowing cannot prevent hoping. The young mother, while deploring her mate's desertion, also sings his praises, foremost of which was his willingness to praise her.[74]

A fifteen-year-old mother in rural Washington described her boyfriend this way: "He was a liar most of the time, but he made me feel good. He was always nice to me so I can't be too mad at him." Her best girlfriend, age sixteen, also has a baby. Of her boyfriend she said: "I'm glad I didn't have to marry him but I wouldn't want to have never met him. He was a nice guy, just not dependable. I kinda thought this [becoming a mother] might happen, but I never thought much about it." A seventeen-year-old from Portland, Oregon, offered this: "I liked it when he was nice to me. I don't know if I ever *loved* him, even though I told everyone I did. I just liked his always wanting to do things for me, and his always saying nice things to me." These testimonials speak to the heart of primitive intimacy. It is not fool's gold, it is real; but the deposit rarely goes to depth, and the mineable reserves are almost always impossible to prove.[75]

Infatuation As An Expression Of Primitive Intimacy

By infatuation we mean a state of powerful attraction where one is preoccupied with the partner so fully that thoughts and feelings about them intrude involuntarily into consciousness, and where other concerns recede into the background, where one longs to be with the partner, where one has an acute sensitivity to the reactions of the partner, where one feels buoyant, vitalized, and swept away and, where one is obsessed with the admirable traits of the partner. Infatuation is intense, passionate, and usually short-lived. Adolescents, especially early and middle teens, confuse it with love; a confusion which derives from the reflexive tendency to overrate self-experience in order to inflate the importance of the self doing the experiencing. The grander my experience, the grander am I.

Infatuation Versus Mature Intimacy

> Some people would never have been in love if they hadn't
> heard love talked about.
> —La Rouchefoucauld

How does infatuation differ from mature intimacy? From love? Generally speaking, and we require considerable latitude here, infatuation is triggered by superficial features rather than substantive ones, grounded in physicality more than in caring, one-sided rather than reciprocal, stagnant rather than growth-fostering, and "pervaded with illusion rather than honest attempts at mutual understanding" (Martin, 1996, p. 13). In sum, infatuation is a stab at intimacy rather than intimacy itself.

Infatuation has a swiftness and an uplifting abruptness which in some ways resembles love, but in other ways falls quite short. With infatuation love comes as a thunderbolt from the sky; lovers are struck, smitten, paralyzed by a force too great, too true, and too glorious to resist, and with it their innocent hopes for unity and union are given wings.

All that he feels is that here is a person whom he likes or trusts, or with whom he feels infatuated...They may be aroused by erotic or sexual advances, although these may have nothing to do with love...Many such relations are carried on under the camouflage of love...when actually the love is only the person's clinging to satisfy his own needs...One of the factors essential to our idea of love—reliability and steadiness of feeling—is absent in these cases. (Horney, 1937, pp. 94-95)

Infatuation can be a cruel introduction to love since it rarely lives up to what is hoped for. Although it may serve as a precursor to intimacy, it is not at all the same as intimacy. What then is it? *Primitive* intimacy.

The Language Of Love

When speaking with adolescents about intimacy (interestingly, they rarely use this word in ordinary conversation), one cannot help but be struck by their fascination with the pronoun "I." This is due partly to their lack of skills in explicit communication, and partly to nervous self-consciousness, but more than anything it conveys the narcissism in which their intimacy is grounded; the language of adolescent love almost always reduces to the language of narcissistic sentimentalism. When listening to teens talk about their relationships one often gets the feeling that each partner has sculpted a patch of identity turf and, having done so, sends out "feeler invitations" for someone to come in and share it. These invitations are a necessary prelude to intimacy, and to love, but unto themselves they are neither. "He was charming; a sweet talker. I was attracted to him because he thought I was hot. He treated me nice." (18-year-old to the question: "What attracted you to the first boy you had intercourse with?")

Teens, for the most part, have difficulty expressing deep emotion, but they have special problems when they share it with someone who is listening intently to what they say, and who holds an emotional interest in exactly how they say it. Teens are better suited to communicate their affection through touch, closeness, fidelity, concern, and possessiveness than through words. Teens feel the power of love, the eroticism of love, the highs and lows of love, but they do so without very much in the way of a language of love:

> Eros requires speech, and beautiful speech, to communicate to its partner what it feels and wants... What one cannot talk about, what one does not have words for, hardly exists. Richness of vocabulary is part of richness of experience ... to make love humanly, the partners have to talk to each other. (Bloom, 1993, p. 25)

What Bloom describes in the abstract teens report in the concrete: "When I love someone and want to know him better, I am afraid to tell him of my feelings for fear that his reaction will disappoint me. He may not love me back.... So, I may stifle my feelings of love because I don't want to handle the disappointment of being refused the real love that I would eventually ask" (DeVaron, 1972, p. 342). But fear is only one reason why teens do not express their love verbally. Intimate language is an art form which requires self-knowledge, self-esteem, and a grasp of which emotions are being suppressed and which are being released. Again, on these counts teens come up short.

Intimacy requires one to reply to the inner feelings of the partner, and a willingness to talk further and deeper about these feelings. Intimacy grows with self-disclosure and then again with the reciprocation of self-disclosure. Spontaneity of language, playful barbs, harmless bantering, and excited rambling all play essential roles. We express our love through the melody and rhythm of words; and whereas adolescents are willing to risk and sacrifice in the hope of achieving meaningful intimacy, they fall short when it comes to speaking their love.[76]

Many youngsters know almost nothing about love as they have not seen it in their household, and neither have they received much of it in their growing-up process; consequently, they lurch into adolescence unskilled at every aspect of love and without knowing how to differentiate desperate clutching from earnest embrace. To compensate for these deficiencies they create fables which persuade them that love is what they have, and through these fables they magically elevate their lesser reality into a greater one.

Sharing In The Pleasure Of The Partner

It helps us to keep our bearings if we recall that mature intimacy requires a concern for the *genuine* needs and the *real* feelings of the partner. Not exclusively, not totally, but convincingly. Sullivan, the first Neo-Freudian to openly investigate intimacy as a psychological phenomenon, claimed (as I noted earlier) that intimacy requires "a clearly formulated adjustment of one's behavior *to the expressed needs of the other person* in the pursuit of increasingly identical—that is *more and more nearly mutual-satisfactions"* (1953, p. 246, emphasis added). Sullivan helped us to recognize the significance of sharing in our partner's achievements, and to be uplifted by the good moments in the partner's life. Brehm, in her excellent work on human relationships, spoke to the same issue: "In close, rewarding, intimate relationships, partners will meet each other's needs, disclosing feelings and sharing confidences, discussing practical concerns, helping each other, and providing reassurance" (Brehm, 1991). Many teens (and all narcissists) have a problem with this elementary fact of intimacy because they cannot share wholeheartedly in the pleasures of the partner. Indeed, these pleasures produce within them an unwelcome envy and an unwanted jealousy.

Adolescents are confused as to how another person can bring pleasure to their loved one; it makes them feel replaceable, and it beckons jealousy, resentment, and a load of other troublesome emotions. These feelings may cause the left out partner to conclude that the other should have *no outside pleasures at all.* This conclusion (and its fabled defense) is typical of primitive intimacy, especially when the male is threatened by the outside pleasure of his female partner.

Mature intimacy is felt in the heart, but it is expressed in action; indeed, it is the action of intimacy, not the emotion of intimacy, which separates its primitive and mature expressions. Mature intimacy is grounded in the action of *giving* oneself in positive and affirming ways; in *caring* for the growth of the partner; in *responsibility* to respond to the partner's needs; in *respect* for the integrity and individuality of the partner; in *understanding* the real needs of the partner so that one can try to improve his or her general welfare. As we move toward integration of these acts of love, we move toward mature intimacy. All of which takes us back to Shakespeare: "They do not love that do not *show* they love."

THE PREDISPOSITIONS THAT SHAPE ADOLESCENT BONDING

Teenagers search for relationships ... where the primary experience sought is not so much the personal bond as it is the sharpness of affect.
—David Wexler

One of the great mysteries of teen relationships is why young people give their allegiance and their devotion to one particular partner. As one scholar put it: "We have a theory of infant attachment, a theory of adult attachment, and a great deal in between left to the imagination" (Waters, 1991). Here I want to briefly investigate two of the forces that speak to the mystery of adolescent bonding, *fidelity* and *particularization.*

FIDELITY

Adolescents are predisposed to attach to a person or to a cause perceived as worthy, special, wonderful, or great. This emotional predisposition I call *fidelity*. Fromm's concept of "the basic sympathy to love" helps us to better understand it. "Love," he claimed, "is rooted in a basic attitude which is constantly present; a readiness to love, a *basic sympathy* as one might call it. *It is started, but not caused, by a particular object*" (1939, p. 519). And it is precisely this final point (that love is started, but not *caused*, by one particular person) which is at the heart of adolescent love. Here are Fromm's own words on this topic:

> Love...is rooted in a basic attitude which is constantly present; a readiness to love, a *basic sympathy* as one might call it. It is started, but not caused, by a particular *object*. The ability and readiness to love is a character trait...The important point, however, is that love for a particular *object* is only the actualization and concentration of lingering love with regard to one person; it is not, as the idea of *romantic love* would have it, that there is only *the* one person

in the world whom one could love, that it is the great chance of one's life to find that person, and that love for him or her results in a withdrawal from all others. (1939, p. 520, original emphasis)

Simon, Eder, and Evans (1992) help us to get a feel for the juvenile expression of the predisposition to love.

For some girls, the onset of their first romantic attraction was the beginning of a continuous state of being in love, often with frequent changes in the object of their feelings. *In fact, simply having romantic feelings may have been more important than the actual boy to whom these feelings were directed.* (p. 42, original emphasis)

This final comment, assuming its basic correctness, speaks volumes to the dynamics of teen attraction. Further to it, the authors report the following anecdote about one of the young girls in their study: "A researcher noticed that a girl had "I love" written on her hand and asked her about it. Although this girl's romantic feelings had no particular target, she explained that she was ready to add the name of a boy as soon as a suitable target was found" (1992, p. 42).

Further to this theme: "When girls realized that a boy they had been going with now liked someone else, they often redirected their romantic feelings toward someone new" (p. 42). The spirit of what we are looking at is recorded in the diary entry of a 16-year-old girl: "Dear sweet, good loving understanding God—hear me, please. I'd love to go on a date with someone SOON" (Kostash, 1987). What is being described here, it seems to me, is the predisposition to attach, to bond, to connect through romance. It is not a predisposition to love, at least not as love generally is understood, but rather as an urge to attach, to affix, or to affiliate in the hopes that love may one day bloom. In sum, fidelity is a natural craving of the adolescent years. The person to whom it is directed is its recipient, but not its cause.

This idea is so rich in its implications that I cannot, as yet, leave it. Because fidelity (the desire to give oneself to someone or to something worthy) lives as a constant readiness it is not *caused* by a particular person, no matter how splendid that person may be, and no matter how much one *wants* the person to be its cause. In this regard, fidelity parallels any number of other organic predispositions; here it is compared with the erotic predisposition:

The erotic person has a basically erotic *attitude* toward the world. This does not mean that he is constantly excited sexually. It means that there is an erotic *atmosphere* which is actualized by a certain object, *but which is there underneath before the stimulus appears.* What is meant here is not the physiologically given ability to be sexually excited, but an *atmosphere of erotic readiness.* (Fromm, 1939, p. 520, original emphasis)

One final thought on a parallel concept—devotion—before we conclude this brief look into fidelity-as-adolescent-predisposition:

> The object of man's devotion vary…He can be devoted to the goal of amassing a fortune, of acquiring power, of destruction, or to that of loving and of being productive and courageous. He can be devoted to the most diverse goals…*yet the need for devotion itself is a primary need demanding fulfillment regardless of how this need is fulfilled.* (Fromm, 1973, pp. 231-232, original emphasis)

From all this it seems to follow that we must take into account three separate forces if we are to understand adolescent bonding: erotic readiness, fidelity, and the desire to share one's love with another person. From these predispositions mutuality and reciprocity eventually evolve, but during the evolution process (which usually lasts three or four years) we have neither mature intimacy nor mature love, but their adolescent incubation.

PARTICULARIZATION

> We impute special value and power to people
> on whom we depend emotionally.
> —Nancy McWilliams

In his classic essay, "On a Certain Blindness in Human Beings," William James observed: "Our judgments concerning the worth of things depend on the *feelings* the things arouse in us." James' message is simple but profound: As our feelings ascend so also do our *judgments* about the particular person associated with them.

Particularization is the belief that the person with whom a love experience is shared is the cause of that experience, and without this particular person, the love experience could never be. Rather than attribute love to themselves, that is, their inner feelings, their warmth, their sexuality, the experience is attributed entirely to qualities within the partner. One result of this attribution is that the partner attains a splendor (and a power) beyond anything known in ordinary friendships.

Love, of course, is a particular and specific experience in which the loved one must possess special qualities (or be perceived to possess them) which ignite passionate feelings in the partner. Love, after all, is directed to a particular individual; it is not generic, it is particular. As Nussbaum put it: "Love is in its essence a relationship with a particular person and that the particular features of the other person are intrinsic to its being the love that it is…Often I will know only that this person is beautiful and exhilarating in some way that I cannot yet describe" (1990, p. 334). Love creates a singular and unique particularity in the lover. Stendhal said that lovers endow their partners with a thousand perfections, and draw from every event proof of the perfection of the loved one (1822/1957).

Particularization is an accentuation of a process already set in motion by love itself. Glorification of the partner is common to falling in love, but particularization takes it a step further by insisting that everything glorious in love is due to the partner, hence one's personal role in the love process is minor. And why not? With real love one sees beauty, strength, character, and virtue where others cannot. Who can be sure that the lover is not as splendid, as heroic, and as powerful as the partner claims?

Adolescents are both excited and frightened by the idea that their love can be nurtured only by some heroic person because without this person love is impossible, and if one is lucky enough to find this person to lose him (her) would be a disaster which must never, ever occur. The young, as often is true for the elderly, may come to believe that only one person can create love and when that person is gone so also is love. Particularization encourages this line of reasoning.[77]

When love is experienced with only one particular person he (she) may attain life-and-death urgency. If the lover is lost, or the relationship broken, an overpowering loss descends, for in losing the person one has forever lost love. Or so it appears. When this is exaggerated by the fable that "my love" is more profound than all other love, the stage is set for the adolescent's willingness to make any sacrifice for the beloved partner. From this fabled scenario heroic loyalty and heroic stupidity are inspired.

A tragic example of the power of particularization can be seen in the following story.

A HUMAN TRAGEDY

TEENAGE LOVERS COMMIT SUICIDE

Sweetwater, Florida (AP)-The bodies of two teenagers were found floating in a canal Tuesday in what police say was a case of a couple who preferred death to being forbidden to see each other.

Police believe the bodies were those of 13-year-old Maryling and 14-year-old Christian, missing since Sunday. Pending autopsies, the bodies were not positively identified.

The teens appeared to have taken their own lives, like Romeo and Juliet in Shakespeare's play about forbidden love, said Sweetwater Det. Ramon Quintero. Both left suicide notes.

"We don't suspect any foul play," Quintero said. "The mother of the girl did not want the boy seeing her daughter. It is very sad."

Family members told police the teens—both honor students at Ruben Dario middle school in northwest Dade County—ran away early Sunday, carrying little money and no extra clothes.

"The children probably drowned themselves," said Quintero, a friend of the girl's family. "Neither knew how to swim."

Christian, 14, left this note in his bedroom:

To everyone:
I can't go on living. I've lost Maryling. That's something that hurts me very deep inside of my heart. I'll remember all of you. None of you will be forgotten. Please don't forget me. I love all of you. I've put my best these 14 years I've been on this hellhole called Earth. I bid farewell to all. Please keep me in your hearts, because I know all of you will be in mine.

I am not leaving you, I'm escaping from the realm of reality into the darkness of the unknown. Because reality is, I can't be with Maryling, and even the strongest man in the world wouldn't resist the loss of a loved one that was held so near and dear to your heart.

Nothing can stop me now. I'm taking my life because without Maryling, I have no life. Funny...Karen was talking about suicide earlier. I never thought it would have anything to do with me. So, say farewell to all. And as the immortal Beethoven once said: "Applaud, friends, the comedy is over." I leave you with the same words.

I love you all,
Christian

Maryling, 13, left this note to her parents:

Mom and Dad:
You'll never be able to understand the love between me and Christian. I feel that without him I can't live. Why is it you were never able to understand me? Or is it that you live to make my life miserable? I love him more than anyone here on this Earth. I'll never be happy without him.

You don't let me see him in this world, so we're going to another place.

I love you all very much. I'd like to ask for your forgiveness, but I know you will never understand me. This is all I want to tell you: I love him and I will always love him very much. But I will never be able to stay on this Earth without him.

Please don't cry for me, this is what I want. I want to feel happy, because right now I'm going to a place where I can be with Christian. Lastly, I'm sorry that I couldn't be with you all.

I love you all very much,

Maryling

From this story of tragic early adolescent love, we move to the more grounded, reasoned, and experience-based statements of a 19-year-old describing her first love.

When I entered my first relationship at 15 the relationship did take on a life-death urgency. I thought that the only reason I was happy was because of my boyfriend, Daren. But this may also be due to the difficult year I had at 14. At that age I never before experienced so much loneliness. I was completely miserable, I had no friends, I was at a new school, my family was broken up. Things were shaping up; when I met Daren things were never better. All I wanted was a true friend and when he gave me that, I attributed all my happiness to him. I can even recall calling him my angel. Still, because I thought he caused my happiness I didn't think of him to be perfection. I saw his faults and I knew the qualities that I disliked. Even with this I thought he was the one who made me happy. With time we began to be more and more absorbed in each other. Then I thought it was him who brought out my sexual desire. With experience and time I've come to learn that I could be just as passionate if I were with someone else I loved. It's inside me—he didn't create it, but I know he helped to bring it out.

These two stories help us to appreciate the range of adolescent love, and to respect the tone it carries at different junctures in the growth process. It also highlights the differences betwen primitive and mature intimacy.

PARTICULARIZATION AS REAL, PARTICULARIZATION AS ILLUSION

Illusions serve love by strengthening attraction through exaggerating the positive and downplaying the negative features of the beloved.
—Mike W. Martin

I do not want to make the case that adolescent love is delusional (as did Schopenhauer and Freud), but I do want to make clear that it is characterized by delusional qualities, some of which are age-based, some of which are grounded in a thought process predisposed to self-enhancing illusions, and some of which flow from the narcissistic spring of adolescent life. In making the case that adolescent intimacy (love) is primitive, I am not advancing the "pathology-passing-for-love" point of view so popular today, nor am I trying to promote the idea of "addictive love" which clutters bookstore shelves. I am merely trying to describe adolescent love for what it is, warts and all.

Like all self-serving beliefs, particularization is, at bottom, an attempt to aggrandize the self. During adolescence imperfections in the self are so painful, and so hard to endure, that fusion with an idealized person is a natural remedy for one's own frailties and limitations. Particularization bestows the partner with qualities worthy of true and total love. And what is better than being loved by someone greater than oneself?

A not very complex principle is at work here: When we elevate someone we love we elevate ourselves. Perhaps nowhere is this more blatant than in the romantic relationships of early adolescent girls. Not unfailingly, but with remarkable consistency, they view their boyfriends as more committed to them than they are, more in love than they are, more virtuous than they are, and more talented than they are. These girls may hold accurate perceptions *in general* but when it comes to their "love" and their "relationships," they often are so amiss as to be delusional. But the delusion is everything, and the girl is nothing without it. At least that is how it seems at the time. Moore and Rosenthal provide us with some interesting background on this:

> We found that young women were more likely to define their sexual encounters as occurring with a regular or steady partner than with a casual partner, while young men were more likely to regard *what must be essentially the same encounters* as casual ... in fact the male interpretation of what is going on may be closer to reality. The girls are interpreting, as an indication of love and commitment, encounters which often turn out to be short-term. (1993, p. 98, original emphasis)

Ayers, in her thoughtful and sensitive work, *Teenage Girls,* claimed "Teenagers are not able, as a rule, to be mature and responsible about sexual relating" (1994, p. 164). Her statement, assuming its essential correctness (which I do), deserves our full attention, because in today's culture about one half of all teens are involved in sexual relationships.

> All my life I've desired to have a "Bosom" friend. One who I could confide in 100%, spend all my time with etc. When this finally happened to me I attributed all my success to her because I felt that she had a tremendous influence in everything I did. I gave her credit for my popularity because she helped me be out-going! Then her father got transferred and she moved away. I immediately made up my mind that I would now have no social life and no friends. I totally doubted my abilities to meet new people because I thought that my best friend was the one who gave me this ability. (17-year-old girl describing the significance of her best friend)

POSTSCRIPT

> The desire for intimacy acts as love's advance guard.
> —Jose Ortega Y Gasset

In this chapter we have considered the idea that early and middle adolescents are not developmentally ready for love or intimacy. More specifically, that adolescents are not emotionally ready for reciprocity and mutuality, that they are not as yet mature enough in their identity for love, that their relationships are shaped by reciprocal rationalization and particularization, and that the intellect which guides their day-to-day operations is shaped by narcissism. My point of view on this topic is, I believe, well-supported by developmental theory and psychological research.[78] But even if it were not, we would still be left with the evidence of our experience which teaches us that early teens simply do not have the maturity of identity or the emotional continuity required of intimacy. The issue is a serious one on all counts because adolescent intimacy is the precursor to sexual intercourse, sexual intercourse to pregnancy, and pregnancy to the depletion of human capital in the adolescent community.

In this chapter I have invited the reader to follow several lines of speculation, which, for convenience, are here briefly summarized:

- Intimacy is a fusion which, in its optimal expression, is characterized by mutuality, by honest communication, and by emotional commitment. In the words of Sullivan, it is "a clearly formulated adjustment of one's behavior to the expressed needs of the other person" (1953, p. 246).

- One is unfair to suggest that "genuine" intimacy is *never* experienced during adolescence; but it seems clear that during early and middle adolescence it is extremely rare. As Sondheimer put it: "The mid-adolescent ... generally remains too self-involved to undertake the mature responsibility of deeply caring for another peer" (1982, p. 224). Along similar lines, research concludes "that older subjects were much more capable of establishing a relationship with another person, of truly sharing experiences and being responsive to their friends" (Gallatin, 1975, p. 127).

  > I was attracted to the first guy because of his status in the school, popular athlete, and his looks and height. The second I wasn't really attracted to at first. I just didn't want to hurt him by saying no. He was attractive however and fun to be with. I don't know what attracted me to Trevor. We just hit it off. We enjoyed each other's company, looks, personalities, and we just meshed really well. (18-year-old girl describing "first attractions")

- Erikson claimed that adolescents must resolve the psychosocial crisis of identity *before* they become intimate. Other theorists, perhaps the most notable being Gilligan (1982), claim that Erikson's understanding of the identity process fits the experiences of males more than females; the "adolescent" experience, is really, in Gilligan's rebuttal to Erikson, the "male-adolescent" experience. Her reasoning goes like this: The experience of being raised female in our culture prepares girls to define themselves through their relationships with others; hence, for girls *intimacy contributes to their identity*. Erikson, more attuned to masculine roles in culture, failed to recognize the importance of this sequence; his claim that solid identity is a necessary precursor to real intimacy does not sufficiently honor the demands (nor the outcomes) of female socialization.

Attaining competence (one of the key demands in the adolescent identity project) requires different skills for boys and girls. Accordingly, Josselson (1987) argues along lines similar to those sketched by Gilligan when she describes the "interpersonal track" which shapes the socialization process of young women in our culture. The implications for intimacy are immediate. For boys "individualizing oneself" is part and parcel of identity as separation from mother is essential for the development of masculinity. For girls, however, feminine identity does not depend on the achievement of separation from the mother. Berman summarized it this way: "Since masculinity is defined through separation while femininity is defined through attachment, male gender identity is threatened by intimacy while female gender identity is threatened by separation. Thus males tend to have difficulty with relationships, while females tend to have problems with individuation" (Berman, 1990, p. 260).

Exciting as these theoretical formulations may be, research findings neither conclusively confirm nor irresistibly refute them, keeping the controversy alive and vital. Research throughout the 1980s and the 1990s has thus far yielded mixed returns; the very extensive and finely detailed research efforts of Dyk and Adams, for example, "found no simple gender difference in the relationship between identity and intimacy" (Cobb, 1992, p. 435).

In this chapter I have placed only slight emphasis on gender differences because I am concerned with the shared commonalities of intimacy. Gilligan, Josselyn, and others have ably advanced their position concerning male-female differences, and in the process they have given us even greater insight into teen relationships. The nuclear ingredients of intimacy, mutual respect, and genuine concern for the needs of the partner, however, are constant, regardless of gender.

- *Fidelity* (the inherent desire to attach and bond) and *particularization* (attributing one's experiences to one's partner) play important roles in adolescent intimacy; any attempt to understand adolescent intimacy without taking them into account, it seems to me, is doomed to failure.

15

The Inherent Selfishness of Youth and its Role in Adolescent Love

The burdens of youth are many, the foremost of which is youth itself. But these burdens gather the weight of a hundred atmospheres when youth encounter the infinite complications of erotic love. The endocrine broth that nourishes adolescent emotionality also percolates the impulse to bond, an impulse quickened by the healthy *and* the unhealthy elements within the developing personality. In this chapter we will look at some of the reasons why the adolescent character conspires against, but does not preclude, mature love.

At this moment those of us who are serious about adolescent love don't know even enough to decide if it originates in the sexual impulse as was first argued by Socrates and later by Schopenhauer and Freud. We so-called "authorities" on adolescent love are in a position of "ignorant expertise," as Allport (1955) liked to phrase the condition, where experts know more and more about less and less. Amidst all this confusion, I have come to believe that those experts who focus on the *experience* of love miss the boat when it comes to adolescent romance. This chapter will try to explain why I think this way; it begins with one final look at Narcissus and Echo, Ovid's ancient symbols of youthful love.

Narcissus was a beautiful young man of mythological antiquity who took love, but did give in return. His self-absorption was so great that his name is now a synonym for impenetrable vanity. He left in his wake the broken hearts and crushed spirits of those who loved him but who, for their love, received nothing in return.

Narcissus is of interest to us for many reasons, foremost being that his self-obsession did not keep lovers at their distance; indeed, they fell before him like roses before a returning conqueror. Those who pursued him, and there were many, kept up their pursuit even though he never surrendered to it. Indeed, they were drawn to him by the very self-absorption that cancelled their own value. The deepest suffering of those who tried vainly to capture Narcissus' love was Echo.

Legend tells us that Echo was a beautiful nymph, fond of the woods and the hills. One day she saw beautiful Narcissus hunting in the hills. She hurriedly followed his footsteps. How she longed to address him in the softest accents, and draw him into conversation. But it was not in her power. She, therefore, waited with impatience for him to speak first, and she had her answer ready. One day Narcissus, being separated from his companions, shouted aloud, "Who's here?" Echo replied in the only way she could, "Here." Narcissus looked around, but seeing no one called out, "Come." Echo answered, "Come." As no one came Narcissus called again, "Why do you shun me?" Echo then asked the same question. "Let us join one another," said the beautiful youth. Echo answered with all her heart in the same words, and hastened to the spot, ready to throw her arms about his neck. But he turned away in anger and disgust. "Not so," he said, "I will die before I give you power over me." All that Echo could say was, humbly, entreatingly, "I give you power over me," but he was gone. She hid her blushes and her shame in a lonely cave, and never could be comforted. Yet, still her love remained firmly rooted in her heart, and it was increased by the pain of having been rejected. Her anxious thoughts kept her awake and made her pitifully thin. They say she has so wasted away with longing that only her voice now is left to her.

At last one of those he wounded said a prayer and it was answered by the gods: "May he who loves not others love himself." The goddess of righteous anger, Nemesis, undertook to bring this about. As Narcissus bent over a clear pool and saw his own reflection he fell in love. And in that instant of mesmerized self-fascination his fate was sealed; and like the narcissists to follow him, he swooned into such self-obsession that all others ceased to exist.

Echo yearned for Narcissus even after he had time and again rejected her, and she did so without even a moment of closeness with him, without the comfort of his touch or caress, and with complete awareness that Narcissus neglected everyone who desired him. Why Echo burned with desire for Narcissus, and wanted nothing more than to be by his side when he showed no interest in her, is an unsolved mystery (which is part of the myth's allure) but there can be no doubt that, at least by modern standards, Echo's love was grounded in an inner emptiness which she desperately hoped Narcissus would lovingly fill. Her relentless pursuit proved to Narcissus his power over her. Rejected and abandoned, Echo withered away, mythology's first anorexic; she starved from an unreciprocated love which she valorized until the moment of her death. (Like many of her adolescent sisters of today she could not differentiate obsession from love.) "The story of Narcissus and Echo is one of self-love that precludes the ability to see, hear, or react to the needs of another" (Donaldson-Pressman, 1994, p. 11).

We simplify unfairly if we believe that Echo was drawn to Narcissus only by his beauty, although his beauty certainly hurried things along. Echo was consumed with the illusion that Narcissus' love would could fill her emptiness. The pathos of Narcissus was his inability to invest in anything outside of himself; the pathos of Echo was her denial that his self-absorption made it impossible for him to love her. Echo "loved" (if this is the right word) to the end a young man who was not only unattainable, but who, by every dignified standard, was unworthy of her love. Echo's obsession is viewed by some as misdirected love and by others as a spiritual deficiency; here (as our focus is on adolescence, and as Echo herself was younger even than Narcissus) her tragedy is not viewed as love at all, but as an illusion encouraged by her immaturity, and her fabled confusion as to what love is all about.[79]

What, after all, did Echo really think she was doing when she put her destiny in the hands of a 16-year-old boy whose primary qualities were selfishness and vanity? Or was she thinking at all? (A question which experts who focus on the *experience* of adolescent love almost never get around to asking.) Was she so lovestruck that she could not see him for what he was? Was she so devoid of vision that she could not foresee the outcome to their coupling? Was there something seductive about Narcissus' boundless self-absorption? If so, what? Was Echo really nothing more than an over-grown child in a young woman's body? (Another question almost never asked by those who focus on the experience, but not the genesis, of adolescent love, because an honest answer destroys the idea that love can develop during early adolescence.) We, of course, do not know for certain the answer to any of these questions, nor can we ever know. But some of us are genuinely concerned with Echo's love for Narcissus because her actions and her perceptions ring as true today as yesterday; we also are concerned with Narcissus because the selfish obsessions, the impervious distance, and the disrespect for human closeness and comraderie which shaped his life are not only alive and well in the adolescent community today, they are, in some quarters, idealized and glorified.

NARCISSUS AND ECHO IN THE
ADOLESCENT COMMUNITY

Lovers accentuate their beloved's good qualities and downplay their flaws.
In that process they are notoriously prone to illusions and self deceptions.
—Mike W. Martin

Despite the failure of Echo and Narcissus to connect in myth, they do so with remarkable regularity in the real world. Why? Because young people are sorting out what it means to be *worthy of love*. But very few early or mid-adolescents know in any real way whether they are deserving of someone else's love, or whether anyone else is genuinely interested in receiving their love. Neither do they know with much certainty if they possess the judgment to know who *is deserving* of their love. These natural deficits inherent to early teens contribute to a certain panic about what love is and what it is not.

Echo Love

My concern is not with love itself, but with its adolescent expression. These are not the same, as I hope has been made quite clear by now. Reciprocal love makes demands on the adolescent character (i.e., self-transcendance) which it rarely can satisfy. During adolescence we see many sides of love, some grand and glorious, some not; among the not is giving one's love to someone who gives nothing in return—Echo love.

Like Echo drawn to Narcissus, girls of today are drawn to initiative, to beauty and to mystery, and as Echo could not initiate her own speech, many young girls today cannot initiate their own ideas or follow their own ambitions; they so lack direction that they willingly, even eagerly, allow another to navigate their course for them. We learn something about this process when we take a look at shy youngsters who are secretive about their yearnings and cravings, indeed all of their feelings. Shy youngsters are awkward in interpersonal settings and often behave inappropriately. They are slow to start conversations, and when they do they speak, they speak less than non-shy people; they make less eye contact, show fewer emotions, and smile less. Shy people, like so many adolescents, are uneasy in social situations, they vascillate beween fear and confidence, between avoidance and approach; they are fearful of being ridiculed or humiliated. They are not paralyzed, but they are inhibited. To venture outward they first must be drawn out of themselves, reassured and comforted, put at ease:

> Most shy people strongly desire to get along with others, to have friends and lovers, and to experience intimacy, but they are afraid that they will make a bad impression and experience rejection, humiliation, ostracism, and anxiety. They are painfully aware of how they might be perceived by others, and they constantly fear that others might see them in a bad light. They focus on avoiding anything that might produce rejection or embarrassment. (Baumeister, 1991, p. 53)

These youngsters are not rare in the adolescent community. They yearn to be rescued from the prison of their own shyness, but first they need to be praised, coddled, and flattered before they can risk sharing themselves. Yet when someone takes the time and effort to seek them out, to meet them on their ground, and to allay their anxieties, their allegiance and loyalty are often given freely. For shy youngsters these first moments of glorious sharing may occur with a partner who has cultivated them for private gain. Narcissists "open" their friends in order to exalt themselves, but in the shy one the experience creates a deep gratitude which expresses itself in fidelity, in adulation and, with surprising frequency, in subservience. For many young Echoes this is the stuff of their first adolescent bondings.

> My first serious boyfriend was when I was 12. He was 16 years old. There was only two years in schools years. He was very caring to me and, at the time, mature. We went out for four months. He was my first boyfriend. I loved him. He wanted me to sleep with him. When I said that I wouldn't he left me for my best friend. I think it was the smartest choice I ever made. For someone that was tall, dark and handsome, he sure was a slimy creep. (18-year-old describing "first attractions.")

Youngsters who cannot experience feelings, who have no zest for life, or who are morose and depressed, are drawn to the few who can arouse their spirit and excite their passion. The allure is in the sizzle, in the thrill of exploding possibility, in the attachment to greatness.[80] But the object of one's devotion sometimes proves to be unworthy. "Unfortunately, the objects of an adolescent crush are not always protective and caring persons. They may, in fact, have been chosen precisely for the allure of their narcissistic aloofness and grandiosity...In the adolescent girl's revering gaze they find a mirror for their narcissistic needs" (Kaplan, 1984, p. 176).

We learn something about Echo love when we consider the low self-esteem for which adolescent girls are rightly known in our culture. Something of a mystery for the past decade or so, is why girls, upon entry into junior high (grades seven through nine) suddenly begin to exhibit what is generally called "low self-esteem." Considerable debate rages about this loss of self-esteem, including whether it even exists. In regard to the shortage of self-esteem among teen girls I would like to offer a few preliminary observations.

Teenage girls in our culture experience low self-esteem because they, as a rule, don't do anything that deserves esteem. Their day-to-day functions are more child-like than adult-like. In our culture, their primary means of escaping their insignificant status are employment, peer popularity, or attachment to a boy. These strategies, as a rule, do very little for genuine self-esteem, and they are, in fact, self-defeating in several ways. Teen employment, except for the poor, is a hoax. The money earned from it, for the most part, is funneled into adventures in esteem purchase. Peer popularity enhances the esteem of early adolescents more than for their mature sisters for the simple reason that as values and goals heighten, the approval of unenlightened peers means less and less. Sexual attachments to boys, for the most part, do not enhance self-esteem because the boys to which girls attach themselves tend to be older, better practiced and more skilled at the power politics that dominate the teen community. When the boys are narcissistic in the way we have described it in "the narcissistic style," this imbalance punishes the girl even more. The Sufi (Muslim mystics acknowledged for their life wisdom) claimed that when the pickpocket meets the saint all he sees are pockets, and this summarizes the plight of girls in the open market of adolescent life. In addition to all this, adolescent girls are hustled into the appearance industry and its hall of mirrors sooner, and with greater force, than boys. These considerations, taken in their totality, create a social milieu which conspires against decent self-respect (a better term, in my estimation, than "self-esteem"). Whereas it is obviously true that some girls attain a dramatic upsurge in their self-esteem from employment, from peer popularity, and from boyfriends, these connections often insult their esteem more than they nourish it.

From this vacuous existence the lure of love, for many girls, is irresistible. Love begins with the finding of it, and for this the adolescent personality is well suited. Even those who cannot speak, like dear Echo, can find it in those, like Narcissus, who do not even speak to them. All of which takes us back to the beginning: Adolescent girls in our culture have low self-esteem because their goals, their values and their behavior are not worthy of esteem. To attain real esteem they must first open their eyes to the emptiness of their day-to-day behavior, then choose goals that are inherently worthy and not mere social contrivances, and finally, they must learn to hold boys to a standard of conduct that enhances the dignity of both partners in the relationship. Until these changes are effected, adolescence will continue to be an emotional wasteland for girls, and their dismal self-esteem will accurately reflect the emotional emptiness of their lives.

Although no eternal truth dictates that every Narcissus must have an Echo to spurn, or that every Echo must have a Narcissus to pursue, this drama is played daily in the adolescent theater. In an arena with few real winners, early and middle adolescent girls are consistently the losers.

BONDING THROUGH GIVING

> To give love is to get love, and to get love is to be assured
> of one's lovableness.
> —Karl Meninger

It was Leo Tolstoy who wrote: "We do not love people so much for the good they have done us, as for the good we have done them." This thoughtful aphorism, like all insights which convey wisdom without explaining it, contains more than a kernel of truth for adolescent bondings.

We can understand the predicament in question (why normal kids are attracted to "the narcissistic style") when we recognize that many teens are compassionate and giving by nature. Giving and sharing are to them simply a matter of human policy, a way of greeting the new and different; in giving of themselves they experience life in an honest and friendly way. *Giving is as natural to them as receiving is to narcissists.* These are the youth Adler (1939) optimistically (but somewhat naively) envisioned all youth to be. Narcissists, as we by now must surely recognize, are the diametric opposite of these gentle souls: Like Narcissus, narcissists cannot give themselves to others but they gladly receive the gifts others bring to them.

Narcissists bond with those who give to them, a fact of their nature which, ironically, encourages their charitable friends to give even more. Because narcissists understand friendship (indeed, all human connections) in utilitarian terms, they do not necessarily respect the person who gives; on the other hand, giving, sharing individuals usually presume that their gifts are appreciated not merely as gifts but as an extension of the giver. They assume that it is *they* (and not merely the gift) that is appreciated. When their gifts bring pleasure they assume that they are part of the pleasure. This presumption is completely without foundation as far as narcissists are concerned. To them friends are providers—necessary, but replaceable, providers. This element of replaceability non-narcissistic youth cannot emotionally or intellectually comprehend. Their lack of experience and their egocentrism prevent them from understanding how someone could be so completely different from themselves; grasping this insight is one of the great learning advances of the adolescent years. The failure to grasp it, quite literally, places one at risk in the presence of those individuals whose human relationships are molded by the narcissistic style.

Holding back the natural propensity to give is not an admirable trait of our humanness, but one that is completely necessary when dealing with narcissists. They take more than anyone can possibly give, and they do it smoothly and naturally because they are "entitled," and because they are heroically special. "They whose motive is utility have no friendship for one another," Aristotle accurately summarized.

The attraction of the narcissistically selfish to the developmentally immature is a significant force in the sexual chemistry of the youth culture. It is the dynamic behind unequal power relationships, especially the early and middle adolescent girl's attraction to late adolescent boys and young men. The young are mesmerized by the power of age and by the functional wealth which comes with it. This fact of juvenile fascination is not lost on 17- to 22-year-old males; indeed, in the youth culture, they have perhaps the keenest eye for it.[81]

The equation gets simpler and sadder: The selfish know what they want and they have a plan to get it. In the teen world this places them in a position of advantage because so many kids have absolutely no blueprint, no compass, no direction. To steer these directionless souls to one's own course is easy; they have no course of their own, yet they are so hungry for a destination that they will take an offered path just to see where it goes.

To help the present line of speculation, let's backtrack for a moment to the differences between the selfishness inherent to the adolescent period (developmental selfishness) and the excessive selfishness inherent to narcissism (narcissistic selfishness). Developmental selfishness is anchored in the natural demands of the developing self and the identity project; it is an exaggerated, but necessary, self-centeredness. On the other hand, in narcissistic selfishness the collective reflexes of narcissism guide behavior. The narcissistically selfish person is always driven by the fear of not getting enough.

Of course, other forces are at work in this complex process. Inferiority plays a role in bringing ordinary kids into the sphere of their narcissistically selfish comrades. How? Narcissists presume that because of their specialness they should associate only with people who are "in a class by themselves"; therefore, the people with whom they associate are granted these qualities (even if only verbally). Because the selfish ones are so heroically special, anyone who flatters their illusions and gives them allegiance automatically becomes greater than the "others" who do not. The fears and insecurities which gnaw at early and middle teens are lessened by the Grand One who, through scorn and contempt, reduces everyone outside their circle to zero. The selfish friend becomes, in effect, the great leveller of social differences; in a world dominated by status and popularity this is no small accomplishment, and one which carries with it certain magnetic powers, as every Echo ever drawn to a Narcissus willingly confesses.[82]

Emotionalism Versus Romanticism

How adolescents think of "love" is severely complicated by the tendency to confuse emotionalism with romanticism; a confusion which leads adults to think that adolescents (especially girls) are "romantics," when, for the most part, they are nothing of the sort, and it leads adolescents to the false belief that they are experiencing romance when they are experiencing themselves. From this confusion springs the fable: "I am a romantic." But to be "a romantic" involves far more than adolescents usually know, and what we typically find is that when they think of themselves as "romantics" they do so to grant themselves a self-absorption otherwise denied.

Perhaps something is to be gained by taking a look at the word and its meaning. In general usage, "romantic" conveys sensuousness, vitality, and an escape from the cold, hard realities of life. In academic quarters romanticism has been defined as a revolt against classicism and neoclassicism, leading to "liberalism" and an emphasis on feeling and originality. Romanticism implies a sympathetic interest in nature, an attraction to spiritualism and mysticism.

Emotionalism is characterized by the tendency to show emotion quickly and easily, and to experience intensely the emotional side of an issue. Emotionalism encourages the warmth of the heart more than the coolness of the mind, and promotes thinking we have labeled "affective logic."

The differences between emotionalism and romanticism are not merely definitional. Emotionalism has as its ground zero the self, its feelings, its sensations and, most importantly, its needs. Romanticism, on the other hand, is an attitude toward life which grows from personal judgments and priorities which side with feeling against reason, with sentiment against impartiality, with subjectivity against objectivity, with imagination against reality, with intuition against evidence, with mysticism against traditional religion, with erotic love against security, with the natural against the artificial, with emotional expression against reasoned discourse, with spontaneity against premeditation, with the new against the established. Romanticism is grounded in the glory of life; emotionalism is grounded in the glory of the self.

While romanticism gives great freedom to emotion and sensuality, it requires much more, including an open and free spirit which embraces the mystery and the sorrow of life. Romanticism is an attitude about how life *should* be lived. Emotion does not make one a romantic any more than compassion makes one a philanthropist or anger makes one a warrior. Emotionality nurtures romanticism and gives it life but this does not make one the other.[83]

POSTSCRIPT

Let me try to pull together certain ideas hinted at so far.

Power and friendship overlap in all teen relationships, but perhaps nowhere does it carry greater significance than in the bondings between youth who are narcissistically selfish and those who are not. Narcissists need the allegiance of peers to handle their own insecurities, a need which makes them court new clients, and to state openly and boldly: "I want you. I need you. I love you." Such overtures are beautiful music to youth who want to share their private pleasures and require only an invitation to dance. What greater way to know that one is worthy than to hear: "I want you. I need you. I love you." If it sounds true, if it feels true, then it is true.

In our analysis of young love we do not want to lose sight of an elementary imperative of adolescent emotional life: to find someone who thinks "I" am wonderful and who will do anything for "me." One the most meaningful experiences of adolescent life is to find someone who is wild about you— someone who will do anything for you, make any sacrifice to share your companionship and joy. The entire process is thrown into a spin by individuals high in narcissism who know how to play the emotional need structure to their own ends. More than anyone they know the importance of covering the nakedness of self-interest with a cloak of calculated sincerity and timely concern, and their "narcissistic style" is remarkably effective among younger brother and sisters as yet unfamiliar with fake knights parading fake virtues.[84]

16

Final Thoughts on the Predispositions that Shape the Adolescent Character

Here, in the concluding chapter, I would like to highlight some of the points, principles, and data that have directed my research, and to share with you some of my general conclusions about the nature of adolescence.

First things first. Adolescents do not have a preordained nature that dictates that they must behave in certain ways any more than the rest of us; but adolescents do possess predispositions which *incline* them toward certain behaviors and *encourage* particular patterns of thinking and, in turn, these behaviors and patterns of thinking shape the youth culture. Predispositions are expressed as inclinations and susceptibilities rather than as hard-wired instincts, and in my attempt to unravel their mystery I have concentrated on three major themes:

1. the predispositions that shape intelligence;
2. the predispositions that shape selfishness; and,
3. the predispositions that shape friendship.

It is my belief that by investigating these age-driven predispositions we can more realistically assess the strengths *and* the limitations of youth.

For those of you who have skipped ahead to the end in order to obtain an overview of the ideas which fill the first fifteen chapters your strategy is only partly effective. The ideas summarized in this chapter have been discussed in greater detail in previous chapters but many important concepts have been left out of this concluding chapter. From the headings sprinkled throughout, it will be easy for you to find the chapter which provides further elaboration of the ideas discussed here.

THE PREDISPOSITIONS THAT SHAPE INTELLIGENCE

The Rise of Intelligence During Adolescence

A major theme throughout has been that adolescent behavior is affected in profound ways by the intelligence inherent to formal thought. A subtheme has been that adolescents, for a variety of reasons, fail to take full advantage of their available intelligence, producing a careless squandering of their intellectual resources. Few adolescents lack the intelligence to negotiate life in a moratorium culture, but almost all lack the ability to rally their intelligence at the precise moment when it is most needed. What confounds us is *why* adolescents only sometimes use the intelligence that graces their nature, and it is to solving this mystery that the first part of this book is dedicated.

If one is serious about creating an environment where adolescents behave intelligently, one must know how they reason and how they try to make sense out of a universe that does not explain itself. The first step in this process is to learn something about the set of operations known as *formal thought*, the name given to the heroic advance in intellectual power that first emerges during early adolescence and brings with it the capacity, as Elkind (1974) put it, "to think in a new key." Aside from puberty, formal thought is the most profound transformation of the adolescent period.

As I have already expressed in earlier chapters, it is vital to grasp the power and profundity of the adolescent's *capacity* for clear thinking because the critical issues of adolescent psychology stand and fall on the affirmative use of this potential. On the other side of the coin, all issues of adolescent misbehavior, truancy, and pathology are judged in relation to their *capacity* for intelligent self-regulation. In the briefest possible condensation, the upswing in adolescent intelligence is caused by a rise in the following competencies:

- **Formal thought increases the adolescent's power of abstraction which, in turn, opens new conceptual worlds.** Adolescents are in the process of exchanging the rigid intellectual apparatus of concrete thought for a more flexible and far-reaching way of thinking which will allow them to negotiate abstract intellectualism. As abstract thought grows the thinker shifts in gradual increments away from the here-and-now to there-and-then, to be guided by more complex maps and to remoter possibilities. Siegler, one of our foremost Piagetian scholars, expressed it this way: "Adolescents begin to see the particular reality in which they live as one of only several imaginable realities. This leads at least some of them to think about alternative organizations of the world and about deep questions concerning the nature of existence, truth, justice and morality" (1986, p. 41).

- **Formal thought stimulates intellectual comprehensiveness.** Not only do adolescents learn to focus on the "larger picture," they embrace a larger range of data when trying to solve a problem; their thought, as a result, is much less susceptible to oversights, and to errors of omission. This increased scope allows them to "plan in considerable detail what they are going to do, and to interpret whatever they do within the total context" (Siegler, 1986, p. 41).

- **Formal thought opens to investigation one's own thought processes.** Adolescent intelligence shines inward illuminating itself. Children have no such introspective bent, so to them a thought is a thought is a thought; adolescents, through the self-analysis prompted by formal thought, realize that a thought may be born to rich or poor parentage. Lacking formal thought, they hold few standards by which to judge whether one thought is any more coherent than another; adolescents learn to distinguish a strong idea from a weak one by standards other than the authoritarian or the autocratic.

- **Formal thought increases the capacity for propositional thought.** A proposition is any statement capable of being believed, doubted, denied, or argued; propositional thought allows the thinker to investigate ideas beyond reality as it is presently understood and to reason about hypotheses—true, false, or unknown. Basically, propositional thought allows the mind to reason about anything and everything.

  Children are not gifted propositional thinkers; they focus mainly on the perceptible elements of a problem, and they tend not to speculate much about possibilities that do not bear directly on the matter at hand. They solve problems with few systematic strategies; they rarely have an organized gameplan. When they solve a problem correctly they often do not know how they solved it, or when faced with a similar problem, they may not be able to beckon the strategies that only a few minutes before were effective. Adolescents are not necessarily gifted propositional thinkers, but they are vastly superior when compared with children.

- **Formal thought fosters future analysis.** Children are not chained to the present, but neither are they free to take flight from it; their intellectual concerns are, for the most part, with the "here and now." Formal thinkers, on the other hand, are liberated from the clock, even the calendar; they glide through light years, infinity, timelessness in ways that concrete thinkers cannot even contemplate. During adolescence immediate time is recognized as a flickering instant of eternal time, and clock time is differentiated from experiential time. The adolescent's transformation to future-oriented thought is profound for many reasons, but most important is that thought is forever primitive until it attains the capacity to transcend the constraints of present time.

- **Formal thought beckons scientific thought.** Formal thinkers form hypotheses, conduct experiments, control variables, describe and record outcomes and, from these steps, they draw intellectual conclusions in a disciplined, formal manner. These mental qualities cause Santrock to observe: "The adolescent's thought is more like a scientist's than a child's...the adolescent often entertains many possibilities and tests many solutions in a planned way when having to solve a problem" (1990, p. 130).

  Formal thinkers come to recognize that patient observation and systematic experimentation are the meat of science, and that disciplined reason and coherent extrapolation are the heart of philosophy. This is the age when the reality of probability replaces the magic of possibility.

In the end we come to see that formal thought permits the thinker to venture beyond the real to investigate the ideal, to peer beyond the physical to investigate the hypothetical, to go beyond fragments to investigate wholes, to think beyond "what is" to "what if," and to transcend the present to wrestle with the future. All in all, these mental skills provide the adolescent with rather impressive intellectual credentials.

The Decline of Egocentrism

As formal thought gains a firmer footing in the adolescent personality, egocentrism loses its grips on the thought processes. This decline in the power of egocentrism sets the stage for an elevation in functional intelligence and an expansion of social interests. In the face of declining egocentrism adolescent life becomes increasingly expansive and other-focused. How? In the following ways:

- the adolescent increasingly recognizes that others have a private existence, and that this private existence has many things in common with their own;
- the adolescent begins to perceive adults as separate individuals with their own private individuality, and not merely as authority figures, providers, or merely "old people";
- the adolescent decreasingly demands that others always see things from his (her) point of view;

- the fable of unique singularity loses ground to the belief that all people share important commonalities;
- the adolescent is able to join social gatherings without assuming that his (her) arrival carries undue significance, thereby lessening nervous, awkward self-consciousness.

In these small steps (along with a hundred others) the adolescent slowly marches away from the simplistic egocentrism of childhood into the more complex egocentrism of adolescence.[85]

In conclusion, I would like to suggest that the following transformations increase intellectual power during adolescence:

- increased powers of abstraction;
- increased comprehensiveness of thought;
- increased power of self-analysis;
- increased ability to backtrack and double-check the thought process;
- increased propositional thought;
- increased power of future analysis;
- increased capacity for scientific and philosophical thought;
- increased capacity for perspective-taking; and finally,
- the migration away from childhood egocentrism.

THE DECLINE OF INTELLIGENCE DURING ADOLESCENCE

Despite its great forward surge, adolescent thinking is not always clear, coherent, or even accurate. Upon close inspection we usually find that the clouded moments occur when the adolescent abandons the system of checks and balances inherent to formal thought; when the adolescent rejects objective reasoning in favor of affective reasoning; when the adolescent shifts attention from the issue at hand to how the issue affects "me"; and, finally, when the adolescent creates fables and illusions to divine unexplained mysteries.

We have now arrived at an important point: Every adolescent needs a collaborator to accelerate the tendency toward objective thought and to decelerate distortion. The most ideal person for this job is an adult who can think clearly and who has the best interests of the young person at heart, whereas the least ideal person is a peer who serves as nothing more than a flattering mirror. In the real world most teens settle for (and often prefer) the latter, and this unto itself promotes second-rate thinking.

In adolescent culture the consequences of positive behavior are nothing compared to the liabilities of negative behavior. Nothing carries the lifetime consequences of having a baby, of dropping out of school, of drug or alcohol addiction, of an automobile or motorcycle accident. Hence, many adolescent-watchers, myself included, believe that the key to teen survival in a moratorium culture is not only the pursuit of positives but, *the avoidance of negatives.* The "avoidance of negatives" simply means the adolescent's ability to escape, evade, circumvent, or somehow miss out on self-defeating outcomes. For every youth arrived at age 20 this involves a considerable degree of luck and good fortune, a healthy dose of adult guidance, and a giant portion of self-directed intelligence. The third part of this formula, self-directed intelligence, is primary to our discussion. In a nutshell, I have tried to demonstrate that clear, coherent intelligence is actualized far less during adolescence than it should be considering its tremendous potential. The failure to actualize intellectual potential is, quite possibly, the most profound limitation of the adolescent character.

Summary

It is time to do a summing up of our basic themes. Although it is impossible to state precisely (and simply) the causes behind the periodic lapses in intelligence, it must be admitted that the following habits reduce functional intelligence during adolescence:

- fabled thinking—the acceptance of illusions, improbabilities and self-magnifying stories as true when they are not; the persistent adolescent fables in North American culture include the fable that "I" am constantly watched, the fable of invulnerability, the fable of total uniqueness, the fable that sexual intercourse will not result in pregnancy, the fable of pure idealism;
- the emotionalization of thought—the fusion of emotion with reason;
- the ascendance of affective logic—thinking where connections between judgments are emotional rather than rational;
- unfair argumentation—angering one's opponent, accepting or rejecting an idea because of its popularity, attributing undesirable motives to the opponent, using incendiary language;
- the manipulation of arguments by unfair and unsound reasoning—including the tendency to use proof by selected instances, oppose a proposition by misrepresenting it, arguing so that no other conclusion is deemed possible, stating one's position over and over without defending the merit of the position, arguing by forced analogy and "straw-man;"
- the fear of reason and the reasoning process—which includes the reluctance to explore ideas calmly and impartially, and the refusal to view reason as an arbiter;
- the emergence of cynicism, nihilism and others "isms" of resignation—which place achievement and failure, virtue and vice, on equal footing.

These habits and predispositions combine to build a mighty barrier against intelligence which holds back the intellectual maturity, not only of particular individuals, but of the entire youth culture.

THE PREDISPOSITIONS THAT
SHAPE ADOLESCENT SELFISHNESS

A hypocritical silence haunts the arenas where the experts annually convene to report and evaluate the research, theory, and paradigms which govern the orthodoxy known as adolescent psychology. The topic avoided is perhaps the one most in need of investigation: adolescent selfishness. The question is an open one, but that is of little consequence as no one seriously addresses it. This sorry state of affairs is corrected slightly in this volume, but my observations on the topic are, most assuredly, preliminary and amateurish.

I have already advanced the hypothesis that adolescent thought and behavior is shaped by three separate expressions of selfishness which I have labeled "developmental selfishness," "narcissistic selfishness," and "the narcissistic style." Before we look at them, we need to introduce a few ideas gleaned from our look at the psychology of narcissism, especially as defined by its 20th century father, Sigmund Freud, and his excommunicated disciple, Karen Horney. I have taken liberally from each of them in order to apply their insights to an area of discourse neither of them chose to investigate: adolescent psychology.

Narcissism and Adolescent Selfishness

Sigmund Freud claimed that narcissism originates in the infant's turning of love away from the world and inward upon the self, thereby making the self the object of its own love. In his words, "The libido withdrawn from the outer world has been directed on to the ego, giving rise to a state which we may call narcissism" (1914). Freud was convinced that infants begin life in a blissful state of *primary narcissism* where no distinction exists between self and world; hence there are no unfulfilled desires, no frustration. Primary narcissism is that stage of development where the infant has not as yet established ego boundaries, and thus experiences itself and its environment as one. In Freud's read it is the most primitive of all emotional states where the infant is bestowed with a grandiose inflation, with feelings of perfection and power. The infant is fused with the mother and the world in wholeness and harmony—a blissful, short-lived state filled with such primal splendor that all of us are driven to recapture its glory.

Primary narcissism, according to Freud, is the stage of psychosexual development where the child's pleasures are concentrated within the self and the body. This is a developmental stage between autoeroticism and object love when distinct autoerotic sensations become fused into one's body, which then becomes a single, unified love object. This narcissistic condition is the libidinal storehouse from which the love of one's self and the love for others emerges. Eventually, primary narcissism is abandoned in favor of ego development, which is to say that self-love is overtaken by love for others. But the love of others does not yield the primal gratification of self-love. Vital to Freud's understanding of narcissism is that shared love is less fulfilling than self-love, a speculation we see borne out time and again during early and middle adolescence.

Karen Horney viewed the entire process differently and for her break from orthodoxy she was dismissed from the New York Psychoanalytic Society, whereupon she founded the American Institute for Psychoanalysis. Horney emphasized social factors far more than Freud (as did all of the Neo-Freudians with whom she collaborated), and she held a more optimistic view of human nature than her pessimistic mentor. Her theories relied heavily on psychoanalytic concepts, but her digressions were significant, especially her belief that neurosis originated in basic anxiety and disturbed human relationships.

Horney did not support Freud's libido theory, which claimed that self-esteem is a desexualized form of self-love, and that persons tending toward overvaluation must be expressing self-love. She believed that narcissism is an identification with the idealized image of the self—an unjustified and undeserving self-inflation, an overdone, relentless self-absorption. She also helped to clarify why certain individuals cling to an idealized image, and her insight is quite helpful to those of us interested in adolescent psychology. "Roughly speaking, a person builds up an idealized image of himself because he cannot tolerate himself as he actually is. The image apparently counteracts this calamity; but having placed himself on a pedestal, he can tolerate his real self still less...He wavers between self-adoration and self-contempt, between his idealized image and his despised image, with no solid middle ground to fall back on" (1945, p.112).

Her contribution to narcissistic theory demonstrates how healthy self-esteem and narcissistic self-esteem are grounded in completely different starting points. She viewed healthy self-esteem as growing from genuine feelings and real actions. Narcissistic self-inflation, on the other hand, is about feeling powerful and great without regard for what causes these feelings. The narcissist, whether adolescent or adult, craves first and foremost the glory of the self triumphant.

The Connections Between Narcissism and Adolescence

Narcissism is the glorification of self-as-island in the human archipelago. As an adult personality trait it borders on the pathological, but as an adolescent trait it borders on the necessary. Throughout this book I have tried to make the case that the psychology of narcissism overlaps in meaningful ways with the psychology of adolescence and that when investigating one, we learn about the other. One discouraging result of my investigation is finding far more of the narcissistic personality in our youth than bodes well for their health or for the health of society.

The psychology of narcissism seeks to understand how our culture can twist the child's natural selfishness into chronic selfishness and, once this corner has been turned, how youth fail to learn to respect others. The study of narcissism has led to the discovery of a basic human principle: As self-priority increases civility decreases. From our study of narcissism we have learned that an *obsession* with self does not produce an appreciation of self, and from our study of adolescence we have learned that when self-pleasure is the only joy, there is soon no joy at all.

The Different Expressions of Adolescent Selfishness

The first expression, *developmental selfishness*, is a healthy and necessary component of human development. When we think of it our thoughts are directed to the natural demands of a developing self, to wholesome egoism, to honest self-pride. The term, for me, carries no negative connotations. Developmental selfishness is the trademark of all healthy kids; without it they have no real sense of themselves as important beings.

Developmental selfishness can be understood as healthy narcissism and as a legitimate expression of productive pride. A healthy self-concept without some narcissism is impossible because we all are characterized by a selfish core. Fromm claimed: "Nature had to endow man with a great amount of narcissism to enable him to do what is necessary for survival" (1964, p. 72). These affirmative expressions, as manifested during childhood and adolescence, I call "developmental selfishness." Narcissistic selfishness is another matter altogether.

Narcissistic selfishness is a radical selfishness. When we think of it we think of an infatuation with the self so extreme that the interests of others are completely ignored. The narcissistically selfish person is anxiously concerned with self; is always restless; is always fearful of not getting enough, of being deprived; and is filled with a burning envy of anyone who might have more. Furthermore, he (she) is unable to give freely but always anxious to take, and the world is viewed from what can be taken from it. The narcissistically selfish person lacks any genuine interest in the welfare of others and has only instrumental respect for dignity and integrity. Because the capacity to care for others is the bedrock of every moral system, narcissistic selfishness is inherently corrosive to morality.

At the risk of being repetitious, I want to once again remind the reader that individuals imbued with narcissistic selfishness cannot handle the give and take of normal human relationships. Their first question at every junction is the same: "Is this for me or against me?" Individuals imbued with narcissistic selfishness are saddled with unworkable presumptions about human relationships which, with the passage of time, harden into the belief that others must always accommodate to "my" needs, that "my" relevance does not need to be earned or proved, that "my" uniqueness not only makes "me" special, it makes "me" superior, and that from "my" specialness flows a river of entitlements.

A Troubling Form Of Adolescent Selfishness: The Narcissistic Style

The selfishness which we find between natural developmental selfishness and pathological narcissistic selfishness I call *the narcissistic style*. The narcissistic style sees life more through the lens of self-interest than social interest, more through monologue than dialogue, more through rights than duties. It is not natural in the same way as developmental selfishness, neither is it pathological, as is narcissistic selfishness; rather, it is an exaggeration of the former and a lessened version of the latter. Like the stream flowing down the mountain, the narcissistic style follows its own course until it is redirected by obstacle or a path of less resistance; it cannot change course on its own and this fact of its nature governs the day-to-day behavior of narcissistic youth.

The narcissistic style is of special interest to us because it represents an adaptation to adolescent life that produces a moral and emotional impoverishment, a diminished spontaneity, and a robotic calculation in personal relationships that is defeating to human decency. Of the three forms of selfishness, this is the most riveting to a student of adolescent psychology as it represents a bridge between the exuberent and natural egotism of developmental selfishness and the pathetic narcissistic selfishness. It also gains our attention because our society, at this very instant, is intent on pushing kids out of their natural developmental selfishness into a sanctioned narcissism. The images which shower youth consciousness are the shallow, superficial, and artificial fluff that the narcissistic style embraces and champions. For all of these reasons the narcissistic style and its psychological profile are under our microscope. The traits we cannot avoid include the following:

- **Excessive entitlement demands.** The narcissistic style is founded on the presumption that "I" am entitled to special treatment and that it is the responsibility of others to provide it. This attitude puts narcissistic youth in an adversarial relationship with those who don't see things that way, but it places them in a position of unique advantage with individuals who, for whatever reasons, see things their way.
- **Insensitivity to the feelings of others.** Individuals with a narcissistic style have very little compassion for others. Their consciousness is monopolized by their own sensations, their own pain, and their own pleasure.
- **Reduced capacity to give love.** The self-priority that shapes decisions and judgments also affects attitudes toward love, most notably in its

predisposition to accept the love of others without giving love in return. Youth who embrace the narcissistic style are not opposed to love in that they enjoy receiving it, but they are opposed to it in that they resist giving it. They are lovers in part but not in whole, a trademark remarkably immune to detection by early and middle adolescents.

- **Diminished moral concerns.** It is generally recognized that every morality involves several preconditions including fear of punishment, the desire to belong and fit into a group, an autonomous conscience, and belief in a higher authority. The morality of individuals driven by the naricissistic style is different, especially on the final two counts. Their morality serves the self, not the other way around. Egocentric priority is their trump card and they play it whenever life deals them a hand they don't want to play. To think of narcissists as completely without morality is too severe—that, after all, would make them psychopaths—but it is fair to report that they occupy only a limited number of floors in the tower of morality.

  Individuals possessed of a narcissistic style admit that honesty is the best policy, but they are inclined to try everything else first. They do not like being thought of as dishonest or disloyal—not because of any genuine moral objections to these vices, but because such perceptions reduce their popularity and lessen their social efficiency.

  Many narcissistic youngsters have what, on first glance, looks like a well-developed morality in that they perceive so many events in good/bad, right/wrong, worthy/unworthy terms. But this is not to say that they are moral persons, if by this we mean that they live by a code of honor, or a belief in higher authority; rather, when we look closely, what we really see is *moralism* rather than morals, *moralizing* rather than morality.

- **Lessened capacity for objective thought.** The narcissistic style, by its very nature, is contrary to an informed and friendly intelligence. The most destructive consequences of narcissistic thinking are diminishment of rational judgment and reduced ability to see the world as it is.

  The narcissistic intelligence is anti-empirical and anti-reason because these are modes of knowing that strive to understand the world as it is, and that validate beliefs through measures of verification beyond the self. The narcissistic style, in contrast, sees things through the lens of self-protection and self-enhancement. This does not mean that narcissists are never empirical or reasoned; in fact, they often are depending on the object of inquiry. The narcissist can be meticulously intellectual, precisely empirical, methodically scientific, and diligently reasoned when the object of inquiry favors or flatters the self, or when the object of inquiry challenges one's security or threatens one's sense of safety.

All narcissists are, to a certain degree, learning disabled; they blur objective reality with a network of prejudices which keep unwanted aspects of reality at bay and, because of this adaptation, they are never able to see the entire picture or have all of the available data at their fingertips. By the nature of their mental operations their decision-making is incapable of a balanced view. Hence, their thought process is disabled.

Whether the narcissistic style has become a dominant youth adaptation to the demands and artificialities of adolescent life is an open question. But any social worker, probation officer, school counselor, or high school coach can point out, without hesitation, clusters of youth who fit this profile.

Self-Importance, Self-Inflation

If we have learned anything about adolescents it is that their good health depends on participating in constructive projects; sharing real feelings; being useful; making meaningful contributions to their family; believing in something greater than themselves; and volunteering freely their muscle, energy, and intelligence. I believe that Ayers was true to the mark when, speaking of teenage girls, she claimed: "Taking care of others helps her think more maturely about taking care of herself rather than merely trying to make herself feel good. When she takes others seriously and tries to do her best, she is more likely to take herself seriously. When she sees people who are more needy than she is, she is likely to see herself in a different light" (1994, p. 74). Unfortunately, as human development would have it, teens are not well-equipped to satisfy any of these prerequisites of mental health on their own. For this they need the guidance, counsel, training, and supervision of adults who understand that youth are entitled to receive, but that they are also obliged to give.

Part of our problem as a society is that we don't value the differences between self-importance and self-inflation. We think that anything that makes adolescents feel good about themselves is a step in the right direction. We are so concerned that teens feel important that we lose sight of *what they feel important about.* Self-importance can never be separate from what one does. And quite frankly, social workers, high school teachers, and parents are exhausted from dealing with youngsters whose sense of self-importance has been warped by consumerism, corrupted by violence, and degraded by pregnancy fables. Youth want to feel important, but they know almost nothing about how to initiate genuinely important behavior; for this they need the assistance of family, school, and society.

If we proceed further in this matter we see that genuine self-importance flows from the worthwhile things one actually does but, unfortunately, in the adolescent community little opportunity arises to build useful products or to assert oneself affirmatively. As a society, in the words of Beatrix Hamburg,

President of the William T. Grant Foundation, "We simply do not provide youth with opportunities to act adult in positive ways." Without meaningful work and constructive participation, young people try to wrangle meaning from consumer goods, from peer approval, and from adventures in intimacy, and the results range from the harmless to the degrading to the self-destructive.

One conclusion to emerge from all this is that youth who do not make real contributions to their family or to their society experience an emptiness they try to fill through narcissistic inflation. This attempt is doomed because the surface sensations and visual images on which narcissistic inflation depend simply cannot nourish the moral, spiritual, and love needs of the adolescent personality.

All youth require a set of social virtues to guide their behavior; without them they get lost in the swirl of surface stimulation and petty distractions that pass for teen life. We may sum up this collection of ideas in a simple formula: As genuine importance increases, the need for narcissistic inflation decreases; and as genuine importance decreases, the need for narcissistic inflation increases.

Broadly speaking, we may conclude that the following predispositions in the adolescent personality, in conjunction with particular circumstances in teen culture, sculpts the adolescent experience:

- an obsession with rights and benefits, receiving and consuming— obsessions encouraged by the fable that "I," simply by merit of being myself, am entitled to receive;
- the attraction to ideologies that claim that society must satisfy the needs of the individual without the individual being obligated to society in return;
- the use of perfectionism as a shield against trying the new, or participating in activities in which one's competence is low;
- the tendency to judge as "bad" those people who merely are indifferent;
- a fascination with the visual, the superficial, the artificial, the immediate;
- a fear of deep friendship—a diminished inclination for mutuality and reciprocity;
- deadness to the feelings of others and a reluctance to extend beyond the circumference of the self;
- inexperience in sharing, giving, and cooperating;
- an intelligence dominated by narcissistic intellectualism rather than by reason;
- the presumption that responsibility is not a legitimate demand on the self;
- indifference to the rights and feelings of others, and the desire to perpetuate this indifference: "The degree to which we blot out things depends on how great our interest is in doing so" (Horney, 1945, p. 133).

The day-to-day realities of culture must also be taken into account when we are trying to decode the tendencies of youth; we are particularly attentive to the following:

- a culture of consumerism which valorizes the adolescent's natural egotism and narcissism;
- a culture that isolates youth from meaningful community projects;
- a culture that does not provide youth with responsible work;
- a culture that does not provide training in honoring social obligations;
- a culture that encourages attitudes of entitlement.

THE PREDISPOSITIONS THAT SHAPE
ADOLESCENT FRIENDSHIP

I would like to begin this segment by briefly stating four important precepts of adolescent bonding:

1. All youngsters need friendship, intimacy, and love, but living alongside these human needs are narcissistic predispositions little concerned with the rightful needs of the partner. Although youth want (and need) to experience meaningful relationships, their narcissism gets in the way of mutuality.
2. More than is recognized by romanticizers of the adolescent experience, friendships require partners to give approval in exchange for it being returned. Convincing a friend that his or her defects are really virtues in exchange for the friend doing the same is what I call "reciprocal rationalization." This is not the pillar that supports teen friendships, but it is a buttress without which many would collapse.[86]
3. Adolescents are inherently attracted to companions who praise their strengths and such attractions result in a profound desire to be in the other's presence because it is there that the liabilities of youthful immaturity are perceived as assets. These bonds are further strengthened by "synchronized self-deception," a choreographed script where partners agree not to criticize each others limitations, immaturities, shortcomings, or defects. Such friends may draft solemn agreements to do nothing that will hurt or embarrass the other, and in this regard the politics of youth are fashioned after the politics of nations.
4. Early and middle adolescents are weak at reading motives, and this weakness increases their vulnerability to exploitation. Deficiency in motive analysis is a primary reason younger adolescents are so easily manipulated by the older ones. The most exploitive bondings in the adolescent community are between late adolescent boys and early adolescent girls. These relationships pass as genuine romance (especially to the teens

themselves) but the older boys' love for the younger girls is not like Dante's for Beatrice or Petrarch's for Laura, it is a bond grounded in the girl's hope that her boyfriend is as grand and glorious as he appears. Sometimes he is, and at an age when the magic of possibility prevails, this is enough to warrant love's gamble.

Teen Employment, Consumerism, and the Artificiality of Teen Life

In the past three decades the most significant transformation in the daily life of teens has been their march into the work force; to be sure, it was not a forced march. Teens and parents agreed that work for pay was a solid idea, although for quite different reasons. Teens wanted the money, whereas parents were motivated by a cluster of well-meaning, but essentially false, beliefs. Notably, that work for pay is good for youngsters and that it helps them "to get their feet wet in the real world"; that work helps kids to better assume responsibility; that working youth contribute to the financial welfare of their household; that extra income inclines young people to "pay their own way"; that learning about work smooths the transition to the harsher world of adult work.

Almost all research conducted in the 1980s and the 1990s failed to confirm any of these optimistic beliefs. Even worse, most research suggests the opposite—namely, that youth employment undermines the quality of education, leads to increased spending on luxury items, leads to increased consumption of junk food, promotes increased alcohol and marijuana use, fosters cynicism toward "lower-level" work, and encourages reliance on consumer goods to enhance self-esteem. These findings have led most researchers to conclude that the benefits of work for pay are remarkably overestimated and its costs are sadly underestimated.

Consumerism is an especially odious "ism" among the young. I do not want to go on about the pathos inherent to 16-year-olds murdering each other for famous-name shoes, but I would ask you to reflect on how easily youth are manipulated into such perversity. Consumerism grows from the commodification of image, and it prospers among those whose image is nothing without commodities. Consumerism, and its collage of ego-bolstering illusions, is embraced by teens at an age when they have neither the life experience nor the mental dexterity to formulate a coherent ethic in its regard.

Adolescent Love, Intimacy, and Romance

I have tried to render meaningful the claim that adolescent intimacy cannot blossom until both partners have attained a certain maturity of identity. This claim is based partly on my assumptions about adolescent development, and partly on empirical research. Dignified intimacy requires *mutuality* and *reciprocity* and a deep and abiding concern for the partner. Sullivan, for example, claimed that intimacy requires "a clearly formulated adjustment of one's behavior *to the expressed needs of the other person* in the pursuit of increasingly identical, that is *more and more nearly mutual satisfactions*" (1953, p. 246, original emphasis). Adolescents rarely can meet the demands of genuine intimacy.

Adolescents reject the belief that intimacy should be reserved for youth of well-defined identity. Indeed, kids with the weakest identity are the ones who most desperately crave it. Because these hopeful youngsters chart their romantic course by a thought process dominated by affective logic, they readily accept the fable that sexual intimacy creates emotional intimacy, that sexual intercourse confirms love. This single instance of clouded thinking becomes, for millions of kids, the most profound mental error in their lives.

Bondings are confused by the adolescent belief that the person with whom an experience is shared is the *cause* of that experience—a circuitous piece of reasoning I call *particularization*. Rather than attribute a fair share of the experience to their own inner feelings, their warmth, or their sexuality, everything is attributed to the partner. In this way the partner attains a splendor (and a power) beyond what is known in ordinary friendships. Particularization is encouraged by the fact that many young people believe that the best within them cannot surface on its own; that it can be elicited only by a special, wonderful person. With that conviction of logic unexamined, the adolescent concludes that the whirlpool of feeling which has swept him (her) away could be caused *only* by the wonderful person with whom it was shared.

Generally speaking, particularization weakens over the course of the adolescent experience, which is to say that each person comes to recognize that something of love comes from within and something of it from without, and that real love is never entirely caused by the person with whom it is shared any more than a hearty appetite is caused by the person with whom dinner is shared. On the whole, however, particularization dominates the young person's perception of love and leads to the kind of love which idealizes the partner and narrows, rather than expands, love's possibilities.

Intimacy, and love are complicated by the uneven levels of maturity in teen society. Some teens have made great strides in their identity quest; they have a solid sense of themselves and they can speak honestly to the question "Who am I?" They have a good idea where they are going, and they have some thoughts about how to get there. Others, quite literally, haven't got a clue. They have nothing that resembles a solid sense of themelves, their growth toward a mature identity has made few real strides, and the primary existential question "Who am I?" is met with platitudes or a blank tilt of the chin. These youth do not live in mutually exclusive worlds; quite the contrary, they share in each other's lives and loves, and in their sharing the primitive ones are pulled upward and the mature ones tugged downward in a youthful dance of convergence and complementarity.

Summary

To sum up, the following developmental immaturities exert a profound influence on friendship patterns and intimacy connections during adolescence:

- *The necessity of peer acceptance* fosters utilitarian and practical friendship during the early years of adolescence; adolescent friendships, especially in the early years, are need-driven and necessity-driven.
- *Zero-sum social thinking* encourages the perception that "your" gain is "my" loss and "my" gain "your" loss; such social bookkeeping quantifies friendship and dampens the free and easy exchange required of its mature expression.
- *Reciprocal rationalization* honors the rationalizations of friends in order to gain greater acceptance by them. It is, at bottom, loyalty grounded in self-enhancement.
- *Primitive intimacy* is the rich, emotive, and profoundly felt connections among immature and underdeveloped identities. Unto itself it is the warm and joyous union of young people one, two, or three years out of childhood.
- *Infatuation* is bonding triggered by superficial features, physicality, one-sidedness, and illusion. Infatuation is encouraged, quite logically, by narcissistic youth driven by the need to be the *object* of infatuation.
- *Deficiency in the language of love* makes it difficult for adolescents to articulate the sensations and feelings associated with it, and this natural limitation of youth, unto itself, lessens their capacity for mature love.
- *Difficulty sharing in the outside pleasure of the partner* dampens reciprocity and impedes mutuality, the cornerstones of mature intimacy.
- *Fidelity* is the adolescent impulse to bond, affix, and attach. The practical consequence of fidelity is that it creates a free-floating inclination to bond once the right bonding object (usually a person) has been found. To assist in this goal, the mind cooperates by making certain candidates appear more worthy than they are, more intelligent than they are, and more decent than they are.
- *Particularization* is the tendency to attribute one's feelings to the person with whom the feelings are shared, resulting in a discounting of one's own role in relationships and an unfair exaggeration of the importance of the partner.
- *The manipulation of "developmentally selfish" youth* (usually early and mid adolescents) by the youth ensconsed in "the narcissistic style." This,

importantly, is not the same as age-based manipulation, where the power imbalance derives primarily from age and aptitude; rather, it is a type of manipulation grounded in completely different motive structures, in differing moral perceptions, and in different degrees of self-priority.

As with our other investigations we must look at the socio-cultural forces that shape adolescent relationships. Those that most diminish adolescent relationships include:

- The artificial nature of a social world rooted in age-segregation and isolation from the larger community.
- The absence of *legitimate* esteem in teen culture.
- The widespread presence of gossip and slander in adolescent peer groups.
- The illusion that the right consumer goods will bring meaningful status and genuine friendship;
- The increased hours adolescents are engaged in work-for-pay, and the negative human qualities and the counterproductive behaviors associated with the workplace;
- A social environment that exploits of early adolescents in dating practices, in gang membership, and in the workplace.

POSTSCRIPT

The single most significant discovery in this investigation is that many of the predispositions of youth are not conducive to their long-term welfare. This does not mean that youth are inherently evil nor, as the Hobbesians, the Freudians, and the Puritans darkly imagined, that youth left to their own resources will naturally sour. But neither does it mean that they will automatically mature into solid citizens; indeed, based upon what we have learned in this investigation, there is every reason to believe that without positive adult guidance most youth will not and many cannot achieve higher levels of maturity.

Notes

[1] Formal operations differ from, yet are similar to, concrete operations. Here is how B. J. Wadsworth explains it:

Functionally, formal thought and conrete thought are similar. They both employ logical operations. The major difference between the two kinds of thought is the much greater range of application and type of logical operations available to the child with formal thought. Concrete thought is limited to solving tangible concrete problems known in the present. Concrete operational children cannot deal with complex verbal problems involving propositions, hypothetical problems, or the future. The reasoning of concrete operational children is 'content bound'—tied to available experience. To this extent, a concrete operational child is not completely free of past and present perceptions. In contrast, a child with fully developed formal operations can deal with all classes of problems. During this stage the child becomes capable of introspection and is able to think about his own thoughts and feelings as if they were objects. (1989, p. 116)

[2] In Flavell's view, *propositional thinking* is the starting point of all advanced intellectualism:

The important entities which the adolescent manipulates in his reasoning are no longer the raw reality data themselves, but assertions or statements— propositions—which "contain" these data. What is really achieved in the 7-11 year period is the organized cognition of concrete objects and events per se (i.e., putting them into classes, seriating them, setting them into correspondence, etc.). The adolescent performs these first order operations, too, but he does something else besides, a necessary something which is precisely what renders his thought formal rather than concrete. He takes the results of these concrete operations, casts them in the form of propositions, and then proceeds to operate further upon them, i.e., make various logical connections between them. (1963, p. 205)

[3] *Dogma* is the patron saint of concrete thought. To analyze it, to dissect, and to evaluate it is the crowning achievement of formal thought.

[4] The conflict between teleology and determinism has not attracted our attention thus far, and here I will digress only briefly to emphasize its relevance to the adolescent

experience. Teleology speaks of being directed toward a definite end, of having an ultimate purpose, especially when these ends and purposes derive from a natural process. Teleology is a belief that natural phenomena are determined not only by mechanical causes but also by an overall design or purpose. Determinism, on the other hand, adheres to the doctrine that everything is entirely determined by a sequence of causes and, as far as human beings are concerned, that one's choices and actions are not free, but are determined by causes independent of one's will. The adolescent's preoccupation with the future derives from the increased mental abilities inherent to formal thought, and from cultural demands to prepare for occupation, marriage, and family.

[5] Quadrel, Fischoff, and Davis (1993, p. 112) remind us: "We do adolescents a disservice if we overestimate their decision-making competence (hence, deny them needed protection) or if we underestimate it (hence, deny them possible autonomy)." Much of the confusion in adolescent psychology is grounded in the tendency to sometimes overestimate and, at other times, to underestimate the abilities of teens.

[6] *Brain development.* Human thought derives from a brain that grows in rhythmic, time-bound progressions. Great advances in our knowledge of the human brain have taken place in the past several decades, including what we know about how it grows during the childhood years.

- *Increased lateralization.* The process by which one side of the brain takes control in organizing a particular mental process or behavior is known as *lateralization.* As children mature, one hemisphere attains dominance over the other which permits greater specialization and increased proficiency of psychological functions. Middle childhood is a time of increased brain lateralization, and it is also a time when more complex thought, and more effective coordination of action take place. For example, complex behaviors such as writing with a pencil, and playing soccer are executed far more effectively in middle childhood. The skills we associate with mid-childhood owe their emergence, in great measure, to increased brain lateralization.
- *Brain size and activity.* The brain increases in size but also changes its patterns of electrical activity during middle childhood. Between ages 5 and 7 the rate of growth in the surface area of the frontal lobes increases rather sharply. The myelination of the cortex nears completion. The brain wave activity of *preschoolers* displays more *theta* activity, which typifies adult sleep patterns; between 5 and 7 years occurs an increase in *alpha* activity, which is characteristic of engaged attention in the adult. As middle childhood advances, alpha activity increases.
- *Brain complexity.* By middle childhood the brain has achieved a structural and neurological complexity almost equal to that of adults. The frontal lobes coordinate activity of other brain centers when the child is forming a systematic plan of action. Since middle children attain greater proficiency at systematic planning during the same time as these changes occur in the frontal lobes, some experts infer that brain development is responsible for this improvement. When we suffer damage to the frontal lobes our behavior is characterized by a weakened ability to maintain our goals, we become more easily distracted, and readily lose our concentration. In many regards, behavior and intellectual functioning

resembles that of the *preschool* child who has not experienced frontal lobe maturity. (Cole & Cole, 1989)

Near the end of childhood the brain attains about 90 percent of its adult weight. Growth in foresightful activity permits more effective transaction of rule-bound games. In addition, the right and left sides of the brain are bridged by neural connections in the corpus callosum, a linkage that brings language and thought into closer working units and, in general, engenders more effective classroom learning.

[7] According to Robert S. Siegler: "Piaget applied the term 'egocentric' to preschool-age children not to castigate them for being inconsiderate, but rather in a more literal sense. Their thinking about the external world is always in terms of their own perspective, their own position within it. Their use of language reflects this adherence to their own perspective, particularly their frequent use of idiosyncratic symbols that are meaningless to other people" (1986, p. 34).

[8] My intent here is not to claim that egocentrism follows clear-cut paths, which Piaget believed, but to indicate that it is lawful and predictable in its progressions.

[9] Here is how a 21-year-old university student described the changing relationship with her parents during adolescence:

Yes, my attitude toward my parents did change during adolescence. As I became older, more mature, my thoughts and perceptions of them were more positive, much more positive. At a younger age, when friends were of extreme importance, and the attitude shared was that parents were more enemies, [who] were "old" and "didn't know anything." I considered my parents "uncool," at times embarrassed to be with them. I refused to see their side in an argument or suggestion. [I was] unhelpful, questioned things—why did I have to do this or that. As I became older, my parents were my best friends and still are. I took a complete turn—now I *want* to hear their advice or suggestions; respect their advice as well as decisions; I help not only with perhaps physical labor but emotional support; I like talking with them, learning from them, etc.

[10] For those readers interested in a more thorough analysis of the adolescent's understanding of the social world I recommend Furnham and Stacey's *Young People's Understanding of Society* (1991). This work, part of the superb "Adolescence and Society Series," edited by John C. Coleman, provides a thoughtful overview of the available data relevant to this topic. Special emphasis is placed on the young person's understanding of politics and government, economics and trade, work and employment, sex and gender, religion and spiritual matters, and law and justice. The prevailing themes of this chapter (especially how the younger adolescent's thinking is influenced by egocentric narrowness) are given solid coverage.

[11] **Perspective-taking.** Selman (1980) claimed that children grow in their perspective-taking in successive stages. He argued that each stage is qualitatively different from the preceding, that each level develops in sequence, and that most children mature through these progressive levels in approximately the same time frame.

Selman's ideas offer helpful instruction on the child's migration away from egocentrism because perspective-taking and egocentrism exist in a converse relationship;

that is, as one increases the other decreases. Therefore, to know about one is to know indirectly about the other.

Age 3-6 years. The guiding principle of the most primitive form of egocentrism, the kind manifested among one-year-olds, for example, is "You see what I see, you think what I think." At age three, children recognize that other people disagree with them, but they have only minimal understanding of the basis for another person's point of view; they recognize the existence of their own thoughts, and the thoughts of others, but often they confuse one with the other. Even by age six, most kids don't think that another person could respond to the same situation differently than they did. Their understanding of others is blocked by a poorly differentiated understanding of themselves.

Age 5-9 years. At this stage children understand that their interpretations of a social situation may be the same as, or different from, another person's interpretations of the same situation. They are aware that different people process information differently, and therefore, that they draw different conclusions, which is itself a considerable achievement. In Level 1 children are able to think from another person's perspective in a very limited fashion. The most significant feature of Level 1 is the child's recognition that each of us formulates ideas through our own individual thought process. At this stage children still cannot judge their own actions from the frame of reference of another person if that frame is different from their own. Another feature of this level is that children realize that others hold different perspectives, but they naively believe that everyone will agree once everyone is given the same information. Since they don't recognize the role of private thought in evaluating information, they mistakenly conclude that information itself molds conclusions. Hence, they have difficulty anticipating when disagreements will arise.

Age 7-10 years. A further advance in perspective-taking occurs when children attain the ability to see their own actions from another person's perspective. This allows them to anticipate other people's judgments more proficiently than in Level 1. Children now recognize that two people may disagree even though the same information is available to both.

Age 10-13 years. This level witnesses the ability to step outside a two-person exchange and imagine how a third person might perceive the interaction. This extention of perspective-taking permits looking at an interaction from two perspectives simultaneously (my own and my parents', for example). In essence, Level 3 allows the child to think about how another person is thinking about him (or her). (It is a necessary precursor to the Imaginary Audience.)

[12] **Egocentrism and conversation.** Egocentric speech tends to lessen when the self is acknowledged on a regular basis. With genuine acknowledgment the egocentric core does not clamor for *excessive* expression.

[13] **Egocentric speech.** Marlene Webber (1991), who spent two years in the streets of urban Canada interviewing runaways, relates a telling tale of harmless, though typical, adolescent egocentrism. In preparing to conduct an interview with a young man, one of dozens whom she interviewed for her book, she had gone to great lengths to explain to him that in her book no names would be revealed, that anonymity would be maintained throughout, and that, in disappointing fact, because of time and space constraints, most of the youngsters she interviewed would never even be included in the book. After these ground rules had been carefully established and agreed to by the young man, an interview followed. Upon its conclusion a friend of the young man arrived; he was introduced to the author with typical egocentric panache: "This is the lady I told ya about that's gonna write a book about me" (p. 9).

[14] **Fables and intellectual distortion.** In human perception distortion takes many forms, and in this chapter we describe only a few. In general, distortions occur when we see others in light of our own needs, desires, and fears. Most typically, these distortions yield three basic outcomes, all of which, to greater or lesser degree, degrade clarity of thought:

- They endow others with characteristics they do not have, or have only to a minor degree.
- They cause the perceiver to be blinded toward positive assets in others, such as friendship or devotion, or cause the perceiver to be blinded toward liabilities such as lying or exploitation.
- They result in the perceiver's being clear-sighted toward certain behaviors within others, and having a keen alertness to certain positive or negative traits. This "clear-sightedness" is focused into specific domains for reasons specific to the perceiver and, as a result, they preclude an overall perspective. These distortions are not blatant misrepresentations but subtle rearrangements and realignments.

[15] "Natural to the thought proces," of course, is not the same as "dominating of the thought process." That such a thought limitation is natural to the adolescent's thinking patterns does not imply that rational, reality-based forces are not also at work at the same time in the same intellect.

[16] Voltaire once suggested that truth is "a statement of facts as they are;" however, during adolescence "facts as they are" are clouded by the very mental operations that attempt to understand them.

[17] Arnett (1992) claimed that adolescent thinking is influenced by "a probability bias" in which youth accurately assess other people's susceptibility to a set of conditions, but do not associate themselves with the same susceptibility.

[18] Some research findings do not support the existence of the fable of invulnerability. A number of researchers have questioned whether it is a plausible explanation for adolescent risk-taking.

Elkind argued that adolescents' personal fable involved a notion of uniqueness so strong that it "becomes a conviction that he will not die, that death will happen to others but not to him." Elkind noted that his theory was largely speculative, being based entirely on anecdotal evidence from his clinical patients. *Although this article has been cited widely, there is little systematic evidence supporting the theory.* (Quadrel, et al., 1993, p. 103, original emphasis)

They further speculate:

The most straightforward account of these results is that adults and teens rely on similar, moderately biased psychological processes in estimating these risks ... both cognitive and motivational procesess could contribute to exaggerating one's safety. On the cognitive side, for example, the precautions that one takes (or at least plans to take) should be more visible than those taken by others, especially for active events (where control is more possible).... On the motivational side, wishful thinking might deflate perception of personal risk. (Quadrel, et al., 1993, p. 112)

Furthermore, in some quarters it is believed that once adolescents understand the relevant facts pertaining to any particular risk, they will avoid exposing themselves to that risk. Those who accept this point of view believe that when teens take risks they do not truly comprehend the danger, either because they do not have the mental power, or because the appropriate information has not been given to them, or it has been delivered in an ineffective manner. Another intepretation is that adolescents understand the risks but choose to ignore them. They may consider the risk acceptable, given the benefits, or they may enjoy the thrill or social status that come with it.

[19a] We know more about the thinking of girls because of their accessibility to research in programs for pregnant teens.

[19b] This is especially true in teen pregnancy. To reinforce the prevalence of this way of thinking, McGuire's (1983) investigation of teen pregnancy is entitled *It Won't Happen To Me: Teenagers Talk About Pregnancy*.

[20] Lauren Ayers expressed it as straightforwardly as anyone. "A young teenage girl has neither the wisdom nor the experience to handle the risks of sexual activity, and the statistics bear out the damage done to young females. The foresight, responsibility, and integrity required for responsible sex come only with maturity and cannot be made to develop earlier" (1994, p. 64).

[21] By grade 10 almost all teens have learned to give morally elevating reasons for their own abstinence, even though they do not always employ these same reasons when accounting for the abstinence of others.

[22] **Self-deception.** One of the ironies of mental progression is that as mental abilities advance self-deception *increases*. With increasing age children grow in cognitive ability, gain in awareness of their social environment, and develop the ability to put themselves in the position of observer. The net effect, according to Feldman and Custrini, is that:

Children come to understand that they can fool both themselves and other people. This is due to their growing realization that discrepancies can exist between their inner experience and their outer experiences. They come to see that they have greater access to their inner psychological experience and thoughts than do other people, and consequently are in a position to manipulate the appearance they present to others. (1988, p. 41)

All of which leads to the conclusion that the capacity for self-deception increases with age:

In sum, there is a cogent argument to be made for the position that self-deception will become more pronounced with increasing age. The research on other-deception shows quite clearly that children become increasingly successful in being deceptive nonverbally toward others and in identifying ... when others are being deceptive. As children's understanding of other-deception grows, however, they are more likely to understand their own instances of self-deception. If this is the case, they are forced to use increasingly sophisticated defense mechanisms to protect themselves. Ability in self-deception, then, is likely to increase with age. *It is ironic indeed that the increased skills in understanding others may act to decrease one's awareness of oneself.* (Feldman & Custrini, 1988, p. 51, original emphasis)

All of which gives us cause to re-examine Ludwig Wittgenstein's observation: "Nothing is so difficult as to not deceive onself."

[23] David Elkind observed that adolescents sometimes seem to behave stupidly when, in fact, they are not stupid at all. Why is it, he asks, that when faced with a simple, straightforward question, adolescents sometimes look at it from a dozen angles, mull it over, and grind it up so thoroughly that they are unable to arrive at any reasonable solution? Why, Elkind, asks, do adolescents often attribute devious, hidden motives to other people when none exist? Such mental convolutions are not the result of real stupidity but of "pseudostupidity." Elkind claimed that this kind of thinking is the consequence of accelerated cognitive growth combined with a lack of experience. When adolescents acquire the more sophisticated reasoning skills which come with formal thought, they literally "think too much" about simple problems, about human motives, about almost anything and everything. As they gain greater experience and their thinking becomes more efficient, "pseudostupidity" disappears. Elkind's idea helps to bring into sharper focus some of the befuddlement of teen thought, but the thrust of his idea is not the same as what I am trying to describe. The concept of pseudostupidity is a more specific concept than the pervasive impediment to critical thought I am discussing.

[24] **Blind spots**. In psychological parlance "blind spots" refer to areas within a person's beliefs, attitudes or perceptions which are resistant to change through objective information or rational arguments. Blind spots protect us from unwanted data, resulting "in an incapacity to bring attention to bear on certain crucial aspects of our reality, leaving a gap in that beam of awareness which defines our world from moment to moment" (Goleman, 1985, p. 15). For young people this "gap in the beam of awareness" is of monumental significance when it blinds them to the relationship between sexual intercourse and pregnancy, or from recognizing the link between alcohol consumption and automobile accidents, or between dropping out of school and obtaining a decent job.

Blind spots prevent adolescents from accurately perceiving their performance weaknesses (such as poor academic achievement), their behavioral shortcomings (such as temper tantrums or undependability) and their character limitations (such as intolerance, prejudice, lying).

[25] Adolescents fear impartial analysis for the simple reason that it is concerned with what is being reasoned about more than with their own needs and wants. When teens emotionalize an argument they lose on the reason end but they gain on the narcissistic end, an exchange rewarded by the fact that narcissism is a more demanding force in their personality than reason.

[26] In the fairly recent past, early adolescence was not a time of great concern as far as health and welfare were concerned because these youth rarely encountered situations where, if critical thought were briefly suspended, they would get into serious trouble. In today's world the story is completely different; drugs, automobiles, sexual behavior, weapons, and gang warfare all place the young person at risk. For today's early-adolescent *the temporary suspension of critical thought* can spell the difference between a successful and a disasterous adolescent career.

[27] **The penchant for argumentation.** In the following passage Albert Schweitzer describes how his adolescent passion for discussion led him into all kinds of difficulties. In *Memories of Childhood and Youth,* he described his penchant for incessant argumentation:

> Between my fourteenth and sixteenth years I passed through an unpleasant phase of development, becoming an intolerable nuisance to everybody, especially to my father, through a passion for discussion. On everybody who met me in the street I wanted to inflict thorough-going and closely reasoned considerations on all the questions that were then being generally discussed, in order to expose the errors of the conventional views and get the correct view recognized and appreciated.... Thus I emerged from the shell of reserve in which I had hitherto concealed myself, and became the disturber of every conversation that was meant to be merely conversation.... If we went to pay a visit anywhere, I had to promise my father not to spoil the day for him by stupid behaviour during conversations. (Kiell, 1964, p. 482)

[28] See *Self-Conscious Emotions*, by J.P. Tangney and K. W. Fischer, Guilford Press, 1995, for a thorough overview of the self-conscious emotions and their influence on thought and behavior.

[29] Consider for a moment the implications of the legal judgment rendered by Chief Justice Berger, in Parham v. J.R., 1979. "Most children, even in adolescence, *simply are not able to make sound judgments concerning many decisions,* including their need for medical care or treatment." When all is said and done, this is the issue behind virtually all discussions of youth in a mortorium culture. Are they, on their own, able to make sound judgments about the vital issues that shape their lives? How we answer this question tells us a great deal about our philosophy of adolescence.

[30] Among the considerations we take into account when surveying the adolescent thinking process is that when they feel that their knowledge is too weak to answer objections put to them they may respond by casting suspicion on the motives behind

the objections. Which is to say, when they cannot handle a problem they attack the person who posed it. Much of their tendency to argue unfairly reduces to this principle.

[31] **Clear thinking and clouded thinking.** *Clouded thinking* is the tendency for thought to become hazy, foggy, blurred, inconsistent, self-serving and, most usually, inaccurate. *Critical thinking* is neutrally reasoned evaluation which requires one to categorize, infer, and deduce. Critical thinkers must, of course, know something about the content in question; for example, to evaluate a reformer's ideas about changing the school system, one must be knowledgeable about the existing school system. Critical thinking, then, relies on having knowledge about the topic to which thought is directed.

Yet this is not all. A critical thinker must also have solid knowledge about how his own thinking process works: "Effective critical thinking requires a person to monitor when she really understands an idea, know when she needs new information, and predict how easily she can gather and learn that information" (Seifert & Hoffnung, 1994, p. 532). Critical thinkers possess enough insight into their own mental operations to know when they are straying from fairness and objectivity..

[32] In simplest language: As self-conscious emotions increase, clear thinking decreases.

[33] "Irrational" means that which is contrary to reason or to the principles of logical thinking. To be irrational is to repeat the same mistakes—to be superstitious, intolerant, grandiose, and perfectionistic.

[34] The adolescent tendency to perceive his (her) own society through platitudes can be seen quite clearly from the research conducted on the younger adolescent's understanding of society. Early adolescents do not comprehend well the social forces of history, nor do they have much insight into the causes of international power struggles. Unflatteringly, their understanding of society and its internal machinery seems to be based as much on platitudes and pledges as on genuine insight.

Having been out of childhood only a few months, early adolescents are inclined to view the world as a place to be run and organized. Adelson, in a thought-provoking essay on the political imagination of youth, offers this not-so-flattering assessment of youthful authoritarianism:

> What accounts for the authoritarian animus among the young? They are, to begin with, preoccupied by human wickedness. They see man as tending naturally toward the impulsive and the anarchic. They are Hobbesian—it is the war of all against all. They do not seen to have much faith in—or perhaps they do not cognize adequately—the human capacity for self-control, or the demands of conscience. (1972, p. 117)

Early adolescents are easy to teach because they believe in the power of authority, because their thought assimilates more easily than it accommodates, and because they possess limited ability to understand ideas too removed from their own experience. They are difficult to teach because they think they know more than they do, because they question better than they understand, because they lack experience in the real world, and because their powers of inference are impeded by cognitive immaturity.

All in all, they are still discovering what they are and what they are not. They are not naturally cooperative, but cooperation is easily learned; they are capable of genuine sharing, but equally capable of genuine selfishness. They enjoy doing the right thing, but they usually require specific instruction before they can recognize it.

[35] **The tendency to intellectual regression.** Adolescence is an era of transition, but these transitions do not flow in smooth progressions; progress proceeds in clutches and spurts interspersed with plateaus and backsliding losses. One outcome of this crab-like cadence is that teens, every now and then, regress to thought modes which worked effectively in childhood but which cannot handle the complex demands of adolescence. Cognitive psychologists refer to this intellectual slippage as "regression to concrete thought." As we recall from materials introduced in chapters one and two, at the "concrete" level of intellectual development children sometimes accept hypotheses as facts and they sometimes reject facts as if they were mere hypotheses. This failure to differentiate "actual facts" from "mere hypotheses" fogs the thought process considerably.

Children believe that because the hypothesis is "mine" it is imbued with its own logical consistency; therefore, it does not seem reasonable to them to change a belief simply because new information contradicts it.

Among mature thinkers, when evidence fails to support a hypothesis, it is nevertheless re-examined on the chance that something was missed. Children almost never follow this procedure. Thus, an eleven-year-old who believes that he is the best baseball player in the 5th grade, and who predicts that he will be the first player chosen when teams are selected, may not alter his belief even when he is chosen last. He may simply interpret the facts in a self-enhancing way (i.e., "The other players are jealous of me," or "I really didn't want to play on this team"). The point here is that the belief is not rejected simply because it is not supported.

Adolescents, much more than children, face evidence when and where it presents itself and, as a result, they rework their beliefs in the light of new evidence. "Maybe the coach is right. I'm not as good as I thought." Nothing heroic here, simply the realignment of a belief to better fit the data; a normal indicator of maturing thought.

[36] **Benign, beneficial and productive narcissism.** Here is how Erich Fromm understood the concept of positive narcissism:

In the benign form, the object of narcissism is the result of a person's effort. Thus, for instance, a person may have a narcissistic pride in his work as a carpenter, as a scientist, or as a farmer. Inasmuch as the object of his narcissism is something he has to work for, his exclusive interest in what is his work and his achievement is constantly balanced by his interest in the process of work itself, and the material he is working with. The dynamics of this benign narcissism thus are self-checking. The energy which propels the work is, to a large extent, of a narcissistic nature, but the very fact that the work itself makes it necessary to be related to reality, constantly curbs the narcissism and keeps it within bounds. This mechanism may explain why we find so many narcissistic people who are at the same time highly creative. (1964, p. 77)

[37] *Self-love versus self-hate.* Some scholars claim that narcissism is not self-love, but a compensation against self-hate. In this view, narcissists are thought to be incapable of relating to the outside world because they fear that their hate will elicit a proportional punishment. According to Margaret Mahler, the child "attempts to save the originally all-embracing narcissism by concentrating perfection and power upon the self ... and by turning away disdainfully from an outside world to which all imperfections have

been assigned" (Kohut, 1971, p. 106). Such hatred is sustained by internalizing everything "good" and externalizing everything "bad."

Self-hatred is more dominant in the narcissist than is self-love. Narcissists have very low opinions of themselves and this is why they constantly seek approbation. *They consider themselves unworthy and unlovable,* and seek constantly to hide this fact from themselves by trying to get the outside world to proclaim them unique, extraordinary, great. But beyond that they suffer from intense, unconscious envy that makes them want to spoil, deprecate and degrade what others have and they lack, particularly others' capacity to give and receive love. (Kernberg, 1978, p. 55, original emphasis)

For all of these reasons, and a few not mentioned, Louis DeRosis claimed: "Essentially, narcissism is a condition of self-hatred, palming itself off as self-love" (1981, p. 343).

[38] **Primary and secondary narcissism.** Some scholars interpret primary narcissism as the infant's all-consuming wish for attention at a time when object-cathexes have not yet been formed, and the entire quota of libido relates to the newly developed ego. *Secondary narcissism, however, refers to the exaggerated feelings of self-importance and self-love that occur later in life.* Most of the focus in this book is more closely related to secondary narcissism than to Freud's original concept of primary narcissism. (See Fenichel, 1945, for further elaboration of the important differences between these two core concepts in narcissistic theory.)

[39] Freud viewed the personality as composed of stratified layers with consciousness at the top; directly beneath is the preconscious stratum, and beneath that the unconscious layer which is the seat of our instinctual impulses, and the depository of our repressed memories and buried anxieties. Not all theorists agree with Freud's specific formulations, but all psychodynamic theories adhere to psychic "layers" or "strata." Implicit to understanding all human behavior is the image of a fluid personality in which energy flows back and forth, and with this flow each stratum weakens or strengthens depending upon whether energy is entering or leaving.

[40] Margaret Mahler described a narcissism where the infant has no recognition whatsoever that mother is the external agent of its own satisfactions; after a few weeks the infant attains a dim recognition that its needs are somehow being satisfied by someone outside the self, but even in this secondary narcissism where the very young child recognizes that needs are being satisfied from outside "they nevertheless are convinced that *their own desires alone are sufficient to assure their presence*" (Monte, 1991, p. 229). In this so-called "autistic state" the child acts out a primitive precursor to adolescent entitlement.

[41] Although more scholars are beginning to recognize the important role of narcissism in adolescent life, this is a fairly recent turn of events. Textbooks of adolescent psychology, devoid of soul and passion as they are, rarely include more than a paragraph on narcissism. In what is generally thought to be the authoritative overview of adolescent theory (*Theories of Adolescence,* 5th edition, 1988), author Rolf Muuss does not include a single reference to narcissism.

[42a] Every new work dealing with narcissism connects, in one way or another, to Christopher Lasch's pioneer treatise *The Culture of Narcissism* (1978) and, in turn, to

the psychological profile born of a narcissistic culture which he described in *The Minimal Self* (1984). In acknowledging the significance of his work, Frosh (1991) reports: "Amongst the various writers who have employed the concepts of narcissism ... it is perhaps Christopher Lasch who has been both most influential and most distinctively thought-provoking" (p. 63). And although his commentary was not directed to youth, his ideas helped us to see more clearly the shallow roles and the empty illusions which shape their lives. Lasch's writings allowed us to better focus on how our culture (a) excites the narcissism inherent to youth and, (b) how it rewards an environment in which narcissism thrives.

[42b] The minor expressions of self-hatred so commonly experienced during adolescence should not be confused with the more profound expressions in which the person actually identifies with the despised self and comes to idealize dependency. During adolescence episodes of self-hate come and go.

[43] Satinover, after searching for a term to encapsulate the narcissistic profile so prevalent in Western culture, settled on "puer Aeternus"—*the eternal adolescent.*

> It is a personality, on the one hand characterized by ... a failure to set stable goals, and a proclivity for intense but short-lived romantic attachments, yet on the other hand by noble idealism, a fertile romantic imagination, spiritual insight and frequently, too, by remarkable talent. (1987, p. 86)

From Satinover's comments it is easy to see how the stuff of narcissism is, to a captivating degree, the stuff of adolescence.

[44] The North American disciples of existential psychology were attuned to ideas which speak to youth, but to my knowledge no one has applied them to the adolescent experience. I found the following precepts of existential psychology especially helpful in my attempt to better understand adolescent behavior:

- Every person is centered in himself (herself) and any attack on this center becomes an attack on the person himself (herself).
- Narrowness and defensiveness are the methods each individual uses to defend his (her) own center. The more the self is threatened (or *perceived* to be threatened) the greater the protective behavior.
- Every person has a character of self-affirmation and a need to preserve centerdness through affirmation. Affirming the integrity of others has an enriching effect on one's own integrity.
- When free of threat we exhibit self-affirming behavior which is less likely to harm others.
- When surrounded by threat we are more likely to exhibit self-affirming behavior which is harmful to others.
- All individuals have the need to participate in the lives of others.
- Participating in the lives of others always involves risk.
- The failure to participate in the lives of others produces emotional emptiness.

(For further development of these ideas, see Rollo May's classic work *Existential Psychology*, 1961.)

[45] **Adolescent irrationality**. We really do not possess any comprehensive explanation of adolescent irrationality. Our understanding of why so many teens (especially mid-adolescents) become pregnant even when they have learned the mechanics of contraception is no more advanced today than it was 30 years ago. Neither do we understand why sexually active young women (19- to 23-year-olds, for example) efficiently avoid unwanted pregnancy while sexually active 15- to 17-year-olds do not? Our understanding of why teens are so influenced by fads, trends, fashions, and why they are so pathetically molded by pop culture is no more advanced today than it was 30 years ago. Our understanding of why teens shoot and kill one another is no more advanced today than it was 30 years ago. In regard to these deficiencies, narcissistic theory has something to offer because it speaks to the irrational, to the selfish, and to the destructive elements in human nature.

[46] **Humiliation and the adolescent experience**. It is nearly impossible to get an adequate feel for the tension which circles and embraces youth without taking into account how deeply humiliation hurts them. To be humiliated is to be made to feel contemptible, flawed, unworthy. Perhaps this is why Nietzsche claimed: "There is nothing for which men demand higher payment than humiliation."

Adolescents are on close terms with humiliation because their social life is one great dance around it. Everyone tries to avoid it, but this is impossible when so many peers bolster their own pride by shipwrecking someone else's. Every adolescent by necessity becomes something of a warrior when it comes to protecting himself against the injury of humiliation.

Everyone knows that to be humiliated is painful, but not everyone knows that to see the humiliation of others brings more than a silent pleasure. Hence, while running away from their own humiliation, youth are fascinated with inflicting it on others. If you fail to recognize this quirk to their nature I suspect that a good deal of adolescent behavior will remain forever a mystery to you.

[47] That adolescents are consumed with the demands of their own development is the starting point of virtually all modern theories of adolescent psychology. The term that I am using here, *developmental selfishness,* is a new one, but the fire behind it was felt by all contributors to adolescent theory. Erik Erikson's concept of psychological stages; Anna Freud's theory of psychosexual development; Peter Blos' second individuation process; Jean Piaget's theory of adolescent egocentrism; David Elkind's personal fable; Robert Havighurst's developmental tasks; Arnold Gessel's reciprocal interweaving; and Robert Selman's theory of perspective-taking each, in their own way, speak to the proposition that adolescence is a developmental period when the individual is consumed by a necessary—and legitimate—self-investment.

[48] With the term *developmental selfishness* I ask the reader for a certain leniency because I simply have not been able to locate a term from self-psychology, from personality theory, from the insufferable expanse of psychologese and creative neologism, which adequately conveys the vital spirit of vigilant self-protectionism which ignites the adolescent experience. I have settled on developmental selfishness, despite its bulkiness, because of its ability to convey a series of ideas rather than only one, and to suggest a connective thread weaving self, selfish, and selfishness into a unified fabric.

[49] What I call *narcissistic selfishness* resembles what Kohut (1971) and Kernberg (1970) called "pathological narcissism," and what Alford (1988) called *regressive narcissism.* To better understand the meaning behind narcissistic selfishness consider this:

In some of us, concerns with "narcissistic supplies," or supports to self-esteem, eclipse other issues to such an extent that we may be considered excessively self-preoccupied. Terms like "narcissistic personality" and "pathological narcissism" apply to this *disproportionate degree of self-concern,* not to ordinary responsiveness to approval and sensitivity to criticism. (McWilliams, 1994, p. 170)

[50] Kernberg believed that unhealthy narcissism arises in early childhood "as a result of chronically cold, unempathic parents who fail to provide the infant with the love and attention necessary for psychological health. Disruptions in the mother-child bond may bring about a refusion of self and object images, resulting in identity diffusion and an inflated or grandoise (narcissistic) self" (Berman, 1990, p. 24). Most theorists believe that in the narcissistic character the real self has never taken hold, therefore, the self-concept remains under the influence of childhood emotional states and the conflicts attendant to . them. The more powerful these childhood emotional states, and the more primitive the conflicts within them, the stronger the narcissistic component to the personality.

[51] Narcissists may respect the feelings of others when it leads to their own gain or gratification. This is not to be confused with respect for people as people. Their respect is what behaviorists call "instrumental" respect since it is grounded in pragmatism more than in empathy, in receiving more than in giving.

[52] Narcissism and high self-esteem are totally different. High self-esteem has nothing to do with praise-crazy self-centeredness. Positive self-esteem doesn't mean "I'm OK; you're irrelevant." Self-esteem is not the same as self-inflation.

Self-esteem means being competent to cope with life challenges; it means trusting yourself. Individuals with positive self-esteem are not enraged when someone points out a flaw in their character.

Narcissism is characterized by an anxious comparison of oneself to others. The narcissist views others as competitors, as threats; narcissism is completely lacking in good will; it is self-based rather than other-based, ego-based rather than reality-based.

[53] What we are here discussing was a source of great conflict between Sigmund Freud and Alfred Adler in their debate on human nature. When Freud originated the concept of narcissism he had in mind "a protective channeling of energy into the self, a healthy self-interest or self-love." Adler postulated (and in this regard his thought is much closer to Karen Horney's than to Sigmund Freud's) that narcissism is an obsessive inward fixation which maximizes self-concern and diminishes social interest. To Adler, the narcissistic attitude is not innate or instinctual, it is a learned response. Adler's version of narcissism deals more candidly with the selfish expressions of narcissism (such as entitlement demands) as he recognized from the beginning that narcissism invariably leads one away from social interest in order to puruse one's own cravings and desires.

[54] Arthur Schopenhauer (who grappled with the inherently selfish qualities within our being as tenaciously as any of the pre-Freudian thinkers) once claimed: "Egoism is so deeply rooted a quality of all individuals in general, that in order to rouse the activity of an individual being, egotistical ends are the only ones upon which we count with certainty." Schopenhauer's statement has been debated in many quarters, but whether one accepts or rejects his view of human nature no one doubts that many of us behave exactly as he described.

[55] Narcissists are obsessed with "respect," but they show it in a way that has little to do with its real meaning. To show respect means to acknowledge the basic integrity or worthiness of a person; to show consideration; to treat with deference. To narcissists, and to many youngsters gripped by the narcissistic attitude, to show respect simply means to flatter, to inflate. When narcissists (or teens embroiled in the narcissistic attitude) complain that so-and-so "shows no respect" we usually find that he (she) does not artificially inflate. The obsession with "respect" often has little to do with genuine respect or real dignity.

[56] Erich Fromm once claimed: "The ability to love depends on one's capacity to emerge from narcissism" (1964, p. 88). In this section we are looking at some of the reasons that support this statement.

[57] See Amitai Etzioni's *The Spirit of Community* (1993) for further elaboration of these ideas.

[58] **The soloist and the choir.** Grovetant, in an informative essay on the integrative demands of adolescent identity (1993), subtitled his essay "Bringing the soloist to the choir." In this article he puts forth ideas which share commonalities with ideas put forth here, especially the tenet that every young self is engaged in a struggle to balance the legitimate needs and demands of the group with the legitimate needs and demands of "me." The key words, however, are not "group" and "me," rather "balance" and "integration." Grovetant writes: "Metaphorically, the interplay required for musicians to produce a coherent, balanced performance is not unlike the interplay required for the orchestration of one's sense of personal identity; both involve blending and integration" (p. 121). Individuals steeped in narcissism enjoy their role as soloists but they fail to grasp that without the choir they have no place to sing. For them "balance" and "integration" mean something quite different than to the choir members, who view the soloist as one voice in a chorus of many.

[59] **Egocentrism and narcissism.** Taking into account our earlier discussion of egocentrism one might be inclined to think that the narcissistic attitude and egocentrism amount to the same thing. This is not so. The egocentrism natural to children predisposes them to anticipate that they will be favored. To young children it is natural that mother provides them with special gifts even when it requires great sacrifice on her part. Egocentrism predisposes children to anticipate that they will be blessed with good fortune, that they will receive the benefit of doubt, and that they will routinely have exceptions made on their behalf. These anticipations permeate their demeanor so completely that when formal thought begins to impress upon them the concept of impartiality, it ruptures their anticipation that they will always receive the lion's share. To anticipate that things *will* fall in one's favor is the precursor to expect that things *should* fall in one's favor.

To summarize, the egocentrism that dominates the world of children is not the same as the narcissistic style observed during adolescence even though they share the common features of self-embeddedness and self-priority. Narcissism is richer in its emotionality, more hostile in its resentments, and more emotive in its self-defense. All narcissists are egocentric but not all egocentrics are narcissists.

[60] Imperviousness is much more than mere denial, and to envision it as denial is to see only one measure of its character. Imperviousness is a mental state which specializes in the avoidance, the omission, the turning away from, the indifference to, the

neutralization of, and the dismissal of data. It is a mental state the adolescent calls upon when reality is painful, or when it stands in opposition to narcissistic cravings. Imperviousness is not apathy, it is profit-yielding inattentiveness.

[61] **Narcissism and its antithesis: social interest.** If a certain selfish protectionism is inherent to our nature does this mean that we cannot also have inherent to our nature a predisposition to give, to share, and to love? Why must one predisposition exist at the expense of the other? (Afterall, many opposites are natural to our makeup, i.e., the needs for independence and dependence, the needs for spontaneity and order, the needs for privacy and community.) Is it not possible that we have a selfish side to our nature *and* a sharing side? There is, in my estimation, much to support this view if we look openly and without prejudice at adolescents and their behavior.

In psychological circles the undisputed champion of the belief that humans are predisposed to share and cooperate is Alfred Adler. Fellow believer David Hume once claimed, "There is some benevolence, however small, infused into our bosom, some spark of friendship for human kind, some particle of the dove kneaded into our frame, along with the elements of the serpent and the wolf." Alfred Adler went much further; he belived that "the spark of friendship for human kind," and the "dove kneaded into our frame," were, in fact, the dominant features of human nature, and to him the "serpent and the wolf" are but necessary inventions to protect our vulnerable selves from a callous, sometimes brutal, environment. Adler believed that all humans possess inborn predispositions for sharing and cooperation which translate into an active propensity toward fellowship and companionship. He was the first of the psychodynamic theorists to claim that we receive greater satisfaction being helpful than being helped.

Adler also believed that it is easy to cultivate a compassionate nature in youth because they are naturally inclined to give. He rejected Freud's theory of narcissism as it could not explain cooperation, sharing, volunteerism, or the broad spectrum of "giving without taking" we observe in all human communities. Adler eventually came to believe that excessive striving for selfish goals is a neurotic distortion of our impulse to cooperate. All in all, Adler's concept of social interest is the diametric opposite of narcissistic selfishness. Whether selfishness comes into being, as Adler suggested, from the blunting of social interest, is a matter still debated by the well informed, and not to be settled here.

"Social interest," as used by Adler, is a translation from the German word *Gemeinschaftsgefuhl*, which means "social feeling" or "community feeling." Adler used it to mean a pervasive feeling of attachment to all humanity and membership in the social community of all people. Adler believed that social interest is an inherent part of human nature. It does not spring forth fully blossomed; it is encouraged through parental love, guidance, and sharing during the first five years of life.

Adler claimed that an obsession with self-aggrandizement is evidence that the initial mother-child relationship was not strong enough or loving enough for the child to progress naturally from self-interest to social interest. Narcissism, again according to Adler, is not a reflection of our nature but a diminishment of it. Narcissistic selfishness is not our starting point as Freud claimed; rather, it is the rupture point.

Because of our hypotheses concerning the egocentric and the narcissistic predispositions of adolescents, it is abundantly clear that Adler's theory of social interest is not our starting point. However, without going into it at this moment, it should also be clear that Adler's ideas are vital to our deliberations on this topic. Why? From our investigations of adolescence a fundamental principle emerges: Youth lacking social interest are left with nothing to guide them except their narcissism. As Adler himself expressed it: "Only those persons who are really trained in the direction of social interest ... will actually have social feeling." "Social feelings," as Adler rightly observed, is not an *inevitable* fact of life; like speech, the mechanics are provided by nature, but the environment must provide training if it is to develop.

[62] Norman Polansky, the noted psychotherapist, encountered similar tendencies among young professionals. He observed: "Just as social work students, most of whom are straightforward people, commonly underestimate the presence of spite as a motivation in clients, they also overlook narcissism" (1991, p. 72).

[63] *Accurate appraisal of peers.* What we have been addressing from a variety of angles condenses to a few basic questions: "Why are teens, under one set of circumstances, inclined to appraise their peers accurately and, under another set of circumstances, inaccurately?" Parallel to this: "Why are teens, under one set of circumstances, inclined to appraise themselves accurately, and under another set of circumstances, inaccurately?" To assist in tackling these questions, Brown, Mory, and Kinney (1994) have assembled thoughtful ideas. Drawing upon principles of social identity theory, Brown, et al., claim that teens: (a) accentuate differences between their own group and other groups, (b) overstate the positive characteristics of their own group, and (c) overstate the negative characteristics of outside groups. These conclusions support the general themes brought forward in Part I of this book; namely, that the adolescent thought process is vulnerable to a host of interpretation biases which get in the way of an objective understanding of their social world.

[64] Some of what is meant by "flattering mirrors" parallels what Jones and Pittman (1982) called *ingratiation* (making oneself likable in another's eyes). On this phenomenon, Sabini makes some interesting observations:

> One way is simply to agree with what other people think. Another is to praise your target's accomplishments, personality, and so on. But these strategies require subtlety to succeed; pushed too far, they give way to their purpose. And they have one further problem. The target of ingratiating behavior is often easier to fool than observers are. (1995, p. 203)

[65] Betrayal hits young people with such crunching force that it shakes their faith in friends and friendships, especially when it comes from a parent, a hero, or a loved one. Betrayal may come from abandonment, as when a friend deserts you or simply forgets you exist; or it may come in the form of rejection, as when one is excluded (symbolically or physically) by peers, parents, or teachers.

Betrayal opens the floodgates to the separation anxiety dammed since infancy. Separation anxiety is the deepest and the darkest of our deep, dark fears. To be betrayed resurrects the painful childhood fears of losing mother or father, and casts into doubt one's desirability.

In her study of runaways who end up as street kids, Webber (1991) reports: "Betrayal is the most common experience among them. Many street youths feel profoundly betrayed by significant adults, usually one or both parents, or surrogate parents assigned by the state" (1991, p. 28).

[66]Teens need to understand that it is possible to earn respect and friendship independently of the consumer goods they flash, wear, or own. Most kids initially reject this message because it is so contrary to the unwritten rules of peer attraction in our culture, and because the opposite message is presented more convincingly by the illusion industry; nevertheless, they need to hear it, and see it in the behavior of adults, before their personal experience can confirm it.

[67]Denby (1996) spoke of the "avalanche of crud" which drowns adolescents in our consumer-driven culture. Individual instances, he claims, cannot convey its subversive power; but its collective impact allows us to see it for what it is.

> Even if the child's character is not formed by a single TV show, movie, or video or computer game, the endless electronic assault obviously leaves it mark all over him...Whether the sets are on or off, the cruddy tone is on the air and in the streets. The kids pick it up and repeat it, and every week there are moments when I feel the spasm of fury that surges back and forth between resentment and self-contempt...The crude bottom-line attitude they've picked up, the nutty obsessive profanity, the echo chambers of voices and attitudes, set my teeth on edge...What American parent hasn't felt that spasm? Your kid is rude and surly and sees everything in terms of winning or losing or popularity and becomes insanely interested in clothes and seems, far, far from courage and selfhood.
>
> Aided by armies of psychologists and market researchers, the culture industries reach my children at every stage of their desires and their inevitable discontent...In this country people possessed solely by the desire to sell have become far more powerful than parents. (1986, p. 85)

[68]Do not be misled by the argument that only middle-class youth spend their earned money this way. Virtually all hands-on professionals agree that low-income youth (teens whose parents have low incomes) spend a greater proportion of their money on junk-food, status items, and brand-name clothing than do middle-income youth.

[69]In Montmeyer (1994), I could not find a single reference to how *normal developmental characteristics* impede adolescent intimacy. This failure, I believe, accords with the unwritten ethos of the 1990s forbidding scholars to explain any phenomenon by an immaturity or a developmental limitation within the person in whom it is observed.

[70]Intimate relationships exist on many planes. In terms of *intensity,* some intimate relationships are intense while others are calm and tranquil. In terms of *commitment,* some relationships are sealed by a strong commitment to longevity while others are brief. In terms of *emotion,* feelings run the gamut from ecstatic joy to agonizing despair. In terms of *sexuality* some intimate relationships are sexual, some are not. Some sexual relationships are psychologically intimate; others are not. In terms of *gender*, men and women (boys and girls) often take different approaches to intimacy. And, as well, intimate relationships exist between same-sex partners and between partners of the opposite sex (Brehm, 1992).

[71]The attentive reader has already observed that I have not put forth a scientific definition of intimacy. My reason for this is simple: The word defies a brief, workable definition. Prager, in her superb book, *The Psychology of Intimacy,* spent the entire first chapter trying to do so, and eventually surrendered. But she did point out something

worth a moment of our time. She writes: "Ideally, a definition [of intimacy] scholars use should be reconcilable with lay definitions. A scholarly definition clearly needs more precision than do lay definitions, but it may not be useful if it excludes many of the experiences the average layperson would call intimate. The risk of deviating too much from lay definitions is that research will be undertaken that has little relevance to people's everyday experiences with intimacy" (1995, p. 14). With this statement I am in complete agreement.

[72] **Pregnancy during adolescence.** Even though we know the incidence of sexual behavior at virtually every developmental level, we have no clear understanding *why* teens are so inept at avoiding pregnancy. Nor do we understand why teens invent, then cling to, irrational beliefs about pregnancy—especially the "It can never happen to me" fable.

Mothers under age 15 experience a rate of maternal deaths two and one-half times that of mothers aged 20-24. Teen mothers also have a higher rate of nonfatal complications than non-teen mothers; the younger the mother the higher the risk for such complications of pregnancy as toxemia, anemia, prolonged labor, and premature labor; teen mothers are 92 percent more likely to have anemia, 23 percent more likely to experience premature birth than mothers in their 20s. Teenage pregnancies more frequently end in miscarriage and stillbirths than pregnancies of women in their 20s. Babies born to teenagers are more likely to be premature, to have low birth weights, to have low Apgar scores, and to die within the first month and within the first year. Low birth weight contributes to cerebral palsy, mental retardation, epilepsy, and is a major cause of infant mortality. The Carnegie Council on Adolescent Development (1989) reports that medical costs for low-birthweight infants average $400,000. (By the time you read these figures they will be much higher.)

[73] The choice of "man" rather than "boy" is a real one in teen pregnancy. Research confirms that more than 50 percent of children born to teens are fathered by adults.

[74] **The adult years following teen pregnancy.** The impact of teen motherhood was effectively summarized by Campbell:

> The girl who has an illegitimate child at the age of 16 suddenly has 90 percent of her life script written for her. She will probably drop out of school; even if someone else in her family helps to take care of the baby, she will probably not be able to find a steady job that pays enough to provide for herself and her child; she may feel impelled to marry somone she might not otherwise have chosen. Her life choices are few, and most of them are bad. (Ginzberg et al., p. 30, 1988)

By age 29 about 50 percent of women who had their first child as a teen had obtained a high school diploma, while over 95 percent of those who did not have their first child until after age 20 had obtained a high school diploma. Mothers without a high school diploma are twice as likely to live in households receiving Aid to Families with Dependent Chldren. Women whose first child was born in their adolescence produce more children in their lifetime than women whose first child was born after adolescence.

Teenage mothers pose a substantial cost to the state. "A major source of new applications/acceptance on welfare rolls is the young teenage mother who, in the absence of a wage-earning male, frequently has no other source of income to cover living expenses for her child and herself (p. 30)." A significant factor for teen mothers is longevity: "Although many adults who go onto the rolls leave within a relatively brief time (less than two years), many teenage mothers remain for a decade if not longer" (Ginzberg et al., 1988 p. 30).

[75] A reproof to those who think of adolescents as masters of their own destiny is that they have such extreme difficulty avoiding pregnancy. Yet, in a few short years, with the onset of early adulthood, they have no such difficulty at all. The "pregnancy pockets" of middle and late adolescence are, for all intents and purposes, a thing of the past by the early 20s. Girls who avoid pregnancy during the critical years of 15-18 rarely experience unwanted pregnancies during later years.

[76] **The fear of intimacy.** Intimacy may trigger preexisting personality weaknesses within one or both of the partners, which have gone unnoticed during previous conditions of casual friendship or pseudo-intimacy. Therefore, intimacy partners not only encounter the stress of adjusting to one another, but they must also come to grips with deficiencies within their own personalities which have been defensively avoided. Intimacy brings joyous connections but it also exposes the dark side of the youngster's personality; hence, it involves both pleasure and pain, a mixture many teens would rather avoid altogether. Abstinence for many is easier than moderation.

[77] "Fame by association" is virtually universal among youth and it works in two ways. Its first expression is seen when the young person finds someone acknowledged by peers, society, or tradition to be great, and then affixes himself (herself) to this great person. The second expression is seen when the young person first affixes to someone and afterward creates a network of justifications which prove that this person is great. The latter habit dominates primitive intimacy, whereas the former dominates hero worship, religious bondings, and other culturally sanctioned attachments.

[78] **Intimacy beyond adolescence.** Researchers investigating what is variously called "maturity," "psychological health," or "competence" recognize adolescence as a starting rather than a finishing point.

Throughout adulthood we increase in our *potential* for symbolization—that is, for putting our experiences into symbolic form, whether words, music, art, dance, or gesture. During adulthood the personality tends to become more allocentric, more attuned to issues beyond itself. As a result, adults seem better able to focus long term energy on a valued goal. In essence, becoming more allocentric entails the humanization of values, and the development of cooperative relationships.

Attaining increased maturity also means becoming more integrated. Coherence and synthesis become more integral to our nature, and a certain internal logic to personal values, ambitions, and actions begins to manifest itself. Closely allied is the adult tendency to become more stable and autonomous. Stability enhances self-regulation and releases energy for other life demands, rendering the person more able to effectively deal with the problems of life, love, and work.

[79] That adults are also attracted to narcissists is a worthwhile topic, but it is not the point of this discussion; our concern is with how the attraction of the young to narcissists is influenced by their developmental limitations, their social immaturity, and their limited ability to read the motives of individuals with whom they are connected emotionally.

[80] Whether feeling is positive and affirmative or negative and depressing is not as significant as feeling itself. In adolescence the quest for feeling is so powerful that *profound feeling becomes an end in itself.* Hence the attraction to whatever, or whoever, produces powerful feeling.

[81] The attraction of younger females (approximately from 13-16 years) to older males (approximately 17-20 years) is one of the most significant attractions in the adolescent community. The developmental differences between these age groups is so great that they virtually always place the male in a position of power (both intellectually and socially) over the female. The human consequences of this imbalance are not totally predictable, but they rarely are to the girl's advantage, and they rarely serve her long-term best interests. Perhaps the most significant issue is pregnancy, of which Musick gives us something to think about:

> Research data indicate that a significant number of adolescent girls are impregnated by males who are at least five years older. Are these pregnancies the result of sexual exploitation or merely of inappropriate dating relationships? (1993, p. 86)

[82] During adolescence the bonds of closeness forged during a two- or three-month period may take two or three years to untangle. The virtues of decency are too deep in ordinary kids for them to walk away from narcissistic peers who would walk away from them in a minute. Hence, they remain vulnerable to their overtures, to their special requests, to their impassioned pleas for one final, special favor.

[83] The failure to see what is plainly evident is sometimes referred to as a "blind spot." The concept has considerable application here. In physiology, the blind spot is the gap in our field of vision that results from the way the eye is constructed. At the rear of each eyeball is a point where the optic nerve, which runs to the brain, attaches to the retina. This point lacks the cells, which line the rest of the retina, to register the light that comes through the lens of the eye. As a result, at this one point in vision there is a gap in the information transmitted to the brain. Here the blind spot registers nothing, and the perceiver perceives nothing.

[84] Much of what we are discussing here has been explored by Gardner's theory of interpersonal intelligence. In Gardner's theory, *interpersonal intelligence* refers to the ability to read accurately the moods and motives of the individuals with whom one interacts, to assess realistically the dispositions and sentiments of other people, and to be able to differentiate the real from the artificial in matters of sincerity and intimacy.

> Examined in its most elementary form, the interpersonal intelligence entails the capacity of the young child to discriminate among the individuals around him and to detect their various moods. In an advanced form, interpresonal knowledge permits a skilled adult to read the intentions and desires—even when these have been hidden—of many other individuals and, potentially, to act upon this knowledge—for example, by influencing a group of disparate individuals to behave along desired lines. (Gardner, 1983, p. 239)

[85] Piaget (1928) believed that all individuals grow through four stages of egocentrism, three during childhood and one during adolescence; he also believed that these stages are time-bound, and that the ability to negotiate them depends on how successfully the previous stages were negotiated. The four stages include:

1. the egocentrism of infants in which the child acquires the ability to differentiate the self from the outside world;

2. the egocentrism of preschoolers in which thinking about the world always begins from the child's position within it;
3. the egocentrism of middle-years children in which the child acquires the ability to perform elementary syllogistic reasoning and to propose concrete hypotheses; and, finally,
4. the egocentrism of adolescents in which the individual acquires the ability to double-check private thoughts, and to evaluate the integrity of abstract ideas.

[86] Few assignments are more difficult than to formulate a coherent appraisal of the adolescent experience in North America. The reasons are many; here I will provide a short list to which readers can easily add further entries of their own:

- Adolescents represent an extremely diverse population; hence accurate generalizations about them are hard to come by.
- The term "adolescent" usually spans ages 13-19; therefore, changes within the same person during the course of adolescence are remarkable. One can make the case (as I did in *The Nature of Adolescence,* 1986) that late adolescents are so fundamentally different from early adolescents that they represent two different developmental stages rather than the extremes of one.
- The most serious youth problem in every moratorium culture is pregnancy, a fact which makes females inherently more vulnerable to dropping out of school, to unemployment, to protracted stays on welfare roles, and to minimum-wage employment.

Despite these differences, adolescents are connected to one another by a cluster of developmental similarities found during no other period in the life cycle, including the physical transformations of puberty, the intellectual transformations of formal thought, the onset of sexual desire, and the departure from childhood.

References

Adams, G. R. & Archer, S. (1994). Identity: A precursor to intimacy, in *Interventions for adolescent identity development*. S. L. Archer (ed.) Thousand Oaks, CA: Sage.

Adelson, J. (1972). The political imagination of the young adolescent, in *12 to 16: Early Adolescence*, J. Kagan & R. Coles (eds.) New York: Norton.

Adler, A. (1939). *Social interest*. New York: Putnam.

Alford, F. C. (1988). *Narcissism*. New Haven: Yale University Press.

Allan, G. (1989). *Friendship*. London: Harvester-Wheatsheaf.

Allport, G. W. (1955). *Becoming: Basic Considerations for a Psychology of Personality*. New Haven. Yale University Press.

American Psychiatric Association. (1994). Diagnostic and statistical manual of mental disorders (4th ed.). DSM-IV. Washington, D.C.: American Psychiatric Association.

Arnett, J. (1992). Reckless behavior in adolescence. *Developmental Review, 12*.

Atwater, E. (1988). *Adolescence*, 2nd ed. Englewood Cliffs, NJ: Prentice Hall.

Ayers, L. K. (1994). *Teenage girls*. New York: Crossroad.

Baker, M. (1985). *"What will tomorrow bring?"... A study of the aspirations of adolescent women*. Ottawa, ON: Canadian Advisory Council on the Status of Women.

Balk, D. E. (1995). *Adolescent development*. Pacific Grove, CA: Brooks/Cole.

Barrett, H. (1991). *Rhetoric and civility*. Albany, NY: State University Press of New York.

Baumeister, R. F. (1991). *Escaping the self*. New York: Basic.

Berman, J. (1990). *Narcissism and the novel*. New York: New York University Press.

Bleiberg, E. (1994, Winter). Normal and pathological narcissism in adolescence. *American Journal of Psychotherapy*, 48 (1).

Bloom, A. (1993). *Love and friendship*. New York: Simon & Schuster.

Blos, P. (1962). *On adolescence*. New York: Free Press.

Branden, N. (1973). *The disowned self*. New York: Bantam.

Branden, N. (1983). *Honoring the self*. Los Angeles, CA: J. P. Tarcher, Inc.

Brown, B. B., Mory, M. S. & Kinney, D. (1994). Casting adolescent crowds in a relational context: Caricature, channel, and context, in *Personal relationships during adolescence*, R. Montmeyer (ed.) Thousand Oaks, CA: Sage.

Bruner, J. (1986). *Actual minds, possible worlds*. Cambridge: Harvard University Press.

Bursten, B. (1977). The narcissistic course, in *The narcissistic condition*, M.C. Nelson (ed.) New York: Human Science Press.

Bursten, B. (1986). Some narcissistic personality types, in *Essential papers on narcissism*, A.P. Morrison (ed.) New York: New York University Press.

Carnegie Council on Adolescent Development (1989). *Turning points: Preparing American youth for the 21st century*. Washington, D.C.

Chomsky, N. (1989). *Necessary illusions*. Boston: South End.

Cobb, N. J. (1992). *Adolescence*. Toronto, ON: Mayfield.

Cole, M. & Cole, S. (1989). The development of children. New York: Scientific American.

Cooper, A. M. (1986). Narcissism, in *Essential papers on narcissism*, Morrison, A.P. (ed.) New York: New York University Press.

Cote, J. (1996). *Generation on hold*. New York: New York University Press.

Csikszentmihalyi, M. & Larson, R. (1984). *Being adolescent*. New York: Basic.

Denby, D. (1996, July 15). *The New Yorker*.

Dennon, L. E. (1961). *The basic writings of Bertrand Russell*. New York: Simon & Schuster.

DeRosis, L. E. (1981). Horney's theory and narcissism. *American Journal of Psychoanalysis, 41*(4).

DeVaron, T. (1972). Growing up, in *12-16: Early adolescence*, J. Kagan & R. Coles (eds.) New York: W.W. Norton.

Donaldson, M. (1978). *Children's minds*. Glasgow: Fontana.

Donaldson-Pressman, S. (1994). *The narcissistic family*. New York: Lexington.

Dusek, J. B. (1991). *Adolescent development and behavior*. Englewood Cliffs, NJ: Prentice Hall.

Elkind, D. (1967). Egocentrism in adolescence. *Child Development, 38*, 1025-1034.

Elkind, D. (1974). *Children and adolescents*. New York: Oxford University Press.

Elkind, D. (1978). Understanding the young adolescent. *Adolescence, 13* (49), 127-141.

Elkind, D. (1985). Egocentrism redux. *Developmental Review, 5*, 218-226.

Elkind, D. (1987). The child yesterday, today and tomorrow. *Young Children, 42*(4), 6-11.

Erikson, E. H. (1946). Ego development and historical change, in *The psychoanalytic study of the child*, Vol. II. R. Eissler (ed.) New York: International Universities Press.

Erikson, E. H. (1956). The problem of ego identity. *Journal of American Psychiatric Association, 4*, 56-121.

Erikson, E. H. (1959). *Identity and the life cycle: Selected papers*. New York: International Universities Press.

Erikson, E. H. (1960, March/April). Youth and the life cycle. *Children, 7*, 43-49.

Erikson, E. H. (1968). *Identity, youth and crisis*. New York: W.W. Norton & Co. Inc.

Etzioni, A. (1993). *The spirit of community*. New York: Crown.

Farris, P. J. (1996). *Teaching, bearing the torch*. Dubuque, IA: Times Mirror Higher Education Group.

Feldman, R. S. & Custrini, R. J. (1988). Learning to lie and self-deceive: Children's nonverbal communication of deception, in *Self-deception: An adaptive mechanism?* J. S. Lockard & D. L. (eds.) Englewood Cliffs, NJ: Prentice-Hall.

Fenichel, O. (1945). *The psychoanalytic theory of neurosis*. New York: Norton.

Fine, R. (1986). *Narcissism, the self and society.* New York: Columbia University Press.

Flavell, J. H. (1963). *The developmental psychology of Jean Piaget.* New York: Van Nostrand.

Freud, A. (1948). *The ego and the mechanisms of defense.* New York: International Universities Press.

Freud, A. (1966). The ego and the mechanisms of defense, in *The writings of Anna Freud.* Vol. 2. New York: International Universities Press.

Freud, S. (1914). On narcissism, in *On Metapsychology.* Harmondsworth: Penguin, (1984).

Freud, S. (1926). *Inhibitions, symptoms and anxiety.* London. Hogarth.

Freud, S. (1932). *The ego and the id.* Vol. 19 of *The standard edition.* London: Hogarth.

Friedenberg, E. (1959). *The vanishing adolescent.* New York: Dell.

Fromm, E. (1964). *The heart of man.* New York: Harper & Row.

Fromm, E. (1957). *The art of loving.* New York: Harper & Row.

Fromm, E. (1939). Selfishness and self-love. *Psychiatry,* 507-523.

Fromm, E. (1973). *The anatomy of human destructiveness.* New York: Holt, Rinehart & Winston.

Frosh, S. (1991). *Identity crisis: Modernity, psychoanalysis and the self.* London: Routledge.

Furman, W. & Werner, E. A. (1994). Romantic views: Toward a theory of adolescent romantic relationships, in *Personal relationships during adolescence,* R. Montmeyer (ed.) Thousand Oaks, CA: Sage.

Furnham, A. & Stacey, B. (1991). *Young people's understanding of society.* London: Routledge.

Gallatin, J. E. (1975). *Adolescence and individuality.* New York: Harper and Row.

Gardner, H. (1983). *Frames of mind.* New York: Basic.

Gardner, W. (1993). A life-span rational-choice theory of risk taking, in *Adolescent risk taking,* N. J. Bell (ed.) Newbury Park, CA: Sage.

Garrod, A., Smulyan, L., Powers, S. I. & Kilkenny, R. (1992). *Adolescent portraits: Identity relationships, and challenges.* Boston: Allyn and Bacon.

Gilligan, C. (1982). *In a different voice.* Cambridge: Harvard University Press.

Ginsburg, G. & Opper, S. (1979). *Piaget's theory of intellectual development.* Englewood Cliffs, NJ: Prentice-Hall.

Ginzberg, E., Berliner, H. S. & Ostow, M. (1988). *Young people at risk: Is prevention possible?* London: Westview.

Goldberg, C. (1980). *In defense of narcissism.* New York: Gardner.

Goldman, R. (1965). *Religious thinking from childhood to adolescence.* New York: Seabury.

Goleman, D. (1985). *Vital lies, simple truths.* New York: Simon & Schuster.

Goleman, D. (1986). Insights into self-deception, in *The pleasures of psychology.* New York: New American Library.

Greenberger, E. & Steinberg, L. (1986). *When teenagers work: The psychological and social costs of adolescent employment.* New York: Basic.

Grice, H. P. (1975). Logic and conversation, in *Syntax and semantics: Vol. 3. Speech acts,* P. Cole, & J. L. Morgan (eds.) New York: Academic.

Grovetant, H. D. (1993). The integrative nature of identity, in *Discussions on ego identity,* J. Kroger (ed.) Hillsdale, NJ: Erlbaum.

Hall, G. S. (1916). *Adolescence.* New York. Appleton.

Hamburg, D. A. (1992). Today's children: Creating a future for a generation in crisis. New York: TimesBooks.

Hamburg, D. A. & Takanishi, R. (1989). Preparing for life: The critical transition of adolescence. *American psychologist, 44*(5), 825-827.

Hewitt, J. P. (1989). *Dilemmas of the American self.* Philadelphia: Temple University Press.

Holmes, J. & Silverman, E. L. (1992). *We're here, listen to us.* Ottawa: Canadian Advisory Council on the Status of Women.

Horney, K. (1937). *The neurotic personality of our time.* New York: W.W. Norton.

Horney, K. (1939). *New ways in psychoanalysis.* New York: W.W. Norton.

Horney, K. (1942). *Self-analysis.* New York: W.W. Norton.

Horney, K. (1945). *Our inner conflicts.* New York: W.W. Norton.

Horney, K. (1950). *Neurosis and human growth.* New York: W.W. Norton.

Ingersoll, G. M. (1989). *Adolescents,* 2nd ed. Englewood Cliffs, NJ: Prentice-Hall.

Inhelder, B. & Piaget, J. (1958). *The growth of logical thinking.* New York: Basic.

Irwin, C. E. (1993). Adolescence and risk taking: How are they related?, in *Adolescent risk taking,* N. J. Bell (ed.) Newbury Park, CA: Sage.

Jones, E. E. & Pittman, T. S. (1982). Toward a general theory of self-presentation, in *Psychological perspectives on the self,* Vol. 1. J. Suls (ed.) Hillsdale, NJ: Erlbaum.

Josselson, R. L. (1987). *Finding herself: Pathways to identity development in women.* San Francisco: Jossey-Bass.

Kaplan, L. (1984). *Adolescence: The farewell to childhood.* New York: Touchstone.

Kernberg, O. (1970). Factors in the psychoanalytic treatment of narcissistic personalities, in *Essential papers on narcissism,* A. Morrison (ed.) New York: New York University Press.

Kiell, N. (1964). *The universal experience of adolescence.* London: University of London Press.

Kimmel, D. (1974). *Adulthood and aging.* Toronto. John Wiley & Sons.

Kohut, H. (1971). *The analysis of the self.* New York: International Universities Press.

Kohut, H. (1977). *The restoration of the self.* New York: International Universities Press.

Kostash, M. (1989). *No kidding.* Toronto, ON: McClelland & Stewart.

Kroger, J. (1989). *Identity in adolescence.* London: Routledge.

Lasch, C. (1978). *The culture of narcissism.* New York: W.W. Norton.

Lasch, C. (1984). *The minimal self.* New York: W.W. Norton.

Lees, S. (1986). *Losing out: Sexuality and adolescent girls.* London: Hutchinson.

Lloyd, M. A. (1985). *Adolescence.* New York: Harper & Row.

Looft, W. R. (1972). Egocentrism and social interaction across the lifespan. *Psychological Bulletin, 78,* 73-92.

Lyons, N. (1990). "Dilemmas of knowing." Harvard Educational Review 60 (2): 159-180.

Maddi, S. (1989). *Personality theories: A comparative analysis.* Chicago: Dorsey.

Manaster, G. J. (1989). *Adolescent development.* Itasca, IL: F.E. Peacock.

Martin, M. W. (1996). *Love's virtues.* Lawrence, KS: University Press of Kansas.

May, R. (1961). *Existential psychology.* New York: Random House.

McGuire, P. (1983). *It won't happen to me: Teenagers talk about pregnancy.* New York: Delacorte.

McWilliams, N. (1994). *Psychoanalytic diagnosis.* New York: Guilford.

Mead, L. M. (1986). *Beyond entitlement.* New York: The Free Press.

Mencken, H. L. (1982). *A Mencken chrestomathy.* New York. Vintage Books.

Meninger, K. (1963). *The vital balance.* New York. The Viking Press.

Miller, P. (1989). *Theories of developmental psychology.* New York: W.H. Freeman.

Millon, T. (1981). Narcissistic personality: The egotistic pattern, in *Disorders of personality DSM-III: Axis II.* New York: John Wiley & Sons.

Mitchell, J. J. (1972). *Human nature: Theories, conjectures and descriptions.* Metuchen, NJ: Scarecrow.

Mitchell, J. J. (1973). *Human life: The first ten years.* Toronto, ON: Holt, Rinehart & Winston.

Mitchell, J. J. (1974). *Human life: The early adolescent years.* Toronto, ON: Holt, Rinehart & Winston.

Mitchell, J. J. (1978). *Adolescent psychology.* Toronto, ON: Holt, Rinehart & Winston.

Mitchell, J. J. (1980). *Child development.* Toronto, ON: Holt, Rinehart & Winston.

Mitchell, J. J. (1986). *The nature of adolescence.* Calgary, AB: Detselig Enterprises.

Montmeyer, R. (1994). *Personal relationships during adolescence.* Thousand Oaks, CA: Sage.

Moore, S. & Rosenthal, D. (1993). *Sexuality in adolescence.* London: Routledge.

Moore, T. (1992). *Care of the soul.* New York. Harper Collins.

Moriarty, A. E. & Toussieng, P. W. (1976). *Adolescent coping.* New York: Grune & Stratton.

Morrison, T. (1977). *Song of Solomon.* New York: New American Library.

Moschis, G. P. (1978). *Acquisition of the consumer role by adolescents.* Atlanta, GA: University of Georgia.

Muller, H. J. (1960). *Issues of freedom.* New York: Harper & Row.

Musick, J. S. (1993). *Young, poor, and pregnant: The psychology of teenage motherhood.* New Haven, CT: Yale University Press.

Muuss, R. E. (1982). Social cognition: David Elkind's theory of adolescent egocentrism. *Adolescence, 17*(66).

Muuss, R. E. (1988). *Theories of adolescence,* 5th ed. New York: Random House.

Nagel, T. (1975). Comment. In *Altruism, Morality and Economic Theory,* E.S. Phelps (ed.). New York: Russell Sage Foundation.

Nelson, M. C., (ed.) (1977). *The narcissistic condition.* New York: Human Sciences.

Nickerson, R. S. (1991). Some observations on the teaching of thinking. In *Enhancing learning and thinking,* R. Mulcahy (ed.) New York: Praeger.

Nussbaum, M. (1990). *Love's knowledge: Essays on philosophy and literature.* Oxford: Oxford University Press.

Olgivy, J. (1995). *Living without a goal.* New York: Doubleday.

Ornstein, R. (1992). *The roots of the self.* New York: W.W. Norton.

Overton, R. (1991). Formal thought, in *Encyclopaedia of adolescence.* New York: Garland.

Pagliaro, A. M. & Pagliaro, L. A. (1993). Knowledge, behaviors, and risk perceptions of intravenous drug users in relation to HIV infection and AIDS. *Advances in Medical Psychotherapy, 6,* 1-28.

Peel, E. A. (1971). *The nature of adolescent judgment.* New York: Wiley-Interscience.

Peterson, A. C. (1988). Adolescent development. *Annual Review of Psychology, 39,* 583-607.

Phoenix, A. (1991). *Young mothers.* Cambridge: Polity.

Piaget, J. (1928). *Judgment and reasoning in the child.* New York: Harcourt Brace Jovanovich.

Piaget, J. & Inhelder, B. (1958). *The growth of logical thinking.* New York: Basic.

Piattelli-Palmarini, M. (1994). *Inevitable illusions.* New York: John Wiley & Sons.

Pipher, M. (1994). *Reviving Ophelia.* New York. Ballantine Books.

Polansky, N. A. (1991). *Integrated ego psychology.* New York: Aldine de Gruyter.

Postman, N. (1986). *Amusing ourselves to death.* New York: Penguin.

Prager, K. (1995). *The psychology of intimacy.* New York: Guilford.

Putney, S. & Putney, G. (1964). *Normal neurosis.* New York: Harper & Row.

Quadrel, M. J., Fischoff, B. & Davis, W. (1993). Adolescent (in)vulnerability. *American Psychologist, 48, (2.)*

Sabini, J. (1995). *Social psychology.* New York: W.W. Norton.

Santrock, J. W. (1990). *Adolescence.* Dubuque, IA: Wm. C. Brown.

Satinover, J. (1987). Science and the fragile self: The rise of narcissism, the decline of God, in *Pathologies of the modern self,* D. M. Levin (ed.) New York: New York University Press.

Schmookler, A. B. (1988). *Out of weakness.* Toronto, ON: Bantam.

Sebald, H. (1984). *Adolescence: A social psychological analysis,* 3rd ed. Englewood Cliffs, NJ: Prentice-Hall.

Seifert, K. L. & Hoffnung, R. J. (1994). *Child and adolescent development,* 3rd ed. Toronto, ON: Houghton Mifflin.

Selman, R. L. (1980). *The growth of interpersonal understanding: Development and clinical analysis.* New York: Academic.

Siegler, R. S. (1986). *Children's thinking.* Englewood Cliffs, NJ: Prentice-Hall.

Simon, R. W., Eder, D. & Evans, C. (1992). "The development of feeling norms underlying romantic love among adolescent females." *Social Psychology Quarterly, 55*(1), 29-46.

Sondheimer, A. (1982). Anticipation and experimentation: The sexual concerns of mid-Adolescence. In *Adolescent Psychiatry,* Vol. X. Ed S.C. Feinstein *et al.* Chicago. Universiyt of Chiacgo Press.

Steinberg, L. (1989). *Adolescence,* 2nd ed. New York: Alfred A. Knopf.

Stendhal (1822/1957). *Love.* (G. Sale & S. Sale, Trans.). New York: Penguin.

Sullivan, H. S. (1953). *The interpersonal theory of psychiatry.* New York: W.W. Norton.

Thornburg, H. D. (1982). *Development in adolescence.* Monterey, CA: Brooks/Cole.

Wadsworth, B. J. (1989). *Piaget's theory of cognitive and affective development.* New York: Longman.

Waters, E. (1991). Learning to love. In M.R. Gunnar & L.A. Sroufe (Eds) *Self process and development: The Minnesota symposium in child development.* Hillsdale, NJ: Erlbaum.

Webber, M. (1991). *Street kids.* Toronto, ON: University of Toronto Press.

Weiss, P. (1980). *You, I, and the others.* Carbondale, IL: Southern Illinois University Press.

Wexler, D. B. (1991). *The adolescent self*. New York: W.W. Norton.
Vygotsky, L. S. (1978). *Mind and society*. Cambridge, MA: Harvard University Press.

Author Index

Subject Index